DIVIDED
EMPIRE

DIVIDED
EMPIRE
Milton's Political Imagery

ROBERT THOMAS FALLON

The Pennsylvania State University Press
University Park, Pennsylvania

Library of Congress Cataloging-in-Publication Data

Fallon, Robert Thomas.
  Divided empire : Milton's political imagery / Robert Thomas
Fallon.
      p.   cm.
  Includes bibliographical references (p.   ) and index.
  ISBN 0-271-01460-1 (acid-free paper)
  1. Milton, John, 1608–1674 – Political and social views.
2. Politics and literature – Great Britain – History – 17th century.
3. Political poetry, English – History and criticism.   4. Milton,
John, 1608–1674 – Style.   5. Figures of speech.   I. Title.
PR3592.P64F33   1995
821'.4 – dc20   94-41636
                                                        CIP

Copyright © 1995 The Pennsylvania State University
All rights reserved
Printed in the United States of America
Published by The Pennsylvania State University Press,
Barbara Building, Suite C, University Park, PA 16802-1003

It is the policy of The Pennsylvania State University Press to use
acid-free paper for the first printing of all clothbound books. Publi-
cations on uncoated stock satisfy the minimum requirements of
American National Standard for Information Sciences – Permanence
of Paper for Printed Library Materials, ANSI Z39.48-1992.

Contents

Preface   vii

1 The Image of Rule   1
     France and the Kingdoms of the Imagination   4
     A Handmaid to Truth   18
2 The Kingdom of Heaven   25
     God the Father   26
     God the Son   42
3 To Reign in Hell   55
     The Great Consult   62
     The Voyage   72
4 Heaven and Hell   83
5 The Lords of the Earth   97
     Prelapsarian Rule   98
     Postlapsarian Rule   103
     Fulfilled All Justice   113
6 Divided Empire   119
     Cosmic Conflict   121
     The Missions to Earth   131
     The Conflict Within   135
7 The Final Things   143
     The Trump of Doom   144
     All in All   155
8 Embattled Humanity   161
     Paradise Regained   162
     Samson Agonistes   169

Works Cited   180
Index   186

Preface

This book is the natural sequel to two earlier works. The first, *Captain or Colonel: The Soldier in Milton's Life and Art,* examines the influence of England's wars on the poetry. Since Milton never served in a military unit, that influence was indirect, a consequence of his experience as a citizen of the besieged city of London and the accounts of battle he heard from others. His experience in political life, on the other hand, was immediate and protracted, and the account of it fills a volume of its own, *Milton in Government,* a study of his decade of service as Secretary for Foreign Languages to the English Republic. In its early stages, that work had a subtitle, "The Making of a Political Imagination," intended to convey my conviction that Milton's experience in public service played a role in shaping the political imagery of his later poems; but an early reader of the manuscript, the distinguished historian, Dr. John Morrill, wisely observed that since the book said little about the poetry, the subtitle seemed to promise more than it delivered. As a result, *Milton in Government* appeared with its colon deleted.

In hopes now of delivering on the promise of that abandoned subtitle, I examine Milton's great poems here, appraising the imprint of those years in office on his creative imagination. During the first three years of his tenure as Secretary for Foreign Languages, until he lost his sight entirely, Milton served the Commonwealth's Council of State in a variety of capacities, most of them "in connection with foreign affairs," as he later put it (*Prose* 4:628; *MG* 25). For the entire decade of his public service his chief function was to prepare correspondence between the English Republic's executive bodies and foreign heads of state and to assist in the processing of documents exchanged in treaty negotiations with continental powers. The accepted language of diplomatic discourse at the time was Latin; thus it was Milton's responsibility to translate English documents into that ancient tongue for dispatch abroad and to render those received by his superiors into English for their consideration (*MG* vii-viii, 20-21, and passim). *Milton in Government* endeavors to demonstrate that the poet was much more deeply engaged in the duties of his office than has been hitherto supposed, that he was responsible for many more documents than the 170-odd which appear in the early manuscripts (*MG* 268-71) and very likely composed a number of them, hence that this experience had a significant influence on his imagination.[1]

That influence, as will appear, was both general and specific. It was general in that Milton conceived of the cosmic struggle between good and evil as a clash of political forces. The poetry is crowded with a host of public figures – kings, counselors, senators, soldiers, and ambassadors – competing for power in a comparable variety of public acts – debate, decree, diplomacy, and warfare. These figures and these acts define traditional political oppositions – the individual and society, loyalty and rebellion, obedience and freedom – the balance of which ultimately determines the quality of any system of governance in any time. They offer, moreover, a wide spectrum of government structures, ranging from absolute monarchy to egalitarian community. The specific influence of Milton's public service is manifest in a wealth of individual images traceable to political events of which the poet was intimately aware. In brief, having lived through two turbulent decades of war and political experiment, Milton came to imagine spiritual matters in terms of the exercise of power; and certain events of those years left such a lasting impression on his imagination that they reappear in lines where art closely imitates life.

Recent studies of Milton's political imagery argue that his stance in the poetry accurately reflects his stance in the prose,[2] or that it is consistent with what is known of his political allegiances,[3] or that it conforms comfortably to prevailing ideologies of his own time or our own.[4] *Divided*

---

1. It should be noted at the outset that William Riley Parker finds this experience of little consequence. He sets small store in Milton's activities as a mere "translator and interpreter for monolingual bosses," as he puts it. Curiously, Parker elsewhere elevates the poet to "secretary for foreign affairs," which somewhat overstates his importance (*Milton, A Biography* 2:945, 1022).

2. David Loewenstein, *Milton and the Drama of History*.

3. Joan S. Bennett, *Reviving Liberty*.

4. Christopher Hill, *Milton and the English Revolution*, passim. The New Historicists are

Empire rests upon a rather different premise: *Paradise Lost* is a poem, not a political testament, one, moreover, whose purpose is to delineate universal spiritual values, not partisan ideologies. Its political imagery, therefore, like all the imagery of the poem, is not an end in itself but serves a larger purpose, as handmaid to spiritual truth. The effort, therefore, to force that imagery into conformity with the poet's polemic political or religious prose, or to insist that it mirrors his lifetime allegiances, serves only to constrict it to the Procrustean bed of this or that narrow ideology *external to the poem* and runs the risk of ignoring, or distorting, the purpose of the imagery *within the work,* that is, its artistic end. As Joseph Wittreich observes, "Ideology, especially when its workings are unrecognized, unacknowledged, distorts and disfigures interpretation."[5] Milton surely drew his political imagery from his experience, whether from the many books he read or from his life richly lived, but it plays a role in *Paradise Lost* quite different from that to be found in his library or his life. Milton drew images of warfare from Homer and Virgil, but put them to a different purpose than did his classical predecessors. So too, the kings and councils of his poetry can be shown to resemble those of his experience; but when they appear in his lines, their purpose there may have little to do with the part they played in his life. Milton's art was obviously influenced by historical events. The object of these pages, however, is to discover, not what the poetry says about the events, but what the events say about the poetry.

To state the book's premise in these spare terms is, admittedly, to run certain risks. It seems almost perverse, on the surface, to propose that the poet's political imagery does not define his political ideology; and readers accustomed to studies that enlist the poetry to paint him in one color or another within the spectrum of political sentiment may find the argument

---

ably represented in Milton studies. Richard Helgerson cites Milton's isolation from public affairs during the writing of his later works, proposing that once the poet abandoned his ambition to assume the role of laureate, "at once poet, prophet, and spokesman of the governing order," his works reflect that decision: they "appear with no sign of a connection between poet and state" (*Self-Crowned Laureates,* 280, 278). Helgerson argues ably for Milton's isolation from his political present after the Restoration but then implies that his works are similarly isolated from his political past, a position that unfortunately leaves the scholar all but silent on the political imagery of the poet's great works. Leah Marcus has written with clarity and insight about *Comus* and the 1645 *Poems* but has not turned her hand to the later works ("The Earl of Bridgewater's Legal Life," "Milton as Historical Subject"). We must regret that scholars of such skill and learning have not ventured studies of *Paradise Lost.*

5. Wittreich, *Interpreting "Samson Agonistes,"* xxv.

unsatisfactory, or even irrelevant. Another risk, of course, is that even the suggestion that life influences art may relegate the present author to a premature grave in the unhallowed ground where lie the late and unlamented "biographical critics." These seemed risks worth taking, however. For the moment, I can only ask forbearance, promising a diligent effort to justify the approach in the pages to come.

Politics

The word "politics" has unhappy connotations for citizens of modern states. In a free and open society it is more often than not uttered with a sneer. Though all can find much to admire in a favorite "politician," one distinguished by high-mindedness and devotion to a local constituency, the profession as a whole does not stand in great esteem. In the eyes of many, public officials are far too prone to become mesmerized by the exercise of power and to view issues of great national moment as opportunities to gain advantage and garner votes rather than as questions of moral significance. Seldom are these public officials lauded as skilled practitioners of "the art of the possible," who engage in the demanding practice of compromise to achieve a worthy end.

In order to avoid the pitfalls of that perception, this study will interpret "politics" in the broadest possible sense, much as Milton did in *Of Education,* that is, as the study of "the beginning, end, and reasons of politicall societies" (*Prose* 2:398). The *OED,* citing that same passage, defines the word as "the science and art of government; the science dealing with the form, organization, and administration of a state or part of one, and with the regulation of its relations with other states." The focus, then, of our concern is, first, the relationship between the governing and the governed within a state, and, second, the competition among sovereign nations for advantage on a global stage.

That some men govern others and that nations compete for power Milton accepted as sorrowful features of a fallen world. The human race found it necessary to form communities and nations "by common league to bind each other from mutual injury, and joyntly to defend themselves" against harm from without; and they established authority within the state to "restrain by force and punishment what was violated against peace and common right" (*Prose* 3:199). In a broader sense, political institutions provide the fallen race with a means of ordering physical existence, keeping at bay the anarchy of social Chaos, which in Milton's symbolic cosmology surrounds the World, all too ready, given the opportunity, to replant "the Standard there of *ancient Night*" (2:986). Milton's poetry, however, is not a discourse on the politics of Man; it is rather a revelation of the love of God and the ways in which fallen humanity can escape the snares of evil and return that love. His theme is governance of the self rather than the state; but he does convey the ordering power of that love in political terms to make it accessible to human understanding.

Milton was ambiguous about conflict, as are we all, yearning for unity yet exhilarated by competition. The narrative voice in *Paradise Lost* is indignant about our squabbles: "O shame to men! Devil with Devil damn'd / Firm concord holds, men only disagree / Of Creatures rational" (2:496-98). Yet in *Areopagitica* the poet delights in the "disputing, reasoning, reading, inventing, discoursing, ev'n to a rarity, and admiration" (*Prose* 2:557) of the citizens of London, and urges that the power of Truth is displayed in contest: "Let her and Falshood grapple; who ever knew Truth put to the wors, in a free and open encounter" (*Prose* 2:561). Human conflict is a legacy of the Fall; and yet, paradoxically, it is the means whereby the race will arrive at its desired end.

To Milton, then, politics was an inescapable feature of the human condition; and he embraced it in both his life and his art. *Paradise Lost* presents Heaven and Hell as political states, and the conflict between them as a contest for hegemony in a political cosmos. By accommodating an inner spiritual conflict to human understanding, the poet depicted the abstract in terms of a struggle for advantage between two powerful rulers. The politics of paradise, lost and regained, may not, therefore, carry a political message at all; it does, however, constitute a narrative structure around which Milton shaped his vision of religious truth, of the struggle between the forces of good and evil in the universe and within the human spirit.

In the minds of seventeenth-century citizens religion and politics were, of course, virtually inseparable. There can be no doubt that they were so in Milton's mind, nor can there be doubt as to which he considered the more significant. As he put it, until "religion [is] set free from the monopolie of hirelings, I dare affirme, that no modell whatsoever of a commonwealth will prove successful or undisturbd" (*Prose* 7:275; see also 1:853, 7:379). He considered the individual soul to be the primary concern of the Almighty; and *Paradise Lost* lays out the path of salvation for wayfaring and warfaring Christians alike, regardless of how they may govern or be governed by their fellows. *Paradise Lost,* again, is not a political statement; it is a beacon of belief for that soul; and though the poet, drawing on his experience in public life, represented his beliefs in a striking series of political images, we are not free to assume that in those images he is defining a political ideology. His theme is how the individual should govern himself, as guided by Scripture, not how men should govern men, concerning which the message of Scripture is most uncertain.

Some two generations ago, Paul Phelps-Morand published *The Effects of His Political Life on John Milton,* which arrived at conclusions on the subject that scholars since have labored diligently to discredit. Drawing on the earlier work of S. B. Liljegren, he depicted Milton as a censor, a forger, and a liar, a writer who probably hastened the death of Salmasius and then callously took credit for his demise.[6] His political prose, further, is offensively polemic, "course and ferocious" throughout, full of omissions, half truths, and outright falsehoods, such as his claim to have visited Galileo. Once he entered political life, Phelps-Morand argued, Milton abandoned the values of his idealistic youth and embraced an arena in which expediency is commonplace and the ends fully justify the means. Unlike Liljegren, however, who found Milton's political activities morally reprehensible, Phelps-Morand considered none of this offensive. It is simply the sort of activity that one should expect from a revolutionary government composed of zealots devoted to building a kingdom of God on Earth, and no moral taint should be attached to a man so persuaded of the hallowed justice of his cause. Indeed, the experience greatly enhanced Milton's later works, especially in the description of Satan as a consummate political and military figure. Of the poet, Phelps-Morand concludes, "Though not Machiavellian in character, he could on occasion, for the Great Cause, stoop to Machiavellian means."[7]

Against this distasteful backdrop, Milton scholars a half-century later are still uneasy about acknowledging the influence of the poet's political career on his great works. Though many of these charges have been dismissed or defused by later studies, some slight stain yet discolors Milton's political activities; and it is feared perhaps that to identify them too closely with his poetry might taint it as well.[8] As a consequence scholars, apprehensive

---

6. S. B. Liljegren, *Studies in Milton.*

7. Phelps-Morand, *The Effects of His Political Life on Milton,* 8–9, 51.

8. The most persistent instance of that anxiety is the frequent insistence that the poet deliberately distanced himself from the Protectorate regime because of a distaste for its policies (*MG* 181–85). This book proposes that the period fed his imagination significantly.

about straying too far outside of the text itself, have been largely content to limit their inquiries to a comparison of the poetry and the prose in an effort to understand Milton's political philosophy. *Milton in Government* was conceived as a work designed to place Milton's political career in somewhat more favorable light; and the present work proposes that his poetry is not tainted, but enormously enriched, by the experience. Scholars, it is hoped, may once again address the influence of life on art without fear of thereby diminishing the art.

A Note on Sources

This book quotes liberally from Milton's prose works, both political and religious, cites extensively his experience in public office, and on occasion refers to his literary sources, but to the purpose only of illuminating the spiritual theme of his poetry, not of constructing a theory of his political philosophy, which many fine minds have already explored.[9]

The modern poet often adopts the stance of social critic, standing outside the established order to see it more clearly and draw attention to its flaws and inequities. Milton is an instance of a poet who played an important role within that order, as a public servant in the government of his country, one, moreover, who left a substantial body of prose articulating in extensive detail a body of political thought that evolved from that experience. He wrote these works in response to pressing historical events, the passage of the Licensing Act, the execution of Charles I, the concerted attacks on the legitimacy of the English Republic, and the impending election of a new Parliament in 1660, among others; and as a result these works are quite specific, vigorously polemic, and notably partisan in their expression of political allegiance.[10] Hence, the prose, like the sonnets, is for the most part

9. When the subject is raised, some names spring immediately to mind: Don M. Wolfe (*Milton in the Puritan Revolution*), Arthur Barker (*Milton and the Puritan Dilemma, 1641-1660*), and the several who contributed introductory essays to the Yale edition of his prose. Although I take issue with them in isolated matters, their works remain unchallenged monuments of Milton scholarship.

10. Scholars like David Loewenstein ("Milton and the Poetics of Defense") and James Grantham Turner ("The Poetics of Engagement") equate the artistic merit of Milton's political prose and poetry. As Loewenstein argues, "There is no divorce at all in his imagination between literary and political discourse" (184). Such studies must be applied with caution. In an altogether commendable effort to heighten our appreciation of the political works, they run

occasional; and to dispense with any discussion of those occasions is to limit both our understanding of their meaning and our appreciation of their achievement. The imagery of the great poems is assuredly drawn from that same experience but it surveys events from a loftier vantage, placing those two or three eventful decades within the grand sweep of cosmic history, and in the final books of *Paradise Lost* in the context of the sorry spectacle of human history. Milton views both of these histories from the perspective of his few decades, standing at a moment in vast time, looking to the past and to the future, interpreting their passage in terms of his own personal instant, in which he finds a microcosm of the cosmic struggle that he believes will prevail until the final day. He read history avidly and found in the past a confirmation of his judgment on his own time. He read Scripture with equal fervor and in the biblical vision of the future he found reason for hope despite the failure of his age to realize the New Jerusalem. He used both history and Scripture in all his works, but to different purposes. In the prose they bolster his argument, reflecting the thought of a politically committed man reacting to the historical moment. In the poetry they embellish that same man's vision of his moment's participation in eternity.

Milton's prose works are an indispensable source of information for what the poet *knew* about the political life of his time. *Eikonoklastes* and the two *Defences* offer a detailed survey of the clash of interests that precipitated the upheavals within the country, and the State Papers constitute a record of his knowledge of events on the wider stage of continental Europe. These works are, then, a rich storehouse of information for the chronicle of Milton's time *as he saw it,* knowledge on which he drew to narrate his vision of cosmic history.

The relationship between *Christian Doctrine* and *Paradise Lost* is another matter entirely, since they both survey the state of the human soul from its creation to its final destiny. But the two works were composed to different ends and employ distinctly different methods. Maurice Kelley draws attention to the distinctions between the two works, the one a "systematic theology," the other a "blank verse epic," but he is so intent on showing them as professing the same body of belief that he is reluctant to pursue the significance of their differences.[11] *Christian Doctrine* is an appeal to reason, its thought imparted in the language of logic. As many have noted, of

---

the risk of diminishing the poetry. The one is argument, the other art. Indeed, insofar as poetry indulges in argument, it is the less art.

11. Kelley, *This Great Argument,* 195-96.

Milton's prose works the one with which it shares the closest affinity in tone
and method is *The Art of Logic*. [12] Milton asserts, time and again, that divine
truth is accessible to anyone who will study the plain meaning of Scripture
and dismiss the sophistries of the theologians. God gave Man reason, and
then revealed as much of his nature as reason could comprehend; and so
much as he did reveal is entirely sufficient for salvation. In his rational
exposition of divine truth, Milton scorns those who pry into the mysteries of
the Christian faith. Forget about such matters, he counsels, just use your
head and you can save your soul. [13]

Paradise Lost, on the other hand, is a work of the imagination; hence it
operates under a different imperative entirely, engaging the dynamic of
poetic expression and appealing to a faculty of comprehension that tran-
scends pure reason. It can do more, it can say more, than a systematic
theology; it can touch deeper chords of our nature, sounding responses
from emotional and spiritual centers that reason has no access to. *Christian
Doctrine* attempts to explain God, *Paradise Lost* to justify him, and to do so
in more than the legal sense. It must satisfy an intuitive perception of justice,
one that when violated can excite pity, fear, and rage in the human breast.
The one, therefore, appeals to reason alone, the other to a reader's emotional and spiritual life as well. The treatise may throw light on the poem,
but it does not interpret it.

I do not personally subscribe to the grim view of the world that perceives
everything as political; but Milton seems to have detected a political dimension to most philosophical, theological, and social questions. These pages

12. For what is surely the earliest such observation, see William B. Hunter, "The Provenance of the *Christian Doctrine:* Addenda from the Bishop of Salisbury," in which Hunter
quotes the bishop to this effect in a work published in 1829 (205n). In a more recent
comment, Maurice Kelley observes that "the *De doctrina* is the presentation of this body
of belief in the manner of a systematic theology, and the principles that directed this
logical presentation are those detailed in Milton's *Artis Logicae*" (*This Great Argument* 195).
Kelley confirms the parallels anew in "The Provenance of John Milton's *Christian Doctrine,*"
154.

13. William B. Hunter has recently questioned the provenance of *Christian Doctrine,* a
position rejected by Barbara Lewalski and John Shawcross ("Provenance"). Gordon Campbell
joined the controversy with "The Authorship of *De Doctrina Christiana*" and Hunter returned
with "The Provenance of the *Christian Doctrine:* Addenda from the Bishop of Salisbury." The
argument continues in his "Animadversions upon the Remonstrants' Defenses against Burgess
and Hunter" and the replies of Christopher Hill ("Professor William B. Hunter, Bishop Burgess,
and John Milton") and Maurice Kelley ("The Provenance of John Milton's *Christian Doctrine*").
For reasons I have personally conveyed to Professor Hunter at some length, despite his many
misgivings I continue to accept the work as Milton's.

will address a number of subjects in his poetry that may seem to some readers marginally political at best: the Holy Spirit (Chapter 1), the Holy Trinity (Chapter 2), divine love (Chapter 4), the innocence of Adam and Eve (Chapter 5), the destruction of the world (Chapter 7), and the divinity of Christ (Chapter 8) – only Chapters 3 and 6 seem unreservedly political. This is not to claim resolution of any of these frequently contested questions about Milton's thought, but simply to add to the debate an ingredient too often missing: the poet's use of political imagery to define these abstractions and accommodate his spiritual message to temporal understanding.

The organization of *Divided Empire* is fairly straightforward. Chapter 1 introduces the method by examining analogies between the French monarchy and Milton's vision of cosmic rule. *Paradise Lost* offers five different patterns of governance, those in Heaven, Hell, Chaos, and the pre- and postlapsarian worlds. Chapter 2 examines Heaven; Chapter 3, Hell; Chapter 4 compares the two; and Chapter 5 addresses the political changes occasioned by the Fall. These are followed by a discussion of the imagery of cosmic conflict (Chapter 6), the political dimensions of Milton's apocalyptic vision (Chapter 7), and the spectacle of human governance figured in *Paradise Regained* and *Samson Agonistes* (Chapter 8).

The use of "Man," "Mankind," and similar gender-specific generic terms may cause some annoyance. I can only plead that I employ such terms as Milton does, and ask an appreciation of the difficulty of remaining entirely correct in such usage while discussing the political art of a seventeenth-century male and the political life of a nation governed entirely by men.

A Note on Documentation

This book draws on material developed at length in *Captain or Colonel* and *Milton in Government*. While mindful of the need to avoid reploughing ground already prepared, I am also conscious of the obligation to offer a complete and self-contained work; hence some restatement of that earlier material is unavoidable. To avoid troubling the reader with the need to juggle two other books in order to make sense of this one, I summarize the historical accounts in sufficient detail to illustrate the parallels between the experience and the poetry. For those desiring more thorough accounts, historical and interpretative passages are cross-referenced to the earlier volumes, "(*CC*)" to *Captain or Colonel* and "(*MG*)" to *Milton in Government.*

Of the two major editions of the prose, the Columbia volumes are cited as *Works* and the Yale as *Prose.*

Intertextual documentation is held to a minimum so as not to render unreadable pages already crowded with quotations. Use is restricted to the following:

1. The poetry, cited by book and line number from Merritt Y. Hughes, *Complete Poems and Major Prose.*
2. The State Papers, cited by reference to the numbers assigned them in *Works* and *Prose,* e.g., "(W1, P5)."
3. The prose other than the State Papers, cited by volume and page number in *Prose,* e.g., "(*Prose* 1:501)."
4. The aforementioned cross-references to *Captain or Colonel* and *Milton in Government.*

The premises of this book would seem at times to place it somewhat at odds with certain modern critical schools of thought, those, for example, which question authorial intent, textual integrity, and the influence of life on art, and especially those which read the political imagery as ideological testament. It is not my intent to quarrel with colleagues with whom I may disagree but for whom I have only the highest regard, some of whose studies have opened up the scholarship to valuable new insights. My chief concern in these pages is to address Milton's works from a perspective not formerly considered at such length, one that when taken in concert with other views, will further enhance our appreciation of the poet's imagination. Hence, textual reference to individual scholars and their works is reserved for those occasions when it serves to illustrate elements of the argument. Agreement or disagreement with current interpretation of Milton's political thought and imagery is, therefore, confined for the most part to footnotes.

I am indebted to a number of individuals and institutions for their encouragement and counsel at various stages of this journey. First, I thank Michael Lieb, who read the manuscript and lent the weight of his scholarship to its early aspirations. Next, I owe much to my good friend, James A. Butler, who stepped briefly out of his Romantic period, where his star shines so brightly, to offer his advice on several chapters. I am especially grateful to the scholars of the Milton Seminar, and in particular Joan Bennett and Susanne Woods, for their challenging response to my first airing of these thoughts. Lee Jacobus was kind enough to read and offer advice on critical sections;

and William Kerrigan has lent the stimulus of his wit and learning throughout. I wish also to acknowledge a debt of gratitude to my colleagues at La Salle for their generous support over two decades of my labors, and to Peter Potter and the staff of the Penn State Press both for their imaginative and meticulous production of these handsome volumes and for their encouragement during the years of composition.

1

THE IMAGE OF RULE

Milton's travels introduced him to a rich array of political structures. Passing through Louis XIII's France in 1638, he went on to Florence, firmly in the hands of the Medici dukes at the time; then to Rome, capital of the Papal States, a Catholic theocracy ruled by the pope; and to Naples, then a part of the kingdom of Spain. On his return he visited ancestral duchies in Ferrara and Milan; spent a month in Venice, ruled by a commercial oligarchy; and stopped in Geneva, a Protestant theocracy. It cannot be said, however, that the young Milton showed much interest in political matters, at least not according to the account of his travels in the *Second Defence of the English People*. He spent in all four months in Florence, a city he valued for "the elegance, not just of its tongue, but also of its wit," obviously more taken with its "private academies" than the public rule of the Medici or the memory of Machiavelli. Indeed, there is little evidence that he was attracted to political matters at all until the "sad tidings of civil war from England" caused him to curtail his European odyssey; and even then he took six months to reach home (*Prose* 4:615-20). During those early years of idealism and innocence, he was far more concerned with the pursuit of knowledge, the cause of religion, the delights of art and poetry, and the pleasures of society, than he was with the intrigues of magistrates, the tedious wrangling of senators, or the decrees of kings.

The decade to follow forced such matters upon him, however, interrupting his plans for quiet study and the slow maturing of his poetic art. The public debate over church government drew him into the pamphlet war; and later he imagined for a moment the real one, that fought by captains and colonels, reaching to his very doorstep. These intrusions turned his mind to the cause of freedom, forcing him to forgo for a time the delights of art, though even here politics was not a central concern. Of the three "varieties of Liberty" that occupied his thoughts, only the first two, "ecclesiastical" and "domestic," engaged his pen. He did "not touch upon" civil liberty, he observes, until a revolutionary tribunal brought Charles I to trial and condemned him to death (*Prose* 4:626).

Up till then, Milton's thought had only hovered around the edge of politics. *Areopagitica* is addressed to the government, of course, one which Milton praises as "mild, and free, and human" (*Prose* 2:559), and it is eloquent in its argument for pluralism; but it is not a political document as Milton used the word, that is, a discourse on "the beginning, end, and reasons of politicall societies" (*Prose* 2:398). It is a theoretical defense of freedom of the press as opposed to the licensing of books, a form of censorship imposed in one way or another by virtually every government of the time, whatever its form. The work is valued for its persuasive plea for diversity and its affirmation of individual conscience, not for whatever small insights it might offer regarding the poet's views on government or the issues dividing the country at the time. As noted, Milton himself identified the work as a defense of "domestic" rather than "civil" liberty (5:624-26). *Of Education* was influenced, of course, by the conflict raging about the poet, which doubtless induced him to define "a compleate and generous Education" as "that which fits a man to perform . . . all the offices both private and publicke of peace and war" (*Prose* 2:378-79); but the tract devotes little space to the issues driving that conflict.

Milton's writings later in the decade have a more immediate focus, to be sure. He composed *The Character of the Long Parliament,* most probably in 1648, as part of *The History of Britain,* from which it was later excised, not to appear until after his death.[1] It is an impassioned cry of frustration at the political divisions and public corruption that have prevented the nation from reaping the harvest of that vast expense of blood and treasure. He is as yet distant from the fray, however, examining that failure in the context of ancient events, comparing it to the inability of fifth-century Britons to assert their independence after the departure of the Romans (*Prose* 5:443). The sonnet to Fairfax, composed at about the same time, echoes his frustration at that same failure and subtly proposes that the commander in chief of the New Model Army do something to rescue the cause. This is not to say that he was unconcerned with the political life of his nation, of which he was certainly aware, but that it failed to move his pen to practical matters of governance. He was an outsider looking in, one who had an interest surely in the public controversies of his day, read of them with some disquiet, and made useful entries in his commonplace book; but when public affairs were thrust upon him by the force of events, he responded in an abstract vein, writing of church matters, of education, of freedom of expression, and of his discontent that things had not worked out as he had hoped.

Had Milton, during these years, pursued his earlier intent to write an Arthuriad, one wonders what shape the epic poem might have taken. It would have been embellished, perhaps, with scenes of domestic tension; and certainly the passages of armed conflict would have been enhanced by the poet's experience with the uncertainties of war and the accounts he heard of battles won and lost; but would the work have been enriched by the spectacle of public figures engaged in the art of governance, or animated by the language of royal compliment and parliamentary debate, the careful rhetoric of league and alliance, and the peremptory pitch of edict and decree?

One would think not. That rich imagery is the legacy of a decade of public service. If John Milton became a "profoundly *political* animal," to use Christopher Hill's provocative phrase, it was the consequence of laboring for years close to the centers of power of the English Republic.[2] The

---

1. Nicholas Von Maltzahn proposes that the *Character* and the first four chapters of the *History* were composed during the six-week period 1 February–15 March 1649 (*Milton's "History of Britain"* 22–48). Austin Woolrych argues against that period for the *History*, and proposes for the *Character* rather some time in early 1660 ("Debate" 942–43). French Fogle, who edited the work for the Yale edition, makes an altogether convincing case for the traditional dating of the composition of the *Character* and the major part of the *History* in the spring of 1648 (*Prose* 426–33).

2. Hill, *Milton and the English Revolution,* 199. Hill suggests that Milton was influenced in his radical political views by his familiarity "with the tavern society" of London (98). Perhaps.

execution of Charles I ushered in the rule of that regime and thrust Milton into the political arena. He was appointed Secretary for Foreign Languages to the revolutionary government in March 1649, and affairs of state became the focus of his thought and energies for the next eleven years. His involvement in treaty negotiations brought him into direct contact with the representatives of a further variety of governments: monarchies (Portugal, Denmark, Spain, Sweden), a minor German county (Oldenburg), and a new republic (United Netherlands). Further, his official letters were addressed to city senates (Hamburg, Bremen), North African potentates (Tetuan, Algiers), a German landgrave, a Transylvanian prince, and a Russian czar.

We may add to this array his experience in his own government during the Interregnum. It was a time of political searching and experiment, as England's revolutionary leaders struggled to fashion an alternative to the traditional monarchy; and the poet found himself performing his public duties under a variety of structures, a Commonwealth in which both executive and legislative power resided in the Parliament, a Protectorate in which the executive was entrusted to a single strong person, and the direct rule of the military for several short intervals, in 1653, 1659, and 1660, when the New Model Army took temporary control of the state. During the Interregnum, then, the poet either experienced or gained knowledge of a rich variety of governing bodies, any number of which could have suggested a pattern for the realms of his great poems.

France and the Kingdoms of the Imagination

From the evidence of *Paradise Lost*, it would appear that of these many political structures, the one that left the strongest impression on his imagination was the French monarchy; and a vivid instance of the relationship between the poet's political experience and the shape of his art may be seen in the parallels between the ruling body of France and the several governments of his later poems.

During the decade of the 1650s, the kingdom of France gave every outward appearance of a nation governed by co-rulers; or so it must have seemed to Milton, at least, who was responsible for preparing the official

---

I would only argue that his experience in government had a more profound influence on his poetry.

correspondence between those rulers and the Lord Protectors of England from 1655 until 1659. On the death of his father in 1643, the five-year-old dauphin became Louis XIV of France. The queen mother, Anne of Austria, assumed power as regent during his minority; but in practice she entrusted the reins of government to her able chief minister, Cardinal Jules Mazarin. In keeping with tradition, when Louis reached the age of thirteen in 1651, he ended the regency; and he celebrated his coronation three years later. During all of these years, however, save for some months of exile during the period of civil conflict known as the Fronde, Mazarin exercised the power of the throne, and indeed continued to do so until his death in 1661. Hence, the protocol of the time required that any letter to the king, who was titular head-of-state, be accompanied by another to the cardinal, who would act on the matter in any event. Milton's thirty-one letters to France, preserved in the seventeenth-century manuscripts of his state papers, include eight pairs of these companion letters; and there is clear evidence that he prepared considerably more than that number (*MG* 151-60). The poet apparently found in the unique pattern of co-rulers in that nation a useful paradigm for the various realms of *Paradise Lost,* in which the political imagery follows, at least outwardly, a like pattern of power-sharing. In brief, all four of the poem's realms, Heaven, Hell, Chaos, and Earth, are similarly governed.

Milton describes a Heaven ruled by two kings. God so presides, of course, but the Son does as well, once he is declared "to be Heir and to be King" (6:708). They reign together, "God and *Messiah* his anointed King" (6:718, 5:664, 6:43), seated on separate thrones, toward which the loyal angels bow with equal reverence, casting their crowns "to the ground / With solemn adoration" (3:350-51). Milton employs this political oxymoron, the Son as both heir and king at once, to brighten the otherwise unpromising prospects of the heir to an immortal father, though somewhat similar arrangements are not unknown in human experience. During his minority, Louis XIV was indeed king, but it may be said that he was only heir to the power of the throne, which was exercised by Mazarin. In Heaven, however, the Son is not kept waiting: "all Power / I give thee," the Father declares, "reign for ever, and assume / Thy Merits" (3:317-19).

The pattern prevails in Hell, where Satan aspires to reign – a goal "worth ambition" (1:262), as he puts it – but his aspirations do not go unchallenged. At the gates of Hell, a crowned apparition confronts him, one who asserts his own right to the throne. Hell is a place, Death proclaims, "Where I reign King, and to enrage thee more, / Thy King and Lord" (2:698-99). The two prepare for armed combat to settle the matter, only to have Sin intervene and disclose their relationship. The issue, therefore, is left unresolved, temporarily leaving Hell a realm with two kings as well.

There are also co-rulers in Chaos, "where eldest *Night* / And *Chaos,* Ancestors of Nature, hold / Eternal Anarchy" (2:894-96). Beside that allegorical monarch "Enthron'd / Sat Sable-vested *Night,* eldest of things, / The Consort of his Reign" (2:961-63), "Consort" here meaning "a colleague in office or authority," without any implication of gender (the *OED* cites these lines as example). Satan addresses the two as equals (2:970) and promises that on his victory he will return the World to their realm, so that they may "once more / Erect the Standard there of *ancient Night*" (2:986).

On Earth, before the Fall at least, Adam and Eve, as "Mankind," rule as equals; according to Raphael, God intends them both to

> fill the Earth,
> Subdue it, and throughout Dominion hold
> Over Fish of the Sea, and Fowl of the Air,
> And every living thing that moves on the Earth.
> (7:531-33)

Adam recalls that at his birth the Creator entrusted the Earth to him and his race: "as Lords / Possess it, and all things that therein live" (8:338-40). Adam and Eve, as "Lords" of the Earth, then, share equally the authority bestowed upon them by God.

Hence, to all outward appearances the various realms of *Paradise Lost* have co-rulers. The actual exercise of power, however, is another matter entirely, for Milton provides further features of these realms which modify the political imagery of the poem, bringing it closer to his readers' experience. The word "modify" is most apposite here. Any ruling body, whatever its constitutional basis, is subject to internal dynamics – family relationships, the vicissitudes of health and age, the rise and fall of trusted counselors – which alter its character in time and modify the image it presents to the world. The presence of such factors in Milton's governments does not "contradict" or "subvert" or "compromise" the image of co-rulers; they complete the figures, adapting them to a reader's sense of reality.

Milton adopts additional characteristics of the French monarchy to accommodate his political structures to human understanding. Ruth Kleinman, in her biography of Anne of Austria, describes the relationship between the queen regent and her chief minister as something more than official. Kleinman dismisses the conjecture that the two were married, though this was not an impossibility as Mazarin was never ordained. Certainly, any public declaration of marriage would have forced him to lay aside his cardinal's robes, however, and he never did. Not so lightly dismissed, however, is the evidence that there was a close emotional bond between them. On the basis of Anne's letters to Mazarin, Kleinman is persuaded that "she loved him," and his to her are equally suggestive.[3] As a consequence, Kleinman concludes, "the relationship created a strong spiritual bond, the equivalent of a family bond, between Mazarin, Anne, and her son. On this fabric Mazarin and Anne built their idyll of mutual affection: godparent and parent were united in a common obligation to protect the interests of the young king."[4] It was a bond, moreover, that prevailed until the cardinal's death.

Of particular interest is the effect of this relationship on the young king. Historians agree that during the years of his minority Louis demonstrated a genuine affection for Mazarin, to whom he deferred not only in state affairs but in personal matters as well. Though officially only Louis's godfather, because of his intimacy with the mother, the cardinal assumed a paternal role in the fatherless boy's life.[5] When Mazarin returned from exile after the Fronde, Anne and he resumed control of the monarchy, and, as Kleinman puts it, "the family triumvirate was once again complete, with godfather, mother, and son reunited."[6] After Louis's coronation the cardinal continued to exercise the power of the throne, as Milton's companion letters confirm; and the queen, while content to remain in the background of affairs, retained a significant voice in affairs. Of the relationship, Kleinman observes, "They acted like a family because they were a family."[7]

Such was the state of the French monarchy during the years when one of Milton's primary functions was the preparation of letters to France; indeed the thirty-one to that country preserved in the early manuscripts far exceed in number those to any other single state – and he was doubtless responsible for more (*MG* 156-60, 264-65). Since over half were addressed in pairs to Louis XIV and Mazarin, Milton was well aware of the power-sharing arrangement within the monarchy; and no one so directly engaged in that correspondence could have been ignorant of the queen's influence with the cardinal and the king, though it would have been altogether inappropriate

---

3. Kleinman, *Anne of Austria, Queen of France,* 226-31.
4. Ibid., 232.
5. Ibid., 230. See also Pierre Gaxotte, *The Age of Louis XIV,* 5. W. H. Lewis takes a somewhat different view in *The Splendid Century,* 7.
6. Kleinman, *Anne of Austria,* 243.
7. Ibid., 230.

to take official notice of it after the coronation. It was essential that the inner circles of the English government understand where the real power lay at a time when the two nations were involved in highly secret negotiations for an alliance; and they had ample intelligence sources at their disposal, among them the reports of René Augier, Parliament's agent in Paris until 1650 and thereafter an assistant to the Secretary of State, and, upon Augier's dismissal in 1655, any number of John Thurloe's intricate web of informants (*MG* 248).

In three of the four realms of *Paradise Lost,* the image of co-rulers is similarly modified by a family relationship (in Chaos alone none is stated or implied). In Heaven and Hell the two are father and son, on Earth husband and wife. Of course, Milton is following Christian tradition in his description of both the celestial Father and Son and the terrestrial Adam and Eve, hence the general pattern of these relationships was probably not inspired by the French arrangement; but the internal dynamics of the French monarchy accorded so well with the biblical model in this regard – and, as we shall see, in other respects as well – that Milton surely found the parallels highly suggestive. It is an instance in which the earthly experience follows the celestial pattern so closely that it may be taken as a significant factor in the shaping of his art.

Without entering here into the controversy over Milton's Arianism,[8] it may be said that in passages wherein the Father and Son appear together, the latter is in every way a model of deference to a senior figure, praising his qualities, respecting his authority, obeying his orders to the letter, and everywhere rejoicing in what is to all appearances a subordinate role in the hierarchy. Their relative status is reflected in the manner of the Son's address, "O Father, O supreme of heav'nly Thrones, / First, Highest, Holiest, Best" (6:723-24) and in angelic hymns to the pair, in which the Son is said to sit "Second" to God (3:409). The Son's status is not static, however; he rises in the estimation of the community of Heaven after his conquest of the rebel angels, for which he is "sung Victorious King, / Son, Heir, and Lord, to him Dominion giv'n, / Worthiest to Reign" (6:886-88), and after his offer to die for Man, upon which God commands the Heavenly host to "Adore him, who to compass all this dies, / Adore the Son, and honor him as mee" (3:342-43). He is, then, King and Lord but at the same time very much Son and Heir.

Although the question of who reigns in Hell is left unresolved at the infernal gates, after Satan's conquest of Earth his status is much enhanced

8. See pages 42-53.

and Death's comparably diminished. The son never acknowledges the father, however – indeed never speaks to, or of, him after their initial encounter – and it is Sin who defines the relationship. She addresses Satan as their "Parent" (10:354) and as "our great Author" who labors for "his offspring dear" (10:236-38), but refers to Death simply as the "Second of *Satan* sprung" (10:591). After that first encounter with his father, Death is for his part so much a slave to his appetite as to little care about dynastic matters:

> To mee, who with eternal Famine pine,
> Alike is Hell, or Paradise, or Heaven.
> There best, where most with ravin I may meet.
> (10:597-99)

He is, in brief, clearly unfit to rule. Thus, whereas the Son in Heaven rises to be honored as king and lord, the son in Hell, who at first claims to be king, is diminished to the status of a sullen "offspring."

Milton characterizes Adam and Eve as husband and wife in keeping with his definition of marriage in *Christian Doctrine:* "a very intimate relationship between man and woman instituted by God for the procreation of children or the help and solace of life" (*Prose* 6:355). They are, as we have seen, co-rulers of the new world, but the family relationship again modifies that status. Milton states clearly that, though "Lords of all," they are in fact "Not equal" (4:290-96); and he goes on to describe the difference in their appearance in terms of a hierarchy of authority. Adam's "fair large Front and Eye sublime declar'd / Absolute rule," whereas Eve's "golden tresses . . . impli'd / Subjection" (4:300-308). As Diane McColley has shown, many passages in *Paradise Lost* emphasize the equality of the two, but the political imagery modifies the relationship, accommodating it to one more traditional in Milton's time and culture.[9] When Raphael appears, Adam goes forth to

9. McColley, *Milton's Eve*, 35, 57. As she puts it "Milton gives Eve equal work, equal talent, and equal opportunity for growth and accomplishment" (129).

McColley proposes, as have others, that the reader first sees the pair through Satan's eyes, hence that their appearance and the characterization of their relationship, "Hee for God only, shee for God in him" (4:288), are not to be trusted. Joseph Wittreich echoes this mistrust in *Feminist Milton*, 86. The entire episode, however, including the view of Eden before the appearance of Adam and Eve and their conversation thereafter, is told from Satan's point of view (4:131-535). We are not free to pluck one phrase out of a passage of over four hundred lines and question its veracity alone, ignoring the rest. It seems unlikely that Milton would have intended the reader's first encounter with Eden and our first parents in the poem to be a false one.

The argument focuses on the ambiguity of the word "seem'd" (4:296). Milton employs the greet God's envoy while Eve retires to prepare an appropriate repast and welcome them later at the entrance to her "Silvan Lodge" (5:377).

The family relationship does not compromise the prelapsarian power-sharing arrangement, however, for though Adam and Eve have distinct roles, he does not rule her, nor does she him.[10] Eve's proposal that they work at separate tasks, had it not resulted in the Fall, would have strengthened the image of co-rulers. The terms of the debate over the issue emphasize their equality. Eve does not pose the question as a petitioner requesting permission to go her own way, which if Adam were to refuse, would certainly alter the relationship. Rather, she raises the issue as one that affects them both: "Let us divide our labors" (9:214), she advises, and the ensuing discussion takes the form of an honest disagreement over working conditions, which once resolved would establish an important precedent for the race, a governing principle for succeeding generations. In the end, they agree, though Adam, admittedly, with some reluctance. The effect is the same, to be sure – she leaves his side – but they arrive at the decision jointly; the debate does not place their equality in question.[11]

Yet another feature of the realms of *Paradise Lost* modifies the image of co-rulers and further identifies them with the French monarchy: each of the governments of Milton's imagination includes a third figure, constituting them essentially as triumvirates. The relative authority of the three figures in France shifted subtly over time. Initially, Anne as queen regent embodied the power of the throne, while Mazarin as her chief minister exercised that power and the boy king served largely as a ceremonial figure. As he grew to

---

same word but a few lines earlier, however, where there would seem to be no ambiguity about its meaning: Adam and Eve are indeed "Lords of all" and entirely "worthy"; and "the image of thir glorious Maker" does indeed shine in them (4:291-93). If Satan's eyesight is entirely reliable in these matters, one must wonder why it should suddenly falter for that brief moment and see them as other than they are.

Eve echoes the line in a later passage: "both have sinn'd, but thou / Against God only, I against God and thee" (10:930-31). Unless one would argue that her judgment is as impaired as Satan's, the phrase "Hee for God only, shee for God in him" must be accepted as a valid characterization of their relationship.

10. Richard Hardin observes that "Paradise is less a monarchy than an aristocracy of two with Adam as *Primus inter pares*" (*Civil Idolatry* 183). In an interesting turn of history, some fourteen years after Milton's death co-rulers mounted the throne of England. William III and Mary II reigned jointly from 1688 until her death in 1695, though it was agreed that the administration of the kingdom was "vested in him for life" (Henri and Barbara Van der Zee, *William and Mary*, 272).

11. As Diane McColley observes, the two engage in a "political debate," one whose "resolution in Eve's moral freedom, is part of the prelapsarian process of working out the government of the human race" (*A Gust for Paradise* 164, 168).

manhood, however, Louis assumed a more active role in affairs and his mother receded into the background of the monarchy. During this transition, Mazarin's authority remained relatively constant, as he adroitly adjusted his office to changing circumstances, at first serving the queen regent and later the king, who remained devoted to him.[12] All the while the three remained a closely knit "family," as Ruth Kleinman puts it, a "triumvirate" at the helm of state.[13]

In *Paradise Lost* this pattern is duplicated, obviously, in the Holy Trinity of Heaven and the unholy one in Hell. And then also, while Chaos and "Sable-vested *Night*" preside over the affairs of their realm, it is a comparably allegorical figure, "high Arbiter / *Chance*" who, as Milton puts it, "governs all" (2:909-10). Their separate roles are not defined, but one can speculate that Chaos acts as titular head and spokesman for a regime that reigns over the realm of "old *Night*" while it is perhaps Chance who "imbroils the fray" (2:908) by which they rule.

As we have seen, the dynamics of the ruling bodies of Heaven and Hell change as well, with the rise in the prestige of the Son most closely approximating the enhanced status of Louis XIV as he grew older. But nowhere is this change more dramatic or more significant than in the shifting relationships among the members of the triumvirate on Earth. That body is not so clearly defined as the others in the poem and indeed seems more distant than they from practical political experience in that it is composed of both natural and supernatural beings: man, woman, and God. The presence of those other trios, however, serves to validate the image in whose changes Milton embodies an essential message for his Christian readers. God, though he designates Adam and Eve as lords of the Earth, makes it clear from the outset that they hold that dignity only as a gift from him. "This new created World" is an "addition of his Empire" (7:554-55) and the first couple rules it only as "chief / Of all his works" (5:515-16). It is significant that, although Adam and Eve "as Lords / Possess" (8:339-40) the World and "throughout Dominion hold" (7:532) over it, they rule only as surrogates of the Deity, who in that sense constitutes the third person of the earthly triumvirate. God, it seems, plans to be an active member of the prelapsarian ruling body. Raphael promises that he will "deign / To visit oft

12. As Batista Nani, the Venetian ambassador, reported, "all his affection seems to go to the Cardinal.... It must be confessed that there is a profound sympathy and submission of spirit and intelligence which incline a great prince to depend on the genius of a particular man.... He sees him several times each day" (Philipe Erlanger, *Louis XIV*, 100).

13. Kleinman, *Anne of Austria*, 230, 243.

the dwellings of just Men" and send his angels as emissaries for "frequent intercourse" (7:569-71) with the race.

The changes wrought by the Fall are dramatic, for in political terms the equality of man and woman is shattered and the triumvirate dissolved. At the cosmic level, God recalls the angelic guards, to that time the most tangible evidence of his participation in the rule of Earth, raises the celestial stairs (3:519-21), and expels Adam and Eve from Eden. God withdraws, not his love, but certainly his presence from the terrestrial realm; and although in the future, "On high behest his Angels to and fro" will pass between Heaven and Earth (3:534), Man will henceforth be deprived of "His blessed count'nance" (11:317), which to behold was for Adam the "highth / of happiness" (10:724-25). Michael comforts Adam with the assurance that "God is as here, . . . still compassing thee round / With goodness and paternal Love" (11:350-53); he will, however, no longer "visit oft the dwellings of just men" (7:570), but be known to them only as an insubstantial "Omnipresence" (11:336). As instructed, Michael secures Eden, which remains under divine protection, a celestial foothold in a world that God surrenders to the rule of Satan and his legions.[14] Eve must henceforth submit to her "Husband's will" (10:195-96), and he is left to deal with the forces of evil as the much diminished and now solitary "Lord" of the Earth.

There is yet another feature of the triumvirate regimes of *Paradise Lost* which identifies them closely with the French monarchy; in the reigning trinities of the poem the third figure is described, at times unambiguously, at others obliquely, as female. History and literature abound with accounts of queens who struggle for autonomy, such as the glorious Eleanor of Aquitaine, whose defiance of Henry II earned her sixteen years of imprisonment, and those who exercise their royal authority to the full, like Shakespeare's wrathful Margaret, who rallies the House of Lancaster while Henry VI mopes about his castle. Milton seems to have preferred the more traditional example of Anne of Austria, who during the years when he was responsible for the preparation of companion letters to Louis XIV and Mazarin, remained an important factor in the government because of the close family ties among the three, but was content to stay somewhat in the shadow of the ruling pair.

The obvious example of a female presence in the triumvirates of *Paradise Lost* is, of course, Sin, who illustrates a quality of those third figures, who,

---

14. See Fallon, *Captain or Colonel,* 145-49, for the postlapsarian status of Eden as a political image.

though part of the ruling body, are satisfied, like Queen Anne, to remain for the most part in the background of affairs. Sin never asserts a claim to the status of wife, consort, or queen, content throughout to be Satan's daughter, revering him ever as her "Parent." In Chaos the third person is Chance; and though Milton nowhere associates that figure with either gender, the impersonal forces perceived as presiding over human affairs are traditionally depicted as female, from the Fates of Greece and Rome, to Dame Fortune of Milton's time, to Lady Luck of our own. It is not too much to say that in the imagination of John Milton and his contemporaries, Chance was such a figure.[15]

When one turns to Heaven, the image is not so clear, for though in his chapter on the Holy Spirit in *Christian Doctrine* Milton consistently refers to the celestial third person with the masculine pronoun, some scholars are persuaded that in *Paradise Lost* the figure is female. This impression derives from an intermediate identification, the assumption that Milton conceived of his inspiration, that is, his muse, as the Holy Spirit. William B. Hunter and Stevie Davies present the case for such an identification. They argue for a trinity of muses, the Father, Son, and Holy Spirit, appearing in different invocations of *Paradise Lost,* the third person most prominently in those to books 7 and 9. Citing Milton's qualification, "The meaning not the Name I call" (7:5), they identify Urania as the Holy Spirit and propose that when the poet explicitly refers to his muse as female in the invocation to book 9, "my Celestial Patroness" (9:21), we are exposed to his true sentiments on the matter. As they note, "Although in Christian tradition the Spirit is ordinarily understood as, or assumed to be, masculine, a substantial tradition exists that associates this person of the Trinity with the feminine gender and more expressly with a mother-principle in the deity."[16]

The argument is persuasive, leaving the distinct impression that the third person of Milton's celestial Trinity is a female figure, sharing power with the two kings but not openly exercising it, in a manner similar to the other

15. Neither "Fortune" nor "Luck" appear in *Paradise Lost.* Milton does not assign genders to any of these abstract forces in the poem. In one instance, "but strict Fate had cast too deep / Her dark foundations," the pronoun, though ambiguous, probably refers to Hell (6:867-70). It is of interest to note that all the realms of *Paradise Lost* are feminine, Heaven (7:499), Hell (2:176), Earth (7:242), and Chaos (2:1038-39). The issue is somewhat complicated in the case of Chaos, however, by an occasional masculine reference to its allegorical ruler of the same name (6:871-73, 10:416-18).

16. William B. Hunter and Stevie Davies. "Milton's Urania: 'The Meaning, Not the Name I Call,' " 32.

triumvirates and much like the role of the queen mother in France during the 1650s.[17]

Earth's triumvirate includes Eve, of course; but God withdraws as a consequence of the Fall, to be replaced after the Resurrection by the Holy Spirit, whose gender on Earth is entirely ambiguous, perhaps deliberately so for Milton's purposes, since the ruling trinity there already includes a female. Although Michael's characterization of the third person as a "Comforter" might imply a feminine identity, its role as armorer of Man's spirit against Satan's "fiery darts" has a more masculine flavor. Hence, despite significant reasons to believe that Milton thought of the third person of the Holy Trinity as female, we can only conclude that he considered the Pentecostal spirit as gender neutral.

These striking parallels prevailing among the various realms of *Paradise Lost* leave the unmistakable impression that Milton conceived of a cosmos informed by a unifying order, a single governing principle stamped upon creation by the hand of God, mute evidence of his presence throughout. In Milton's teleological design all things *are* God, and all created things brought into being *ex Deo;* and the poet, it appears, was enough a creature of his age to feel that all existence, created and uncreated, should somehow reflect its participation in the Divine Being, even to the imagined structures of cosmic governance.

This impression of a single governing principle is confirmed by the hierarchical pattern of the cosmic courts. Although Milton's vision of the ruling bodies of his realms owed much to his knowledge of the French monarchy, the model for his court hierarchy lay elsewhere entirely, in the complex numerology of the medieval system of cosmic order, the Chain of Being, most familiarly exemplified by the intricate structure of Dante's *Comedia* with its meticulous arrangement of the universe into threes, nines, and tens.[18] According to this doctrine, God ruled over a universe of nine spheres, the seven known planets, the stars, and the *primum mobile,* though some accounts include a tenth, the Crystalline. In the medieval synthesis, this model was duplicated throughout the Chain of Being in a series of correspondences reflecting the indelible mark of the Deity, even to the political structures of human society. The Tudor monarchs adapted the scheme to their own political ends, most familiarly in the representation of

17. I am indebted to my manuscript editor, Andrew Lewis, who informs me that the Holy Spirit is grammatically feminine in Aramaic.

18. See, e.g., canto 11 of the *Inferno,* where Virgil explains the complex structure of Hell (*Divine Comedy* 1:145-51), and cantos 1 and 2 of the *Paradiso,* where Beatrice describes the order of the universe (*Divine Comedy* 3:23-25, 39-40).

Elizabeth I presiding, as the *primum mobile,* over a sphere of fixed stars among which shine her nobles, heroes, and councilors, below which come seven more, naming the exemplary qualities that mark her as a queen fit to reign.

This model may be seen in Milton's Heaven, where the angels observe a protocol as elaborate as any prevailing in the courts of seventeenth-century Europe. London, Paris, and the papal court of Rome, to mention only capital cities that the poet visited, were the scenes of courts populated by a colorful array of greater and lesser nobility, whose behavior toward one another was governed by a protocol determined by wealth, lineage, power, and proximity to the throne. Robert West observes that though Milton is imprecise in defining the order of the angels, he makes reference in *Paradise Lost* to the traditional eight degrees – seraphim, cherabim, thrones, dominations, virtues, powers, principalities, and angels. The absence of archangel from the list, West explains, arises from Milton's use of the term, not as a degree but as an "office" or function. Of the four figures referred to as "archangel" – Michael, Raphael, Uriel, and Satan – the three good angels are so designated when they are sent on specific missions, at which times they conform closely to the literal meaning of the word, as "chief messengers" of God.[19] When one adds the Godhead to the eight orders, the sum is the mystical nine; and when it is considered that Heaven has two kings, the result is ten, symbolic of completion and perfection.

This same hierarchy prevails in Hell, where Satan appeals to "the fixt Laws of Heav'n" to reconstitute political order in the demonic realm (2:18-19). He addresses his followers with the same honorifics, "Thrones, Dominations, Princedoms, Virtues, Powers" (10:460); sits in consultation with "The Great Seraphic Lords and Cherubim" (1:794); and returns to Hell disguised as a member of the lowest order, a "Plebian Angel" (10:460). Satan presides over this hierarchy as the ninth order, and initially at least Death's claim that he is "King" completes the sum, once again, to ten. This translation of the Heavenly orders to Hell would seem a natural narrative development and would not draw notice were it not for the fact that Milton duplicated the numerical pattern in that other metaphysical realm of *Paradise Lost,* a

19. West, *Milton and the Angels,* 47. West offers a detailed analysis of the hierarchy (132-36) and summarizes Milton's practice as follows: "In writing angelological passages in *Paradise Lost,* Milton was never controlled first by considerations of the 'science'; his lines on angels are always poetic fiction before they are angelology, and in them doctrine, conjecture, and fancy coalesce in equal authority as poetic fiction, though separately they remain of very unequal weight as angelology" (180).

kingdom of his own devising, whose ruling structure could have taken on any number of alternate shapes. There the co-rulers, *"Chaos* and *ancient Night,"* preside over a court attended by a similar hierarchy of eight: Orcus, Ades, Demogorgon, Rumor, Chance, Tumult, Confusion, and Discord (2:964–70). It seems evident, in brief, that the cosmic pattern of governance was a matter of conscious design on the poet's part.

Eden has no such display of political hierarchy, since within the time frame of *Paradise Lost* its population never exceeds two; but in keeping with the cosmic pattern prelapsarian rule may well have mirrored Heaven, had its lords not sinned. Michael tells Adam that Eden would have been

> Perhaps thy Capital Seat, from whence had spread
> All generations, and had hither come
> From all the ends of th' Earth, to celebrate
> And reverence thee thir great Progenitor.
>
> (11:343-46)

In time, of course, the earthly courts did assume that same design, evolving into the elaborate pattern of Renaissance rule with a king attended by a hierarchy of nobility, dukes, earls, viscounts, knights, and "plebian" subjects.

When the actions of men or angels precipitate a departure from this divine order, there are dire consequences. When Satan challenges the dual monarchy of Heaven, and in consequence the ruling Trinity, threatening to replace it with himself as *single* ruler, he and his followers are banished to Hell. Adam violates the design when he submits to the will of Eve and as a result must rule alone for a time without the tangible presence of God, supported only by a wife who as punishment for her sin must thereafter be submissive to his will. He is the much diminished solitary lord of an enslaved and corrupted planet to be populated in time by a race the spectacle of whose depravity Michael reveals to him. Deviation from the governing principle is, moreover, a mark of distance from God's favor. Satan returns to Hell as its sole "Emperor" (10:429), having cast all opposition into shadow by the success of his exploits. He effectively dissolves the triumvirate in Hell by enticing Sin and Death to leave the realm, occupy Earth, and reign there as his "Substitutes" (10:403), thereby adroitly disposing of the only other claimant to the throne. The rule of Satan in Hell, then, persists as a defiant departure from the cosmic order, with comparably grave consequences. The infernal triad is often described as a parody of the one in Heaven, an interpretation called somewhat into question by the political imagery of the poems. Satan's regime in Hell is indeed a mockery, not, however, in its imitation of the rule of God, but in its deviation from the power-sharing design of the cosmic trinities. In his obdurate violation of that pattern, he becomes the undisputed ruler over a kingdom of pain and darkness, one doomed in time to fail.[20]

Whenever such deviations occur, forces are soon set in motion to restore the design according to the governing principle of the cosmic plan. The disruption of the triumvirate on Earth provides a vivid example. Prior to the Fall, as we have seen, God, man, and woman form a trinity of political authority presiding over the terrestrial domain, with the Deity ruling that "addition of his Empire" from his celestial throne, operating through his vicegerent creatures, Adam and Eve. When that order is shattered by Man's disobedience, it is quickly replaced by one of like design. Satan, now the great "Emperor" of Hell, rules Earth through his vicegerent "offspring," Death and Sin, who, like the deposed pair, are male and female. Thus, through no conscious design of the Devil, the divinely conceived trinity is replaced with its demonic equivalent.

This unholy triumvirate will exercise unrestrained control on Earth so long as Adam remains the solitary lord of an enslaved race; but his harsh condition is contrary to the cosmic order and, as Michael tells Adam, inimical to the divine intent, hence not destined to last. In time the rule of the demonic trinity on Earth will be opposed by a comparable triumvirate, reconstituted when God rejoins the race in the form of a man. His coming will renew the authority of Adam's progeny and restore the dignity of woman, since in the scheme of things a second Eve is to become the vessel of the seed whose "Sire [is] / The Power of the most High" (12:368-69). Although the Messiah will return to his throne above after his Resurrection, the terrestrial triumvirate will prevail when Heaven's third person joins man and woman as Earth's third person, "a Comforter . . . who shall dwell / His Spirit within them" and arm them "with spiritual Armor, able to resist / *Satan's* assaults" (12:486-92).

---

20. In *CC* 168-72, I argue against the parodic reading. It may not escape notice that my views on the Holy Spirit have changed somewhat, as a result of mature reflection (170).

A Handmaid to Truth

The parallels between the French monarchy and the realms of *Paradise Lost* are not analogous in every detail, of course, nor do we expect them to be. As Milton himself observed, "who would claim that things which are analogous must correspond to each other in every respect?" (*Prose* 6:547). The creative imagination, although retaining the larger contours of the original inspiration, molds and shapes its materials to meet the immediate needs of the narrative. Hence, none of these governing bodies agrees in all respects with the triumvirate in Paris, nor does any one faithfully mirror the others. Sin and Death, for example, do not participate in the governance of Hell, nor does the Holy Spirit in Heaven; and in Chaos, Chance, who as part of the triumvirate "governs all," is also listed in the court's lesser hierarchy, reappearing there to achieve the necessary eight attendants on the king (2:965). In Heaven the co-rulers are male figures, on Earth man and woman, and in France man and boy. One could go on.

A great deal of modern commentary dwells on such differences, depending on the disparity between realms to arrive at conclusions about Milton's political philosophy and allegiances. Arguments are based on the premise that he embraced political acts and institutions he associated with Heaven in *Paradise Lost,* and condemned those he attributed to Hell. The similarities between the governments of Heaven, Hell, and France surely leave conclusions derived from such a premise open to question. It is the analogies which are of primary significance in that they illustrate how the artist uses his sources in Scripture, literature, and life. The selection of material to alter or omit is driven by the artist's intuitive perception of the immediate demands of his art, not the compulsion to pass judgment on his sources. Were the analogies parallel in every detail, the art would be dismissed as slavish imitation, transparent satire, or mere caricature. Thus, although different in detail, the realms of *Paradise Lost* are analogous in significant respects, a striking instance of close correspondences between a historical design of rule with which Milton was obviously familiar and the political imagery of his poetry.

These parallels between experience and art make it difficult to dismiss the proposition that the one did indeed influence the other; but they cloud our understanding of the poet's political philosophy and allegiances. Despite the cosmic pattern of trinities in the poetry, we cannot conclude that Milton thought the French monarchy a model political structure. His public writings have little to say about France at all; and whatever his private views on that nation, they probably changed during his tenure in office. During the first half of his public service he cannot have thought well of the French. The Commonwealth pursued a vigorous, though undeclared, naval war with its neighbor, and Paris became a hospitable haven to Queen Henrietta Marie, Louis XIV's aunt, and the English royal family. During the Protectorate, however, the two nations were on much more amicable terms; Cromwell entered into a close commercial and military alliance with France against Spain, and Charles II was forced to find lodgings elsewhere.[21]

Further, although the Holy Trinity may have set the pattern for Milton's poetic realms, nothing else from his pen would indicate that he thought the triumvirate an ideal constitutional structure. He certainly had no sympathy for the rule of "King, Lords, and Commons"; and although it would be tempting to conjecture that his political thought foreshadowed the separation of powers among the three branches of government defined in the U.S. Constitution, in fact, his settlement, as outlined in *The Readie and Easie Way,* was of an altogether different design (*MG* 196–97). Further, Milton's study of history would have persuaded him that an institution of co-rulers is disastrously unstable, an inevitable prelude to civil war.[22]

On the other hand, neither should one feel free to conclude, in view of Satan's obdurate departure from the cosmic pattern of triumvirates in *Paradise Lost,* that Milton believed a single person rule intrinsically evil, however comfortable such a deduction might be to some students of the poet's political thought.[23] He castigated some kings, of course, and tyrants of any color; but he also applauded Oliver Cromwell's assumption of power in 1654 and served the Protectorate loyally during its five-year existence; and in 1660 he pressed a similar role on General George Monk as a means of preventing the Restoration.[24]

It seems evident, therefore, that Milton's political images do not encode a judgment on the various regimes of his day, nor do they reflect his preference for one form of government over another. This being the case, one may

21. Charles first removed to Cologne, then briefly to Brussels, and finally set up his impoverished court in Bruges (Antonia Fraser, *Royal Charles,* 141-52).

22. The Roman triumvirates of 55 and 43 B.C. would have alerted him to the dangers, certainly.

23. Austin Woolrych, "Milton and Cromwell," 210-12; Barker, *Milton and the Puritan Dilemma,* 62; A.S.P. Woodhouse, *The Heavenly Muse,* 115-16; Mary Ann Radzinowicz, *Toward "Samson Agonistes,"* 146.

24. I have argued at some length that Milton was not opposed in principle to the rule of a single person, but was most adamant against one particular such person, Charles II (*MG* 202-5).

reasonably ask, what do these images tell us and why are there so many of them? Modern commentary on a poet's political imagery invariably attempts to position the artist somewhere within the ideological spectrum. In our politically minded community, the artist is either for us or against us; and in the case of a great poet like John Milton, we much prefer him for us. Thus, for generations the critical imagination has been burdened with a heavy obligation to assure readers that Milton is on the side of the angels, the good ones of course, that his God is right and good, his Satan wrong and – well – wicked, that the poet is politically impeccable in his prose, and, further, that the poetry mirrors faithfully, though in a more allusive way, the sentiments to be found in his political tracts.[25] Scholars feel obliged to label a work, and its author, with one or the other of the ideological tags fashionable in the artist's time, or in our own.[26] Such commentary can be skillful and enlightening, but that obligation necessarily limits the critical imagination to a narrow range of inquiry.

When applied to Milton's works, moreover, this method only ends in confusion. When Satan sounds like Oliver Cromwell, whom the poet praised unreservedly, and God Almighty for all the world like the king of England, one is hard-pressed to know where to place the poet within the political spectrum of his day. One can deconstruct, of course, analyze silences, and read between lines to locate the poet on the proper ideological wavelength; but one is forced to exercise such ingenuity only because the lines keep telling us something we are reluctant to acknowledge. Milton's God is an absolute monarch, but since the poet clearly had little sympathy for absolute monarchs, it is difficult to reconcile his figure of the Almighty with his political preferences. But, as we shall see, since *both* Cromwell and King Charles were models for his splendid Devil, *and* for his God as well, all that ingenuity seems pointless.

25. See, e.g., Joan Bennett, who argues that the figure of Satan conforms closely to Milton's image of Charles I in *Eikonoklastes* (*Reviving Liberty*, 33-58), and David Loewenstein, who finds a consistent theory of history running through both poetry and prose (*Milton and the Drama of History*).

26. Hill, e.g., describes a Milton in full sympathy with the more radical elements of English society in the mid-seventeenth century, and by inference the twentieth as well (*Milton and the English Revolution*). Keith Stavely observes that "the politics of Milton's prose style is the opposite of democratic" (*The Politics of Milton's Prose Style* 115). In "Dating Milton," Jonathan Goldberg cites recent studies of the poet that identify his works as "bourgeois," "Marxist," or "capitalist," and reflecting the "feudal economics of a lord-servant relationship" (202-5). Goldberg thinks such ideological labels inappropriate but his dismissal comes at a heavy price, the rejection of any objective historicity of the author, or of his text. There are surely less drastic alternatives.

Such readings are led astray from the outset by the assumption that *Paradise Lost* is a political testament, in the same way that *Eikonoklastes* is a political testament, that is, the poet's statement of his position on the ideological issues that divided his age. Both works are crowded with political figures; but it is abundantly clear that Milton composed the poem and the tract for very different purposes, the one to justify the ways of God, the other the ways of the English Republic. In *The Readie and Easie Way* Milton urges his readers to adopt a particular form of government; but if we examine the governments of *Paradise Lost,* everything we know of him would persuade us that he would have been more inclined to embrace the one in Hell, where there is a degree of representation, open debate of issues, and decision by ballot, rather than the celestial structure, in which an absolute monarch rules by inalterable decree. This is not to imply that Milton was of the Devil's party, knowing full well, but to argue that the political structures of *Paradise Lost* do not reflect the poet's political allegiances.

David Quint's *Epic and Empire* is only the most recent of scholarly studies to interpret Milton's poems as a commentary on the political divisions of his day, or our own. Quint's is an immensely learned and challenging work; but it narrows its focus when it finds *Paradise Lost* "a poem of defeated Puritan republicanism and liberty," the fall of Adam and Eve comparable to the fall "of the English Commonwealth," and Satan's conquest of the World a criticism of "the building of European empires in the 'new world.' "[27] Quint's work similarly defines *Paradise Regained* as a political testament: Jesus is "identified with the republican cause" and his rejection of the kingdoms a reflection of the poet's "fear of central state authority." Milton is no quietist but is "carrying on as a polemicist against the Restoration" in a poem that is essentially "a fight against monarchy."[28]

If one approaches a work of art in the conviction that its lines encode a commentary on the artist's time and that the critic's task is to decipher that message, the range of critical inquiry will necessarily be limited and the response to its artistic qualities muted. Commentaries that propose a direct, unmediated transference of ideological conviction in one-to-one analogies between prose and poetry, or between experience and poetry, arguing from

27. Quint, *Epic and Empire,* 250, 271, 281.
28. Ibid., 326, 328, 326, 334. Similarly, Laura Knoppers finds in Milton's later works a commentary on Restoration politics, particularly the "spectacle of state," which, she argues, he "challenges and replaces" with the "paradise within" (*Historicizing Milton* 10).

the premise that God is good and Satan wicked, ignore the subtleties of the creative process.

In the act of creation, Milton surely made use of any experience within the range of his imagination, but no single event or figure necessarily appears in his work encumbered with all the connotations associated with it in real life. *Paradise Lost* is a poem designed to depict in narrative form a set of spiritual beliefs; and one would be hard-pressed to cite a law of aesthetics, or of logic, no matter how attractive the notion may be, which mandates that a poem on a *religious* theme must in all respects mirror the poet's *political* ideology. Certainly, Milton's political experience left its imprint on his art, especially in the case of a long poem packed with political imagery. An artist, however, has a unique role, that of illuminating rather than simply reflecting reality; and a great artist has the genius not only to transcend contemporary realities but to reshape them into a larger vision. But before an artist's experience is transformed into art, it must first pass through the forge of the imagination. In the case of a minor artist, whose forge may be cool and imagination tepid, the text may indeed emerge as a mirror image of cultural context or personal political ideology. For consummate artists, however, the forge is white hot; they melt down and reconstitute experience to their own transcendent purposes.

But, it may be reasonably asked, if the political imagery in *Paradise Lost* does not make a political statement, what sort of statement does it make? As we shall see, Milton sought to convey in the figure of Satan a sense of the power and deviousness of the forces of evil, and the threat they pose to individual salvation; and to that end he conceived of the very author of evil as an imposing military and political leader. In depicting God, he reached for imagery that would reflect the splendor of the divine nature, the creative power of the Almighty, and his love for Mankind. To fashion such compelling figures, he drew on his memory of *all* the political and military leaders he had encountered in his life and his study, regardless of whether he approved of them or not. In *Paradise Lost,* then, politics and religion are inextricably linked; but the political imagery, like all the imagery of its lines, serves as handmaid to spiritual truth.

This study will proceed, therefore, on the premise that although Milton certainly drew on his experience in public service to shape his political imagery, he did so primarily as a means of bringing the spiritual message within the compass of his readers' temporal understanding. *Paradise Lost* deals with resolutely intractable material, the ways of immortal gods, the minds and hearts of perfect humans, and the endless reaches of space, concerning which the poet attempts to weave a narrative accessible to readers whose world is ordered by, among other things, kings and magistrates. He employed the knowledge he gained of the monarchs, protectors, warriors, and senators of his time to construct a narrative framework on which to shape his testament of religious truth, much as a sculptor molds his clay upon a wire mesh or an architect constructs his building about a skeleton of wood or steel. The politics of the poem is, in brief, a means, not an end.

On this basis, there is no obligation to formulate a perfect equation between life and art; and the critical imagination is liberated to explore the influence of one upon the other without having to accommodate them ideologically. If Satan exhibits some of the qualities of Cromwell, we need not feel compelled to deduce from the similarities that Milton thought Cromwell wicked;[29] or if God is depicted as a king, we should not feel obliged to contemplate the possibility that the poet was a closet monarchist.[30] Nor, if we are convinced that Milton admired Cromwell and detested Charles I, will we be forced to twist the text of *Paradise Lost* to make its meaning conform to the poet's known political preferences.

To return to the subject at hand, the triumvirates of *Paradise Lost,* it is doubtful that Milton's vision of cosmic political order was inspired solely by his familiarity with the unique features of the French monarchy. It is far more likely that the recurring pattern in the governments of *Paradise Lost* was originally determined by the necessity to incorporate into a Christian poem the traditional design of the Holy Trinity. The discussion of Milton's perception of that doctrine will appear in later pages; for the moment it need only be observed that Heaven's Holy Trinity was central to Christian thought in the seventeenth century and could not be ignored in a Christian poem. Once Milton had made the singularly daring decision to interpret that mysterious entity in political terms, adapting a doctrinal abstraction of Christian teaching to the narrative demands of an epic poem and to the temporal understanding of its readers, he quite logically extended the principle of a tripartite God in Heaven to shape all his imaginative realms, reflecting the basic unity of a universe derived from the single substance of the Deity. It is in the particulars of Milton's poetic triumvirates that one detects the influence on his imagination of the French arrangement: the co-rulers, the family relationship, the female presence, the balance of authority among the three members, and the change in that balance over time.

29. William Empson remarks archly that his early readers "must have been agog to know whether Milton intended satire against Charles II or against Cromwell" (*Milton's God* 74).

30. Malcolm Ross, *Milton's Royalism,* 50.

Once Milton had determined to portray the Trinity as a political body and depict the governments of his poem as hierarchical structures, he drew on his knowledge of the French triumvirate to adorn the figures. Again, the political imagery of *Paradise Lost* serves as handmaid to the religious theme.

That Milton made use of his knowledge of world affairs to enrich the fabric of his later poems there can be little doubt; but it was not his purpose in doing so to pass judgment in his lines on the policies of England, or of France, or to depict temporal political institutions as serving on one side or the other of the cosmic struggle between good and evil. His, he said, was a "higher Argument"; and he applied his experience in government to a purpose larger than the encoding of a parochial commentary on his own times or a justification of his political allegiances. Succeeding chapters will explore Milton's use of one of the most pervasive of human experiences, that of governing and being governed, to describe the spiritual state of beings in realms far distant from that experience, in Heaven, Hell, and an unfallen World, descriptions in which the poet, "to compare / Small things with greatest" (*PR* 4:563-64), labored to accommodate the divine intent to human understanding, the better to justify God's sometimes incomprehensible ways to men.

2

THE KINGDOM OF HEAVEN

At some point in the genesis of his epic poem, Milton decided that if the ways of God were to be justified, the Deity would have to speak for himself. It was a deliberate choice from among a number of possible narrative alternatives, made some time after he had compiled the list of possible characters and plots listed in the Trinity Manuscript. God does not appear in any of them, nor does the Son. In the scenarios that most closely resemble the final poem, "Paradise Lost" and "Adam unparadiz'd," the only supernatural characters he considered were Michael, Gabriel, Lucifer, and a chorus of angels; and whatever qualities of the Deity he might have planned to display were to be enacted by a series of allegorical figures, Justice, Mercy, Wisdom, and Heavenly Love. In deciding to portray the Father and the Son as dramatic characters in the narrative, Milton incurred risks that other poets preferred to avoid – Dante for one was content to describe Heaven as a dance and the Deity not at all – and centuries of readers have expressed themselves dissatisfied for one reason or another with the decision, beginning with Joseph Addison, who otherwise full of praise for *Paradise Lost,* observed that "If *Milton's* Majesty forsakes him any where, it is in those Parts of his Poem, where the Divine Persons are introduced as Speakers."[1]

God the Father

A poet sufficiently daring to portray the Judeo-Christian God as an anthropomorphic figure in a historical narrative faced a daunting task, for to Christians the Deity is at once a theological entity, a moral principle, and a spiritual abstraction. Milton assigns the values traditionally attributed to him, which to the poet represent as much of his divine nature as he wishes to reveal to Man. According to that tradition, God made Man in his own image; and since we are, therefore, adumbrations of the divine being, we can contemplate the ineffable in terms of the human condition. He has come within the range of our perception in many guises, the Loving Father, the Stern Judge, the Merciful Lord, the Creative Artist, and possessed of many qualities – he is an "Omnipotent, / Immutable, Immortal, Infinite, / Eternal King" (3:372-73), one who is as well omniscient, omnipresent, and invisible.

A good part of the dissatisfaction with the figure arises from the image of Milton's God as a king, an "all-powerful King" (2:851), "matchless King" (4:41), "all bounteous King" (5:640), and "Eternal King Omnipotent" (6:227). There are few such overt political references in *Christian Doctrine,* save for an occasional citation of 1 Timothy 6:15, "King of Kings and Lord of Lords" (*Prose* 6:145, 230), though Milton is clearly open to the possibility: "If God attributes to himself again and again a human shape and form, why should we be afraid of assigning to him something he assigns to himself?" (*Prose* 6:136). Once the poet had determined to "assign" to God the qualities of a monarch it followed that, as an absolute being, he could not be described as anything less than an absolute monarch.

---

1. Addison, *The Spectator,* 1 March 1712. Addison continues, "One may, I think, observe that the Author proceeds with a kind of Fear and Trembling, whilst he describes the Sentiments of the Almighty. He dares not give his Imagination its full Play, but chuses to confine himself to such Thoughts as are drawn from the Books of the most Orthodox Divines, and to such Expressions as may be met with in Scripture." Equally familiar are Pope's complaint that Milton makes God sound like a "school divine," and Blake's observation that "Milton wrote in fetters when he wrote of Angels and God" (*The Poetry and Prose of William Blake* 35).

This image of the Deity has troubled scholars for generations, in particular those who strive to accommodate Milton's poetic figure to what is known of his political allegiances, for he seems to have had little sympathy for kings. The political trappings with which the poet surrounds his monarch are doubly troublesome. Milton seems intent on showing God "every inch a king," his powers limitless, his sway sublimely imperial, his decrees inviolable law, his subjects bonded to him by an amalgam of boundless love, their voices raised in hymns of consummate poetry. In Heaven's court God rules by decree, as did King Charles I for eleven years between Parliaments and Oliver Cromwell as Protector;[2] and once his words are uttered, they become inalterable law. He demands absolute obedience from his subjects and those who fail to obey are cast into permanent exile or condemned to death. Angels do not debate his law; Abdiel chides Satan for presuming to do so, "shalt thou dispute / With him the points of liberty?" (5:822-23). There is no parliament in Heaven, only an elaborate hierarchy of angels; and laws are announced at assemblies of the entire population "by Imperial summons call'd" (5:584), as when God exalts the Son. Though he is responsive to spontaneous gatherings, as when "in multitudes / Th'etherial People ran, to hear and know" how Man fell (10:26-27), the King of Heaven seems to prefer more formal assemblies. He does delegate authority at times, as when he places Michael in command of his armies and Gabriel in charge of the sentinels of Eden; but each of his subjects, whatever his function, is responsible only to the Almighty.[3]

His court is brilliant:

> Ten thousand thousand Ensigns high advanc'd
> Standards and Gonfalons, twixt Van and Rear
> Stream in the Air, and for distinction serve
> Of Hierarchies, of Orders, and Degrees.
>   (5:588-91)

His subjects await the word, circling the celestial throne in solemn order:

2. Cromwell assumed the royal prerogative. David Masson lists eighty-two decrees issued by the Lord Protector during his first eight months in office (*The Life of John Milton* 4:557-66). Cromwell called two Parliaments (one for two sessions) but they sat for a total of only fourteen of the fifty-six months of his tenure and spent the bulk of that time debating constitutional issues.

3. Kitty Cohen, among others, has traced the figure to its Old Testament sources and found it entirely compatible ("Milton's God in Council and War").

> Thus when in Orbs
> Of circuit unexpressible they stood,
> Orb within Orb, the Father infinite,
> By whom in bliss imbosom'd sat the Son,
> Amidst as from a flaming Mount, whose top
> Brightness had made invisible, thus spake.
>
> (5:594-59)

After the decree, his courtiers "dance about the sacred Hill" and feast on "Angels' Food and rubied Nectar." There is no need for court entertainment in a society where "They eat, they drink, and in communion sweet / Quaff immortality and joy" (5:19-38). But most of all the angels sing, echoing in celestial harmonies praises of their divine ruler: "Thee Father first they sung Omnipotent, / Immutable, Immortal, Infinite, / Eternal King; thee Author of all being, / Fountain of Light" (3:372-75), and "Great are thy works, *Jehovah,* infinite / Thy power; what thought can measure thee or tongue / Relate thee" (7:602-4). These are all, it will not escape notice, communal activities; the angels sing and dance and eat together in union, unlike the fallen ones, who when Satan leaves differentiate themselves into separate groups, some exercising in games, some practicing their military movements, some singing epic songs, some engaging in philosophical debate, and others exploring their horrible new home (2:521-628).

As we have seen, there is a strict hierarchy among the angels, as elaborate as that in any earthly court. At the pinnacle of power sit Father and Son, below whom degrees of authority are determined by proximity to the throne, the most honored being "the sev'n / Who in God's presence, nearest to his Throne / Stand ready to command" (3:648-50). The chief angels perform the traditional feudal ceremony of homage to their Lord: "lowly reverent / Toward either Throne they bow, and to the ground / With solemn adoration down they cast / Thir Crowns"; and then, presumably after a ritually regal gesture acknowledging their allegiance, they are "Crown'd again" (3:349-52, 365). When angels meet, the lower orders offer due deference to those above them in the hierarchy. We learn of these customs, to be sure, chiefly when Satan perverts them to his own ends; but they were apparently in common practice. Satan encounters Uriel in the guise of "a stripling Cherub" whose manner is properly deferential to "one of the sev'n." As he leaves, Satan bows "low / As to superior Spirits is wont in Heav'n / Where honor due and reverence none neglects" (3:736-39). Later outside of Eden, Gabriel acknowledges the customs but accuses Satan of hypocrisy in his observance of them; he "Once fawn'd, and cring'd, and servilely ador'd / Heav'n's awful Monarch" while concealing ambitions "To dispossess him, and thyself to reign" (4:959-61).[4] Milton deplored the "base necessitie of court flatteries and prostrations" in *The Readie and Easie Way* (7:428; see also 425-26), but prior to the loss of his sight he had doubtless observed similar behavior among the favor seekers who prowled the halls of Westminster Palace.[5]

In *Christian Doctrine* Milton considers at length the various attributes of the Deity, according to the evidence of Scripture (*Prose* 6:138-52). Of the many cited, those most frequently mentioned in *Paradise Lost* may be distinguished by how they relate to the human condition: they are either a negation or an extension of the state of mankind. Among the former, which Milton refers to as "negative attributes" (*Prose* 6:149), are those celebrated by the angelic choirs, "Immutable, Immortal, Infinite, / Eternal," all of which human beings are *not*. We are changing, mortal, finite, and temporal, or put otherwise, we age, die, and remain fixed in space and time. Such negative qualities are difficult to demonstrate in poetry and prose, and writers are often reduced to simply attributing them to a figure and letting it go at that. They may draw attention to life as their readers live it and ask them to imagine a being unlimited by conditions that confine their existence. Reading thus requires a elastic exercise of the human imagination, an effort Milton clearly thought within the capacity of his fit, though few, audience.

Other attributes are more readily rendered in narrative, those such as omniscience, omnipresence, and omnipotence, which are not negations but enlargements or extensions of human qualities. We know ourselves to possess knowledge, to be present in space, and to exercise certain physical powers, and so can attribute to God these same capabilities in absolute measure. Milton shows the Deity omniscient in scenes where he foretells the Fall and instructs Michael on human history, "reveal / To *Adam* what shall come in future days, / As I shall thee enlighten" (11:114-16). We learn of his omnipresence when he appears in at least two places at once during the days of the Creation, when "he also went / Invisible, yet stay'd" (7:588-89).

4. Gabriel may be somewhat overwrought in reinterpreting Satan's former ritual deference in the light of his later apostasy. There is no evidence that the thought of disobedience entered his consciousness prior to God's decree, though some have so proposed, e.g., Empson, *Milton's God,* 72.

5. In *Historicizing Milton,* Laura Knoppers finds in Milton "a distrust of ceremonious spectacle" (110); hence she attributes such displays "of lavish magnificence" in *Paradise Lost* to Satan (106). To pursue her argument, however, Knoppers must ignore the splendor and elaborate ritual of Heaven's court.

Omnipotence is another such divine attribute; and since Milton most frequently chose to represent it in *Paradise Lost* as the exercise of political and military power, it deserves our close attention. A reader can plausibly project his experience under the limited sovereignty of an earthly king to imagine the sway of an absolute monarch over an infinity of souls. Or, to put the matter in more general terms, we know ourselves capable of creating and destroying within the limits of our material existence, and so can imagine a regal being possessed of that power in the absolute, one capable of making and unmaking our universe with a word. Poetically, such a figure can be described as one who can bring order out of chaos and part the water from the land with a single gesture, or as one who can unleash at will the force of a thousand hurricanes and as many Etnas, to mention only cataclysms with which the poet's contemporaries would have been familiar. Such power the human mind can grasp, especially present generations, who have witnessed the mushroom cloud.

Omnipotence is the only attribute of the Deity that is essentially political, in the sense that it involves the exercise of power to impose one party's will upon another. Milton essays only one demonstration of God's absolute power, the expulsion of the rebel angels from Heaven; and even in that instance he qualifies it, as if to underscore how far language is unequal to the task. The Son unleashes but "half his strength" (6:853), though this in itself is subtly deceptive: Milton must have been aware that, even as half of infinity is still infinite, so also half of omnipotent power is still omnipotence.[6] The image is essentially military, the final act of a war, embellished with fire, lightning, thunder which shakes the Empyrean, and arrows that pour forth from the many eyes of the Chariot of Paternal Deity. The reader experiences omnipotence chiefly in terms of the effect it has on Satan's legions, who are impressively powerful in their own right, having fought God's armies to a standoff during two days of battle. All God's "War" routs them, however:

> they astonisht all resistance lost,
> All courage; down thir idle weapons dropp'd;
> O'er Shields and Helms, and helmed heads he rode

6. It may be assumed that Milton knew what he was doing. The human mind has played with the idea of infinity since the time of Zeno of Elea, but only as an informal notion. It was not reduced to a theory demonstrable by the formal logic of mathematics until a German, Georg Cantor, offered proofs in the late nineteenth century. But one need not be a mathematician to realize that half of endless is as endless as the whole.

> Of Thrones and mighty Seraphim prostrate.
>   (6:838-41)

They are utterly demoralized by the cloud of arrows, "that wither'd all thir strength, / And of thir wonted vigor left them drain'd / Exhausted, spiritless, afflicted, fall'n" (6:850-52); and to escape the terror they rush, like a "Herd of Goats," to the edge of Heaven and throw themselves into the abyss. Milton cites other instances of the exercise of omnipotence, the creation of the World in book 7 and the various descriptions of the Deity's destructive power on the Final Day; but only in this episode does the reader gain some sense of its awesome dimensions.

The figure of God as a king and Heaven as a political state, one, moreover, split by civil war, has caused considerable discomfort among scholars in the present century. William Empson finds Milton's "treatment of God so strange that it rewards inquiry" and concludes his inquiry with the observation that the figure reminds him of no one so much as Joseph Stalin.[7] The only redeeming feature of the King of Heaven, according to Empson, is that he plans to abdicate, which, as we shall see, is a serious misreading.[8]

What did Milton think of kings? An examination of his public statements on the institution of monarchy may serve to relieve some of the reader's discomfort with the figure of God in the poem. In his prose works Milton frequently states that he has no quarrel with kings, insisting that it is the tyrant he abhors (*Prose* 4:535, 561, 652). He takes pains to define such a ruler as one "who regarding neither Law nor the common good, reigns onely for himself and his faction," and is careful to distinguish one from the other: "Look how great a good and happiness a just King is, so great a mischeife is a Tyrant" (*Prose* 3:212, also 4:562). He protests that in his works he only "seemed to have attacked kings," citing the approval of Queen Christina of Sweden to underline his sentiments (*Prose* 4:655).

---

7. Empson, *Milton's God,* 91, 146. Empson also finds himself in agreement with Phelps-Morand that "Milton described God from his experience of Cromwell" (144).

8. Ibid., 130. If this work is cited somewhat more frequently than others, it is because it illustrates the opportunities open to the critical imagination once liberated from the confining necessity to demonstrate the rather obvious observation that Milton's God is good and his Satan evil. Empson, of course, rather perversely goes to the opposite extreme, declaring "the traditional God of Christianity very wicked" and finding perhaps too much to admire in Satan; hence, while delighting in some of his provocative readings, I find as much to contest as to applaud in the work. My position, as stated above, is that the poet employs the political imagery to other purposes entirely.

Indeed, in all his political writings the only living monarch he mentions by name is Christina, for whom he has only praise (*Prose* 4:556-57, 603-6, 655); and the only one he cites with disapproval is the unnamed Catholic "Emperor of Austria" (*Prose* 4:649). His tracts are bare of reference to Philip IV of Spain, Louis XIV of France, John IV of Portugal, Charles X of Sweden, and Frederick III of Denmark, or of lesser, but no less absolute, rulers, the elector of Brandenburg, czar of Russia, count of Oldenburg, and landgrave of Hesse, to mention only some of those he would have come to know in preparing his Letters of State (*MG* 251-58). He preferred to cite Scripture and history, chiefly ancient, as evidence for points of argument; and this omission of contemporary allusions may be readily explained. During his years in public office, the Republic was either pressing for diplomatic recognition from its continental neighbors or actively negotiating with them to secure commercial or military agreements. In the months prior to the publication of *A Second Defence* (30 May 1654), for example, England was pursuing treaties with the kingdoms of Spain, Denmark, Portugal, and Sweden; and it would have been impolitic for a public official to comment in print on any of the several monarchs of these nations, whatever he may have thought of them.

The Readie and Easie Way is, of course, a venomous attack on "Kingship"; but Milton's invective is directed at the House of Stuart, and to a lesser degree the House of Orange, presided over at the time by the widowed Mary, Charles II's sister (*Prose* 4:570, 629; 7:446). Though released from the diplomatic considerations which restrained him in earlier tracts, he still condemns no kings, save for those English and Dutch.[9] His denunciation of the Houses of Stuart and Orange cannot be said to constitute a sweeping dismissal of the institution of monarchy. He certainly approved of a free commonwealth as the best form of government for England, as that most likely to encourage liberty of conscience, but was never evangelical in urging it on his continental neighbors, since the great majority of them were ruled by crowned heads, who would have taken ill any such suggestion. Each to his own, he seems content to say, and our choice is a republic.

However questionable the evidence of Milton's prose works may be in defining his opposition to the institution of monarchy, there can be no doubt of his rejection of the Stuart kings, whom he considered irredeemable tyrants. Modern scholars, as we have seen, have struggled with the apparent

---

9. He does refer briefly to the corrupting influence of the French court, and to "*Popish* and *Spanish* plots" (7:426, 457), but mentions no living monarchs.

contradiction between the ideological positions of the poetry and the prose, some, like William Empson, resolving the differences by turning *Paradise Lost* on its ear, others, like Malcolm Ross, by turning the poet on his ear. Two more recent book-length works address the subject quite sensibly, adopting the poet's own stated position on the issue by acknowledging that Milton did not reject *all* kings but reserved his condemnation for those who used their power tyrannically. I cite them here because both are works of exhaustive scholarship and enlightened inquiry, and because they illustrate the ingenuity required of an inventive critical imagination attempting to come to terms with the figure of the King of Heaven. Both authors are highly respected in their field, and rightly so, for whatever my reservations on isolated matters, their works have added significantly to our understanding of Milton's political thought.

In *Images of Kingship in "Paradise Lost,"* Stevie Davies proposes four kinds of kings, three of which, the absolute monarch, like Charles I, the Turkish sultan, and the Roman emperor, she argues, Milton's God is not. He represents, rather, the ruler in an ideal feudal relationship in which king and subject enjoy a balance of mutual responsibilities and the monarch reigns only as *"primus inter pares."*[10] Milton, she concludes, approved of feudalism "in its pure form."[11] Davies's scholarship is comprehensive and her argument ingenious; but the attentive reader of *Paradise Lost* will surely be troubled by her conclusion that Milton's "Omnipotent,... Eternal King" of Heaven (3:372-74) rules as the first among equals.

In her impressive *Reviving Liberty,* Joan Bennett finds Milton's Deity "an absolute monarch voluntarily accountable to law" and therefore "worthy of his subjects' praise," unlike the tyrant who exercises his power arbitrarily.[12] Bennett's argument is persuasive in bringing to our attention Milton's distinction between a just king and a tyrant and in characterizing his God as a monarch who may be considered just because he abides by his own decrees. The difficulty, of course, lies in those decrees; and Bennett's argument seems to beg the question of the poem, that is, whether *they* are just or not. God may certainly be said to keep his word and so may be absolved of arbitrariness; but the same may be said of any tyrant. In January 1655, the duke of Savoy issued the Edict of Gastaldo, directing that his Waldensian subjects either vacate their homes or convert to Catholicism; and three months later he adhered resolutely to his decree by massacring

10. Davies, *Images of Kingship,* 162.
11. Ibid., 130.
12. Bennett, *Reviving Liberty,* 9, 60.

those who refused (*MG* 139-40, 215-19). In like manner, God creates the universe according to the natural law, from which he declares himself unwilling to depart. It is a law, moreover, whose provisions call for absolute obedience to his will, for any violation demands the ultimate punishment: "Die he or Justice must" (3:210). The Almighty dispatches Raphael to warn Adam and Eve of the dangers threatening them, whereby the narrative voice declares him to have "fulfill'd / All Justice" (5:246-47).

So God doesn't change his mind; but it is precisely his merciless adherence to the law that stands most in need of justification. The law of which he speaks was of his own making, and the Almighty may be accounted just only if his law is just. Adherence to it is another matter. An omnipotent being surely has choice, and can exercise it or not. Implicit in such statements as "Die he or Justice must" and "I else must change / Thir nature" (3:125-26) is the understanding that God could go either way – he *could* let Justice die and has the power to change Man's nature, but chooses not to. It is both the making of and the adhering to the law that want justification; and God's accountability can be of little comfort to the faithful when it necessitates their death. It is precisely the voluntary nature of God's judgment that is so disturbing. If he could have spared us, why didn't he, instead of falling back on "the Law" to absolve himself of responsibility? After all, the duke of Savoy said as much: "I have decreed their death and so it must be done. It's out of my hands." This is a tyrant talking. Bennett's argument for accountability does not make God any more palatable.

These works, arguing from the unstated premise that all things associated with God must be good, equate political evil with absolute power and good with authority less than absolute. In the present instance Milton's God is said to be a just ruler because, in the one case he is but the first among equals, and in the other a king accountable to the law, or what might be called today a constitutional monarch. The suggestion that God is anything less than absolute would seem to run counter to Milton's professed beliefs; and the proposal that there are limits to the power of the Almighty of *Paradise Lost* must leave the reader uneasy.

There is, in the end, no way to avoid the impression that Milton's God is an absolute monarch who governs in ways that the poet roundly condemned in earthly kings. He is treated like a king, sitting at the pinnacle of a political hierarchy punctilious in its observance of deferential ritual, his subjects standing before him in awed silence or singing his praises in exalted hymns. He sounds like a king, issuing decrees that have the force of inviolable law, demanding unquestioned obedience, commending those who obey and condemning those who defy him to death or eternal pain. He acts like a king, assembling the entire population of Heaven by summary edict, elevating his son to the dignity of royal heir, sending his armies into battle, and celebrating the defeat of his enemies. Louis XIV's "L'état, c'est moi" could have been inspired by Milton's God, who not only rules the universe but *is* the universe: "I am who fill / Infinitude, nor vacuous the space" (7:168-69). But, given Milton's firm belief in an "Omnipotent, ... Eternal" God, it was impossible for the poet to present him otherwise. Once he decided to depict the Deity as a political figure acting in a political arena, to make him anything less than absolute would have been contrary to the poem's larger purpose.

Milton judged a monarch by his acts and words, not by the aura of his office; and his chief quarrel was with those who cloaked themselves in authority by divine right, depicting themselves as rulers over their subjects and kingdoms in appropriate imitation of God's reign over the angels and the universe. This was, so went the theory, the divine order of things, with the king acting as God's anointed vicegerent in the human sphere, and he should be obeyed as such. Any king who claims such dispensation Milton brands an idolator, and a people who abide him guilty of "a civil kinde of Idolatry in idolizing their Kings," so ready are they "to fall flatt and give adoration to [his] Image and Memory" (*Prose* 3:343-44); they are, as he puts it again, "an inconstant, irrational, and Image-doting rabble" (*Prose* 3:601).[13] Governments, he argues, grew "from the root of *Adams* transgression" not from any divine ordinance; and rulers are not "anointed" by God but designated of necessity by the people as "thir Deputies and Commissioners" to "restrain by force and punishment what was violated against peace and common right" (*Prose* 3:199).

It may be said, however, that Milton seems to have ornamented the court of Heaven somewhat too lavishly. Although it would not have been entirely decorous to depict the King of Heaven as the presiding officer of an executive committee, like the president of the Commonwealth's Council of State, the poet might be faulted for embellishing the celestial scene with a bit too baroque a hand. One might attribute such excess to poetic enthusiasm, the artist carried away with imaginative energy; but in the instance of a poet

---

13. See also *Prose* 4:369-70, 551; for a recent study of Milton's sentiments, see Hardin, *Civil Idolatry,* 164-201.

so conscious of his art and deliberate in his design, one must consider alternative reasons for this display.

In his celestial court Milton described a spectacle of rule so grand that it put the aspirations of earthly kings to shame. Insofar as they seek to imitate the grandeur of Heaven's realm and to approach the transcendentally absolute of the King of Kings, as we have seen, they stand condemned of the sin of idolatry, as do their subjects who join in the charade, since all are seen as worshiping the image of God rather than God himself. When Milton chose to describe Heaven as a political state, he had to make use of the practices and protocols of the very monarchs he deplored in order to accommodate his vision of divine government to the understanding of his mortal readers.[14] In doing so, he defines a Heavenly court, which so far surpasses the glories of earthly monarchs that their pretensions can be seen as but a pale imitation of the divine, and they can be unmasked for the pitifully inadequate idolaters they are. The Kingdom of Heaven had to be seen as the most splendid imaginable with all the institutions of royal rule carried out to their most dazzling extremes, its subjects more numerous, their praise more exalted, their obedience more unswerving, their knees more willingly bent, and their devotion more profound than any earthly monarch could possibly command. The court of Heaven represents everything to which those monarchs aspire; and Milton describes it in these terms so that the shallow masque of manners that they and their courtiers enact may be seen for the feeble, shoddy, threadbare mimic of Heaven's glories that it is. He knew what he was about; in showing how God rules, he drew a picture of government truly sublime and warned temporal rulers not to reach for it.

God possesses power in the absolute, that is, at all levels of existence, even to shaping an ordered universe out of the anarchy of Chaos and then dissolving it with a word. Such power can be represented either as latent or kinetic, that is, as a potential to act or as the act itself. The courtly ceremonies that revolve about the person of a king are designed to demonstrate his power to control the lives of his subjects. In the seventeenth century that potential was displayed in court masques, formal processions, coronations, and the elaborate protocol of address, all trappings of office which celebrate the latent power of the monarchy. He exercised his royal authority kinetically through the legal establishment with arrests, imprisonments, and public executions; through the political system by calling and dismissing Parliaments,

---

14. Hardin describes Milton's "loathing for church and state rituals" (*Civil Idolatry* 207; see also 166–67).

appointing public officials, and apportioning government revenue; and through the employment of armed might, either against his own subjects or other nations. To depict an all-powerful God, the poet must magnify these features of earthly political authority to represent his absolute sovereignty over all created subjects and hegemony over all states.

How much of the structure of the Kingdom of Heaven derives from Milton's political experience it is difficult to say. There is no evidence that he ever saw a king, but he did live under the rule of English monarchs for all but eleven of his sixty-six years; and he was familiar with the ceremonial deference shown lesser nobility, doubtless observing ritual honors rendered the earl of Bridgewater on at least one occasion during his inaugural progress as Lord President of Wales. In Italy he was warmly welcomed by other figures accustomed to such deference, Giovanni Battista Manso, marquis of Villa and lord of Bisaccio and Panca, and Cardinal Francesco Barberini, the chief counselor to the pope. Of perhaps more significance, prior to his blindness Milton's duties as translator at official audiences familiarized him with the elaborate courtesies of diplomatic protocol. In *John Milton's Writings in the Anglo-Dutch Negotiations, 1651-1654,* Leo Miller gives an account of the extravagant ritual observed in the reception of foreign ambassadors in that era. When Leo ab Aitzema, the envoy from Hamburg and the Hanse Towns, was received by the Council of State on 27 February 1652, Sir Oliver Fleming, the Republic's protocol officer,

> three times made reverence (a sweeping bow?). Aitzema took off his glove and, speaking in Latin, handed his letter of credentials to Fleming. Aitzema put his glove back on; his head having been uncovered, he put his hat back on, the others put their hats on, and he proceeded to deliver his message in Latin. Lisle responded in English, of which Aitzema had a good grasp. Again there were three bows, and Aitzema withdrew.[15]

There is no evidence that Milton was present on that particular occasion; but prior to his blindness he regularly participated in such ceremonies, translating the Latin for less learned Council members.

After his blindness, Milton's chief duty was to prepare letters to a number of the crowned heads of Europe, as well as to a variety of princes, dukes, electors, governors, prime ministers, landgraves, and pashas. He was skilled,

15. Miller, *John Milton's Writings,* 7.

certainly, in the ritual of address required in approaching such figures, the semantic stroking of elaborate compliment and unrelenting praise, the deferential language of petition and the subtle phrases needed to move them to favorable action.

Some few passages from these letters will illustrate the poet's familiarity with this protocol of praise. In the late summer of 1657, Cromwell sensed that Frederick William, the great elector of Brandenburg, was showing signs of renouncing his treaty with Charles X, king of Sweden; and he sent an envoy, William Jephson, to both rulers with the mission of bolstering the alliance between them. Jephson's letter of credential is a model of compliment to the elector, but it is mild compared to the one that followed closely upon it. Cromwell, apprehensive that Jephson would arrive too late, sent another by swifter means, in which he praises extravagantly Frederick William's adherence to the treaty in the face of all temptation to abandon it. The language may seem almost bizarre to modern ears, but it illustrates the protocol of praise that Milton was called upon to observe in international correspondence. The letter mentions that Jephson is enroute but that the Lord Protector wants to assure the elector personally of his appreciation for "your great Vertues" and to demonstrate "our own good will and Affection." It goes on:

> Nevertheless, That we may not seem too superficially to have glided over your transcending deservings of the Protestant Interests; we thought it proper to resume the same subject, and pay our Respect and Veneration, not more willingly, or with greater fervency of Mind, but somewhat more at large, to your Highness. And truly most deservedly, when daily Information reaches our ears, That your Faith and Conscience, by all manner of Artifices Tempted and Assail'd, by all manner of Arts and Devices Tempted, yet cannot be shaken, or by any Violence be rent from your Friendship and Alliance with a most Magnanimous Prince and your Confederate.

He concludes with a prayer to "the God of Mercy and Power, that so signal a Prowess and Fortitude may never languish or be oppress'd, nor be depriv'd the Fruit and due Applause of all your Pious Undertakings" (W101, P135). Ironically, even as Milton was penning these elaborate phrases, Frederick William was abrogating the treaty with Charles and joining the forces arrayed against him (*MG* 168).

One further example will suffice to illustrate how Milton's experience with diplomatic correspondence schooled him in the art of political praise. Each of the pairs of letters to Louis XIV and Cardinal Mazarin had to engage in a special quality of elaborate compliment. Since it was distinctly possible that they read each other's mail, neither could be acclaimed at the expense of the other; and the praise had to be sustained at times over a series of letters, calling for an extended vocabulary to avoid repetition. In one sequence addressed to Louis XIV in May–June 1658, Cromwell is concerned with the capture of Dunkirk by an Anglo-French army and its transfer to English control (*MG* 153–56). He sent, as an envoy to the king, his son-in-law, viscount Fauconberg, with letters of credential that extol

> the Court of so great a Prince, celebrated for the resort of so many Prudent and Courageous Persons, more nobly prepar'd for great Performances, and fully Accomplish'd in whatsoever may be thought most Laudable and Vertuous.
>
> (W113, P146)

Before the capitulation of the town, Cromwell predicts that "your Majesty, by your Military Prowess, will now take speedy Vengeance of the *Spanish* Frauds" (W116, P148); and after its fall, he thanks the king for the news:

> By so speedily repaying our profound Respect to your Majesty, with an Accumulation of Honour, by such an Illustrious Embassy to our Court; you have not onely make known to us, but to all the People of *England,* your singular Benignity and Generosity of Mind, but also how much you favour our Reputation and Dignity.
>
> (W118, P154)

The companions to these letters, addressed to Mazarin, are even more exuberant. Cromwell commends Fauconberg to the cardinal's "Favour and Goodwill; whose single Prudence and Vigilancy, Supports and Manages the grand Affairs of that Kingdom" (W114, P147). The envoy is instructed to

> wish your Eminency long Life and Health in our Name, and to return Thanks to your Eminency, by whose Fidelity, Prudence and Vigilancy, it chiefly comes to pass, that the Affairs of *France* are carri'd on with such Success.
>
> (W115, P149)

After the victory, Cromwell observes that young men may benefit from Mazarin's

> Example of Civility, Candour, and Friendship to us; since there are not more conspicuous Examples of extraordinary Prudence and Vertue to be imitated then in your Eminency; from whence they may learn with equal Renown to Govern Kingdoms, and manage the most important Affairs of the World.
>
> (W119, P155)

Thus spoke kings to kings, princes to princes, lords to lords, and ambassadors to heads of state. Some of Milton's experience with the protocol of praise may be seen in passages depicting the court of Heaven, where the elaborate custom of address, the deference shown both Father and Son, the hierarchy, the celebrations, and the hymns to the Almighty reflect his familiarity with such symbols of rule. These hymns far surpass in grandeur and beauty any praise that might reach the ears of earthly monarchs, however, and Mary Ann Radzinowicz, with her usual grace, has explained why: Milton drew his inspiration for his lines from the Book of Psalms, illustrating once again by how far God's glory exceeds their own, and how shallow and idolatrous are their poor efforts to imitate the Most High.[16]

The details of his Heavenly court, one must assume, Milton gleaned primarily from his books, though his participation in audiences for foreign envoys and familiarity with the protocol of praise customary in the diplomatic correspondence of his age may account in part for the elaborate deference shown Heaven's King. Another influence may have been the court of the Lord Protector, accounts of which doubtless came to his ears, though it is unlikely that he ever stood in attendance there. Oliver Cromwell, on assuming the mantle of Lord Protector, grew grand as time went on, having attained with the title a power all but regal. Indeed, at one point he considered accepting the crown, to be deterred only by opposition from the Army. He moved into Whitehall Palace, left untenanted during the Commonwealth period, adopted Hampton Court as an alternate seat, reestablished monarchal offices in the state bureaucracy, the Exchequer and Secretary of

---

16. Radzinowicz, *Milton's Epics and the Book of Psalms,* 148–56. The influence of Psalms would seem to outweigh that of Milton's experience in addressing the monarchs of Europe but his duties in preparing the letters reinforced the propriety of including such passages and contributed to the political tone of the hymns. See also Barbara K. Lewalski, *"Paradise Lost and the Rhetoric of Literary Forms,* 160–72.

State, and presided over a court increasingly marked by regal decorum.[17] What Milton thought of all this we can only surmise, but he was certainly aware of the trend.

Milton may, indeed, have never seen a monarch; but he wrote enough about kings during his public life to demonstrate a familiarity with court life, which he deplored for its ostentatious wealth and false display. In *The Readie and Easie Way* he warns his countrymen of the royal court that will be imposed upon them should they exchange a free commonwealth for the monarchy. The passage is long, but the language delicious, and paraphrase would not do it justice:

> A king must be ador'd like a Demigod, with a dissolute and haughtie court about him, of vast expence and luxurie, masks and revels, to the debaushing of our prime gentry both male and female; not in thir passetimes only, but in earnest, by the loos imploiments of court service, which will be then thought honorable. There will be a queen also of no less charge; in most likelihood outlandish and a Papist; besides a queen mother such alreadie; together with thir courts and numerous train: then a royal issue, and ere long severally thir sumptuous courts; to the multiplying of a servile crew, not servants only, but of nobility and gentry, bred up then to the hopes not of public, but of court offices; to be stewarts, chamberlains, ushers, grooms, even of the close-stool; and the lower thir mindes debas'd with court opinions, contrarie to all vertue and reformation, the haughtier will be thir pride and profuseness.[18]

As for the king, he

> will have little els to do, but to bestow the eating and drinking of excessive dainties, to set a pompous face upon the superficial actings of the State, to pageant himself up and down in progress among the perpetual bowings and cringings of an abject people, on

17. Antonia Fraser describes the elaborate decorum of Cromwell's court "on much the same lines if not to the same degree as that previously enjoyed by the King" (*Cromwell, The Lord Protector* 456-62). By 1659, the annual budget for "His Highness' Household" had reached £100,000, and for "His Highness' Privy Purse" over £23,000 (*MG* 134n).

18. Although there was surely no "chamberlain . . . of the close-stool" appointed in Cromwell's court, one of these useful items (a chamber pot) was secured, in red velvet, for the Lord Protector's comfort (Fraser, *Cromwell,* 459).

either side deifying and adoring him for nothing done that can deserve it.

(*Prose* 7:425-26)

Thus, Milton used the very practices that he deplored in temporal monarchs to create a King of Heaven so glorious and a court so splendid that it put his idolatrous imitators to shame.

God the Son

The praise afforded the Son, "in him all his Father shone / Substantially express'd," introduces ambiguities about the figure of the same order as those that trouble readers about Milton's representation of the Father. The relationship between the two has been a matter of controversy ever since the first publication of *Christian Doctrine* in 1825, from which it was discovered that Milton was not entirely orthodox in his concept of the Trinity. Maurice Kelley has meticulously examined *Paradise Lost* and *Christian Doctrine;* and though acknowledging that allowances must be made for the differences between "a poem" and "a systematic theology," he finds in both evidence of Arian heterodoxy.

It is difficult to escape the conclusion that in *Christian Doctrine* Milton rejects the central belief that the Father and the Son are coeval. He describes God's "external efficiency" as manifest in three ways, through generation, creation, and the government of the universe (*Prose* 6:205); but the only instance of generation cited is the begetting of the Son.[19] A case for the eternal existence of both could perhaps be mounted on the basis of a fine distinction between generation and creation; but Kelley will have none of it and, citing *Christian Doctrine,* book 1, chap. 5 (*Prose* 6:209-10), he summarizes the evidence: "The Son was begotten as a consequence of a decree; and since the decree must have been anterior to the fulfillment of it, the Son was born within the limits of time, and is consequently not eternal, as is the Father."[20] Subsequent scholars have questioned Kelley's conclusions, in

---

19. There is a distinguishable difference between *Christian Doctrine* and *Paradise Lost* in these matters. In Milton's chapters on creation and government (*Prose* 6:299-381) it is everywhere God who acts, although he creates "through Christ" (*Prose* 6:267) and the Son is acknowledged to be "the head" of the angels (*Prose* 6:345). In the poem, as we shall see, the Son is consistently depicted as the active agent in the exercise of these powers.

20. Kelley, *This Great Argument*, 96, 11, 84.

response to which, for example, William B. Hunter unequivocally states that "we may positively assert that Milton was not an Arian" and C. A. Patrides argues that the "subordinationism" implied in the Father-Son relationship does not necessarily identify Milton as an anti-Trinitarian.[21]

The argument of *Christian Doctrine* arises from Milton's belief that although God is incomprehensible, he has revealed as much of his nature as is necessary for salvation. In Scripture, as Milton explains, "he has adjusted his word to our understanding, and has shown what kind of idea of him he wishes us to have" (*Prose* 6:136).[22] God has made himself accessible to human reason and the faithful need only reason properly to comprehend him. The work is dotted with the language of logic – "It would follow from the first hypothesis," "contradiction in terms," "the fact can be reasonably deduced," "inconsistent with reason," "laws of opposites" (*Prose* 6:211, 212, 222, 219, 264) – as Milton urges his readers to think clearly about what the Bible says. As a consequence, he takes literally, as he does all Scripture, the biblical designation of Father and Son, concluding that if the father begot the son, by definition he must have preceded him: "By GENERATION God begot his only Son, in accordance with his decree. That is the chief reason why he is called Father."[23]

Thus *Christian Doctrine,* but *Paradise Lost* is not a "systematic theology" interpretable by the laws of logic; it is rather a work of the poetic imagination, a historical narrative of metaphysical events, embellished with imagery and language that do not lend themselves to the doctrinal certainty of a treatise that calls upon the exercise of reason alone. Kelley acknowledges the difference, of course, but never pursues the distinction, arguing throughout that the two works are doctrinally compatible, in brief, addressing *Paradise Lost* as if it were indeed a "systematic theology."[24] Again, *Christian Doctrine* is a rational exposition of divine truth; *Paradise Lost* is a work of art that employs exalted language, elements of music, and figures of imaginative sweep to reach beyond the rational faculty and say more than reason can

---

21. Hunter, "Milton's Arianism Reconsidered," 50; J. H. Adamson, "Milton's 'Arianism,' " 60; and Patrides, "Milton and Arianism," 71-77.

22. See also 6:133: "Admittedly, God is always described or outlined not as he really is but in such a way as will make him conceivable to us. Nevertheless, we ought to form just such a mental image of him as he, in bringing himself within the limits of our understanding, wishes us to form."

23. *Prose* 6:205. See also 6:167 and 6:264, where Milton chides those who think otherwise: "If Father and Son were one essence, which, because of their relationship, is impossible, it would follow that the Father was the Son's son and the Son the Father's father."

24. Kelley, *This Great Argument,* 98, 195-96.

express, evoking the emotions that life entails – fear, joy, wonder, hope, love, hate, and the sad sense of loss – wherein the reader may find a truth inaccessible to any treatise or testament.

A poem dares to do more than a treatise. At one point in *Christian Doctrine* Milton observes: "Anyone who asks what God did before the creation of the world is a fool; and anyone who answers him is not much wiser" (*Prose* 6:299); but in *Paradise Lost* he is perfectly willing to play the fool, devoting over a thousand lines to such events. Again, he advises caution in contemplating the mysteries of faith: "We should let mysteries alone and not tamper with them. We should be afraid to pry into things further than we were meant" (*Prose* 6:421). The Holy Trinity is a mysterious entity, seemingly without counterpart in human experience; hence it should not be surprising that when Milton, interpreting Scripture as literal truth, reduces that mystery to the rule of reason, he finds it wanting. He rejects the teaching that the Holy Spirit and the Son are of the same essence as the Father. The three do constitute a Holy Trinity of sorts, but they are not one in the same sense that God is "ONE" (*Prose* 6:146); nor are they equal in power, for "the Son undoubtedly comes after the Father . . . in rank" and the Spirit after them both (*Prose* 6:219, 298). In *Paradise Lost,* as we shall see, these distinctions all but dissolve; the poetic images make it possible to conceive of the three as "ONE." The poem, again, can say more than the treatise. A poet, as Milton claims, who is instructed by the Spirit that "from the first / Wast present" (1:19–20), his mind irradiated by "Celestial Light," has the power to "see and tell / Of things invisible to mortal sight" (3:51–55), things beyond the reach of reason. It is not surprising that a poet so guided should claim keener insight than a logician or a theologian, or believe that art can achieve more than the rational mind can aspire to.

The impression of Arianism arises from how the Father and Son function both as political agents operating within a historical narrative and as abstract articles of faith, two perceptions not entirely compatible. In the narrative frame the two appear as separate beings situated in a familial context with the Son properly respectful of the Father, acting only at his direction. It is chiefly in the imagery that defines their relationship and in the hymns of praise addressed to them that one finds the two depicted as one.

As an expression of theological doctrine, we learn of the Son from what others say about him; and in these descriptions Milton appears to be an acceptably orthodox trinitarian. It is true that the angelic choir celebrates him as "of all Creation first / Begotten Son"; but in the same breath he is also the "Divine Similitude, / In whose conspicuous count'nance, without cloud

/ Made visible, th' Almighty shines" (3:383-86). Actually, both descriptions are articles of faith for the angels, who were not present at that first "Creation" and, having never seen God, simply accept the "Similitude." The Father is a surer guide in such matters and he nowhere says that he "created" the Son, who is rather "My Word, my wisdom, and effectual might" (3:170). During the war in Heaven, God refers to him as the

> Son in whose face invisible is beheld
> Visibly, what by Deity I am,
> And in whose hand what by Decree I do,
> Second Omnipotence.
>
> (6:681-84)

The Almighty directs him to create the World, explaining that "my Word, begotten Son, by thee / This I perform" (7:163-64); and on returning from the judgment of Adam and Eve, he is into God's "blissful bosom reassum'd" (10:225). The narrative voice is even more explicit: in the Son "all his Father shone / Substantially express'd" (3:139-40), a characterization worth repeating, "Resplendent all his Father manifest / Express'd" (10:65-66). This imagery leaves the overwhelming impression that the two are one, and the Son is the Father "express'd," that is, made known to his creation. The Deity is "invisible / Amidst the glorious brightness where thou sit'st / Thron'd inaccessible" (3:375-77), known only to his subjects as a voice; and the Son represents those qualities of his nature which he chooses to reveal through action.

The two are one in a theological sense, but their identity serves a narrative need as well: the poet must have the Son if he is to define the Father adequately.[25] The challenge is to create an anthromorphic figure who is at the same time omniscient, and this is a challenge indeed.[26] The difficulty is that any attribution of human qualities to the Deity has the effect of diminishing his divine nature; hence Milton's efforts to create a dramatically satisfying character in a historical narrative often result in a theologically unsatisfactory Almighty. It is no simple matter to represent an omniscient

25. As Anthony Low has observed, "The Father's character, then, is defined to a large extent by his son, who is his visible manifestation" ("Milton's God" 32).

26. Dennis Danielson defines Milton's artistic problem as resolving the apparent contradiction between the beliefs "that certain actions are humanly virtuous and praise-worthy" and "that in fact they result from divine agency" (*Milton's Good God* 80). The same may be said of evil actions, such as Satan's rebellion.

being in the midst of joy or sorrow or anger, or a king seeking vengeance against a trusted lord whom he has known will betray him from the first moment he pledges fealty. A Henry V may with reason rage at the treachery of a Scroop whom he had loved, who as the king charges, "didst bear the key of all my counsels, / [And] knew'st the very bottom of my soul" (2.2.96-97); but can such wrath be justified in a god with sure foreknowledge? Such a Deity should be serenity itself; and indeed Milton is quite skillful in occasionally hinting at the human qualities in the Almighty without jeopardizing the divine equanimity that should accompany omniscience.[27] In one episode, God seems to voice anxiety at Satan's impending invasion, but the Son catches the ironic mockery of his remarks and responds to his feigned uncertainty with appreciation (5:719-42). If Milton's Deity displays anger, it is distinctly subdued; he is not the Old Testament God of wrath, who at times seems to be caught by surprise at just how pigheaded his chosen people can be. His instructions to Michael before the war in Heaven are delivered without rancor, as are those to the Son after the Fall: "I intend / Mercy colleague with Justice" (10:58-59). He seems not quite the serene omniscient, however, when he announces his intention to repopulate Heaven in order to deprive Satan of any satisfaction from his rebellion. If the Deity appears somewhat petty in these sentiments, they are at least recognizably human.[28]

Such efforts are less than successful, however; and for the most part it is the Son who demonstrates the qualities of the Father that draw him within the sphere of human understanding. The Son appears as a prominent figure in four episodes of *Paradise Lost,* and in each he demonstrates a different quality of the Godhead. In the war in Heaven, he displays the Almighty's power. When Man's fate is proclaimed, he reveals divine love, offering "mee for him, life for life" (3:236) to redeem the race. The revelation of God's creative energy fills an entire book of the poem; and both his justice and his mercy are disclosed in the judgment passed on Adam and Eve.[29] The Son, in brief, *is* the Father, that aspect of him which does not "dazzle Heav'n" and

---

27. Roland Frye has drawn attention to the iconographic tradition of Heavenly figures engaged in combat with various forces of evil. The painting usually depicts the moment of victory, but the angel or saint shown displays no sign of physical exertion, nor is there any sense of triumph. Any outward expression of emotion was considered unseemly, for to display uncertainty, or anxiety, or even satisfaction at the victory was considered an indication of wavering faith. See Frye, *Milton's Imagery and the Visual Arts,* 53-54.

28. As Danielson observes, "God's hating and punishing sin is emphatically consistent with divine attributes" (*Milton's Good God* 154).

29. In "Kingly States: The Politics in *Paradise Lost,*" Stephen Buhler proposes another quality of the Deity, "his willingness to serve the people," citing the example of the Son, who is

which the "brightest Seraphim" may approach without veiling their eyes (3:381-82).

The "systematic theology" and the epic poem, the one appealing to human reason, the other to the imagination, do not then always agree in doctrinal detail. A vivid example is their separate approaches to the naming of the Son as "Jehovah." In *Christian Doctrine* Milton goes to great lengths to demonstrate that when the Son is called Jehovah in the Bible, the faithful should not conclude that he and the Father are of the same essence, for, he argues, that title is used very loosely in Scripture, at times referring to angels and at others to two separate persons at once (*Prose* 6:250-60). In *Paradise Lost,* on the other hand, the title appears in a hymn of praise addressed to the Son upon his return from the Creation, one in which the language is so ambiguous as to give the distinct impression that the Father and Son share a single nature:

> Great are thy works, *Jehovah,* infinite
> Thy power; what thought can measure thee or tongue
> Relate thee; greater now in thy return
> Than from the Giant Angels; thee that day
> Thy Thunders magnifi'd.
>
> (7:602-6)

The first three lines obviously allude to the omnipotent God, "what thought can measure thee or tongue / Relate thee," and those that follow to the Son, whose return after the Creation is compared to his return after the War in Heaven; but "thy works," "Thy power," "thy return," and "Thy Thunders" make no distinction between the two. The hymn addresses them as one. The Son, here again, *is* the Father.

The political imagery of *Paradise Lost* illustrates the Son's role in defining the Father. In the narrative of the poem, the first event in Milton's chronology of cosmic history is the anointing of the Son:

> This day I have begot whom I declare
> My only Son, and on this holy Hill

---

praised as "Worthiest to reign" after he has volunteered to serve (50). Buhler contrasts him to Satan, whose concept of kingship is based "not so much upon service provided by the ruler as upon homage offered by the ruled" (60). The contrast works well when drawn between Satan and the Son, but seems to have little relevance to Milton's God, whom Buhler hardly mentions.

> Him have anointed, whom ye now behold
> At my right hand; your Head I him appoint;
> And by my Self have sworn to him shall bow
> All knees in Heav'n, and shall confess him Lord.
>   (5:603-8)[30]

God's decree represents a radical change in the government of Heaven, whose structure until that time may be inferred from the response of the angels to the new order. Before that announcement it is evident that God as the King of Heaven ruled by decree, but that he was known to the angels only through those decrees. To the Heavenly host he is but a voice emanating from a bright cloud, establishing the laws that govern their existence. Prior to his declaration it is apparently known that he has a Son, who is identified as the Word, though it should not be implied from this designation that the Father's speaks through the Son, at least not in *Paradise Lost,* where the Deity speaks distinctly for himself. There is nothing in the poem, however, that would lead one to conclude that the Son, prior to that decree, had an existence separate from the Father. All that is known of the earlier relationship is that the Son was the manifestation of God's creative efficiency, the agent by which the realm of Heaven and its numberless subjects were brought into existence. Nothing would indicate that he had an essence or a substance distinct from God's.

That great decree changes everything, however, for it proclaims a new role for the Son, one he will assume with an identity entirely his own. Prior to his elevation the angels had been ruled by God himself, with the lordly seraphim and cherabim standing close to the throne of the Almighty, answering directly to his voice. Now Heaven has a new "Head"; the Son will henceforth stand between the angels and their God, in a place where none had stood before, initiating his own "Vice-gerent Reign," and, as is immediately apparent, assuming the dignity of "King anointed." God shows himself aware that this new office in the governance of Heaven is so revolutionary in nature that it will invite opposition; and he inaugurates the new order by drawing attention to one of the laws of Heaven of which his subjects are doubtless well aware, that disobedience will be punished by exile "Into utter darkness . . .

---

30. The word "begot" has been the subject of some misunderstanding. In *Christian Doctrine* Milton defines it as having "two senses . . . one literal, with reference to production; the other metaphorical, with reference to exaltation" (*Prose* 6:205). It is generally agreed that in *Paradise Lost* Milton means it in the metaphorical sense. See Kelley, *This Great Argument,* 94-98.

without redemption, without end" (5:614-15). This much of the decree, we may assume, constitutes nothing new.

The Son's new status in the hierarchy of Heaven is soon confirmed by Satan, who resents the consequent diminution of his own political position.[31] His reaction is comparable to that of a powerful nobility when a court favorite is placed between them and the king, interrupting their direct access to the throne. Rebellious political forces of Milton's day, reluctant to confront the monarch himself, professed themselves devoted to his safety and dignity, and in their campaign to undermine his authority sought first to depose his most trusted advisers. One of the first acts of the Long Parliament was to demand the trial and execution of the king's chief minister, the earl of Strafford; and when the French nobles gained the upper hand during the Fronde, they insisted on the exile of Mazarin. As Satan tells his followers, the Son has now "to himself ingross't / All Power, and us eclipst under the name / Of King anointed" (5:775-77), rendering their titles meaningless. Paying "Knee-tribute" to God is humiliating enough, he claims, but to do so to two kings, "To one and to his image" as well, is unacceptable to free beings (5:782-84).

Satan's characterization of the Son as the Father's "image" introduces yet another innovation in the governance of Heaven. The Son, hitherto God's Word in creating Heaven and the angels, now appears to his subjects for the first time. God draws attention to him "whom ye now behold / At my right hand," presumably a position of honor he had not visibly occupied until that time. Abdiel confirms the innovation in his debate with Satan, allowing that though the angels knew of "the Word" by which "the mighty Father made / All things," that is all they knew of him. He stands before them now, however, visibly manifest, and *in the form of an angel;* he has been, as Abdiel argues, to "One of our number thus reduc't," ascending his throne the better to "exalt / Our happy state under one Head more near / United" (5:843, 829-31). In political terms, God reduces the possibility of resentment of the new office by manifesting the Son, and by association himself, for the first time in a shape like their own, the Godhead "reduc't" to the form of an angel, to accommodate his nature to the understanding of his subjects.[32]

It is difficult to identify the Son with the Godhead, however, when he is so

---

31. As Stephen Buhler notes, "To Satan, the Son is a usurper; he has been allowed to appropriate a great deal of angelic order and degree" ("Kingly States" 57).

32. Albert C. Labriola, " 'Thy Humiliation Shall Exalt,' " 32; Danielson, *Milton's Good God,* 223.

much "the Son," and the political "Heir" to the divine throne, and when he pays God all the elaborate deference due an elder sire. The political imagery of *Paradise Lost* depicts him as an agent of the Deity, subordinate to him, obeying his commands, performing duties as "Vicegerent." It is not an easy task to show a son coequal and coeval with a father, especially when the father is "Omnipotent" and "Infinite"; and it is particularly difficult to depict the heir to a throne occupied by an immortal king. Milton confounds the artistic challenge by having the two engage in conversation, both private and public, during which the Son is very much a son, respectful, obedient, loving, and deferential. He is not without his devices, of course, displayed when God predicts the fall and death of Man. The Father descants on justice, glory, predestination, and sin, after which the Son picks up on what seems a chance remark, "O Father, gracious was that word which clos'd / Thy sovran sentence, that Man should find grace" (3:144–45) and asks whether Man will be irredeemably lost. God answers with more justification, concluding with the stern "Die hee or Justice must" unless there be one who will die for him. The Son draws his attention once again to his earlier remark, "Father, thy word is past, man shall find grace" (3:227) and offers himself as the means whereby God may fulfill his promise. The impression that this exchange is a set piece is offset by the Son's shrewd manipulation of the Father's own words to focus on the quality of mercy. No one would ever call it an argument between the two, but it is clear that the Son must be circumspect in prompting the Father to allow the merciful side of his nature to prevail. This, then, is the risk Milton takes in depicting the two in conversation; one is clearly subordinate to the other and their discourse has the faint ring of a generation gap. They sound like advocates, not in disagreement, but with different agendas for Man, the one pleading justice, the other mercy, the one death, the other life.[33]

Pursuing the family relationship dictated by biblical convention and Christian teaching complicates the task of maintaining the theological doctrine of the Trinity. Milton's political imagery cuts both ways. As we have seen, on the one hand, the Son is heir to the throne of Heaven; on the other, he is already a king. In its ritual design, the exaltation of the Son at the great assembly of angels resembles nothing so much as the designation of an heir, even though God's words declare it a coronation: "your Head I him appoint;

---

33. C. A. Patrides observes that the difference between Father and Son is evident only during "their verbal exchange," and that when "the Godhead acts beyond the confines of Heaven the distinction between the two persons is abruptly dropped" ("Milton on the Trinity" 12).

/ And by my Self have sworn to him shall bow / All knees in Heav'n, and shall confess him Lord" (3:606-8). The war in Heaven is, to all appearances, orchestrated by God to provide occasion for the Son to demonstrate his right to that dignity. "For thee I have ordain'd it," the Father confides, "To manifest thee worthiest to be Heir / Of all things and to be King / By Sacred Unction, thy deserved right" (6:700-709); and it certainly achieves all he could have desired. The Son returns to the sound of choirs that sing him "Victorious King, / Son, Heir, and Lord, to him Dominion given, / Worthiest to Reign" (6:886-88).[34]

Thus, Milton balances the seeming contradiction of declaring the Son heir to the throne of an immortal father by describing him as a king already. He is never called a prince, not even the traditional "Prince of Peace"; that rank is reserved for the angels, one of whose degrees is a "Princedom," though only Michael and Satan are specifically referred to by that title. The Heavenly choirs sing with equal exuberance for both Father and Son: "never shall my Harp thy praise / Forget, nor from thy Father's praise disjoin" (3:414-15). And, as observed earlier, both are enthroned. With traditional feudal ceremony the angels show them common respect: "lowly reverent / Toward either Throne they bow, and to the ground / With solemn adoration down they cast / Thir Crowns" (3:349-53).

Milton obscures the inequality inherent in the family relationship in his use of theological, as well as political titles. In his account of the six days of Creation, the two are so intermeshed that they are virtually indistinguishable. In Genesis, God but "says" a thing and it is so; but in *Paradise Lost* Milton pursues the theme of the Son as God "substantially express'd" by making him, here called "the Filial Godhead," the creative agent of the Deity. The language is ambiguous, however. On the first day, it is the Son as "omnific Word" who silences the Deep, turns the golden compasses, and intones the words of creation. On subsequent days, Milton has "God" and "th'Almighty" speak the words; and if the first day is intended as precedent, these titles then attach to the Son. When the time comes for the creation of Man, however, Milton is faithful to the biblical text, which makes use of the plural pronoun: "And God said, Let *us* make man in our image, after our likeness" (Genesis 1:26; italics mine), which leaves the distinct impression that they are working as one. The poet embellishes the verse by attributing the words to God in conversation with the Son:

---

34. Perez Zagorin observes perceptively that "In the civil war in heaven the rebel Milton had to be a royalist" (*Milton, Aristocrat and Rebel* 127).

> th'Omnipotent
> Eternal Father (For where is not hee
> Present) thus to his Son audibly spake.
>   Let us make now Man in our image, Man
> In our similitude.
>
>   (7:516-20)

By interpreting the text as a conversation between Father and Son and adding the parenthetical justification for doing so, "(For where is not hee / Present)," Milton casts doubt on which of the two speaks the words on the previous days, save, as noted, for the first, where it is clearly the Son. The work done, "The Filial Power" returns to "th'Imperial Throne / Of Godhead" and Milton explains that the Father has indeed accompanied the Son, "for he also went / Invisible, yet stay'd (such privilege / Hath Omnipresence) and the work ordain'd, / Author and end of all things" (7:585-91); and we may be assured that the Father was not simply looking over the Son's shoulder as he was about his business. When on the seventh day he is "from work / Now resting" (7:591-92), it is unclear who has been doing the work; the syntax of the passage is so equivocal that it might have been either one.

The pattern prevails in later episodes. When the Son descends to Eden to judge Adam and Eve, the narrative voice refers to him throughout as "God," even "the Lord God" (10:163). Admittedly, for Adam the Son *is* God; but the effect Milton achieves by his ambiguous use of these titles is, again, to identify the two figures so closely with each other that it is difficult to distinguish between them.

Whatever the theology of *Christian Doctrine,* therefore, in *Paradise Lost* the Father and Son are one, both voice and agent in enacting the will of the Deity, and at the same time two distinct figures depicted in a familial relationship. In dividing them Milton is faithful to biblical tradition; in joining them he resolves an artistic dilemma – how to represent the Almighty. In *Christian Doctrine,* Milton the theologian is somewhat contradictory, at one point arguing that since God chose to present himself in human guise, we should not hesitate to accept him as such: "If God attributes to himself again and again a human shape and form, why should we be afraid of assigning him something he assigns to himself." At the same time, however, he questions the practice of ascribing "human feelings to God" (*Prose* 6:136, 134). The theologian may reasonably ponder the apparent inconsistency of ascribing human form to the Deity and yet denying him human feelings; but the poet can have it both ways. He must do so with some care, however; Milton is in enough trouble giving God a voice and to do more would reduce the figure to a Deity restricted to time and space, "a contradiction in terms," as he puts it. He surrounds the figure with the trappings and ritual of a splendid monarch, a court which celebrates that voice in exalted hymns legitimizing its decrees; but the poet dare not depict his God as acting. Indeed, the only instance in which he seems to meddle directly in the affairs of his creation is his orchestration of the war in Heaven, where he limits the strength of the angels and withholds one-half of the loyal host from battle; and the criticism which that passage has attracted, stretching back to Dr. Johnson's well-known complaint about the "confusion of spirit and matter," gives some notion of the dangers to be encountered by introducing an intrusively imminent God into the narrative.[35]

It is the Son who acts, assuming the mantle of a king, defeating the rebel angels in battle, creating the World, forming Eve from Adam's rib, and conversing with Man in the Garden. It is a brilliant solution, doctrinally correct as long as Father and Son are seen as one, and artistically decorous since Milton's Christian readers will identify the figure of the Son with the Messiah, who, though God, was a human like themselves. As God, the Son can create a universe; as Man he can reign in regal state, accepting from his throne the homage of a splendid court. As God, he can destroy that universe; as Man he can ride into battle and defeat his foes with a rain of arrows. As God he is king already, as Man he is heir to the throne. As God he can judge, as Man he can love. By depicting the Son as the Father "substantially express'd," Milton can show him acting both for and as God, thereby preserving the mystery and awe appropriate to a "Omnipotent, / Immutable, Immortal, Infinite, / Eternal" being; by figuring the Son as separate and subordinate to the Father he can bring such a being within the compass of human understanding. The political imagery thus plays a dual role. Milton describes a court whose splendor warns earthly kings against aspiring to absolute rule; and in representing the "King and Heir" of Heaven acting in ways familiar to the temporal reader, the poet makes the Deity accessible to human comprehension without sacrificing his incomprehensibility.

---

35. Arnold Stein, for example, finds the account "terribly funny" (*Answerable Style* 20); and John Wooten sees the angels as "absurdist comic actors" ("The Metaphysics of Milton's Epic Burlesque Humor" 259). See *CC* 201-7.

3

TO REIGN IN HELL

The difficulty that centuries of readers have had with Milton's Satan is that he runs afoul of our moral sense, or at least our understanding of the poet's moral sense. The Devil is the Father of Lies, so goes the response, hence everything he says must be untrue; he is the Architect of Evil, hence all his actions must be wicked; he is the Monarch of Hell, hence he must be the worst of tyrants, a ruthless, self-serving dictator who rules over his dismal kingdom with absolute sway, terrorizing his subjects into servile submission. Evil is foul, so he must be ugly; it is corrupting, so he must stink; it is destined for defeat, so all his designs are futile, his efforts ridiculous. Such, indeed, was the allegorical figure of medieval iconography, a hairy-shanked, cloven-hoofed, horned monster, thwarted at every turn by the forces of good, skewered by serene angels with golden lances and outfaced by faithful saints armed with the dazzling light of their sanctity. So he was, at least until the Renaissance, when artists like Marlowe offered a very different figure indeed, a sophisticated, slick-talking man-about-town, a delightful companion, disarmingly candid about his fallen state and insatiable thirst for souls, a master of amusing tricks, corrupt certainly, but quite charming in his corruption.

Milton takes the figure a step further; the devilishly attractive Mephistopheles is elevated to heroic stature, a resolute commander, undaunted by defeat, who rallies his shattered forces and returns to battle. Again we think – Milton can't mean it. He must be saying something else. Scholars have twisted and turned in contorted interpretations of Milton's message, assuring us that the poet was not of the Devil's party, knowingly or unknowingly, and that in this towering figure he encoded a harsh criticism of his own times. Since this is the Devil, so goes the thought, Milton must be condemning everything even remotely associated with him. Since he displays all the qualities of an Achilles or Aeneas, the poet must be making mock of his literary antecedents who composed in the epic tradition. Since he is a warrior figure, the poet is registering a protest against war.[1] Since he seems to reflect the qualities of Oliver Cromwell, Milton is registering his distaste for the Lord Protector.[2] Since the Devil is a consummate politician, the poet is declaring his disgust with public life and his regret that he had ever taken part in it.[3]

Simply stated, the problem for Milton's readers is that they find entirely too much to admire in his Devil; the figure defies expectations by engaging our sympathy. His speeches reflect a dauntless spirit:

What though the field be lost?
All is not lost; the unconquerable Will

1. Stella P. Revard, *The War in Heaven.* As she puts it, "Milton makes his angels take on the demeanor of classical warriors in order to discredit the ethic of heroic battle.... He makes Satan into an epic hero ... to show what was wrong with the conventional epic hero. He allows his angels to raise heroic battle in Heaven ... to demonstrate what is essentially perverse in the ethic of typical heroic poems" (197). David Quint finds *Paradise Lost* "a general criticism of the earlier epic tradition" and Milton aligned with the "anti-Virgilian, anti-imperial epic tradition" (*Epic and Empire* 264, 326). John Steadman is quite explicit: "Thus the closer Satan resembles Achilles and Odysseus, the more forceful is Milton's condemnation of these Homeric heroes" (*Milton and the Renaissance Hero* 170).

2. As Empson observes, it is uncertain whether he was satirizing Cromwell or Charles (*Milton's God* 74). Perez Zagorin, for example, feels obliged to defend Milton's loyalty to Cromwell in response to Blair Worden's suggestion, in "Milton's Republicanism and the Tyranny of Heaven," that the parallels between Satan and the Lord Protector imply criticism of the latter. Zagorin insists that "nowhere in Milton's later writings, moreover, is there any indication ... that he reversed his opinion of Cromwell as a great and virtuous leader" (*Milton, Aristocrat and Rebel* 128n).

3. Stein, *Answerable Style,* 131.

> And study of revenge, immortal hate,
> And courage never to submit or yield.
> And what is else not to be overcome?
>   (1:106-7)

Though plagued by despair, he refuses to submit to it, charging his followers not to abandon hope:

> For who can yet believe, though after loss
> That all these puissant Legions, whose exile
> Hath emptied Heav'n, shall fail to re-ascend
> Self-rais'd, and repossess thir native Seat.
>   (1:631-34)

The narrative voice enhances the impression, describing a courageous warrior who "durst defy th' Omnipotent to Arms" (1:49) and an inspiring leader who by the force of his example rallied his shattered soldiers from off the burning lake and, moving among them, "gently rais'd / Thir fainting courage, and dispell'd thir fears" (1:529-30). He is an imposing figure, commanding in size; and though he no longer dazzles with his former celestial brightness, the shadows make his countenance somehow more human:

>   his face
> Deep scars of Thunder had intrencht, and care
> Sat on his faded cheek, but under Brows
> Of dauntless courage, and considerate Pride.
>   (1:600-603)

Undeterred by the frightening spectacle of Chaos, "the hoary deep, a dark / Illimitable Ocean" (2:891-92) or its "noises loud and ruinous" (2:921), he undertakes a perilous voyage, "his Sail-broad Vans / He spreads for flight, and in the surging smoke / Uplifted spurns the ground" (2:927-29). William Hazlitt best voiced the impression Satan makes upon the unwary reader:[4]

> Satan is the most heroic subject that ever was chosen for a poem; and the execution is as perfect as the design is lofty. . . . His aim was

---

4. Stanley Fish has alerted us to Milton's designs upon the unsuspecting reader. The insights of *Surprised by Sin* have become so assimilated into modern critical assumptions about *Paradise Lost* that they often go undocumented.

no less than the throne of the universe; his means, myriads of angelic armies bright, the third part of the heavens, whom he lured after him with his countenance, and who durst defy the Omnipotent in arms. His ambition was the greatest, and his punishment was the greatest; but not so his despair, for his fortitude was as great as his sufferings. His strength of mind was matchless as his strength of body; the vastness of his designs did not surpass the firm, inflexible determination with which he submitted to his irreversible doom, and final loss of all good. His power of action and of suffering was equal. He was the greatest power that was ever overthrown, with the strongest will left to resist or to endure.[5]

Puzzled by Satan's appeal, Christian scholars have resolved their dilemma by proclaiming the figure pathetically inept, his pretensions absurd in the light of his ultimate fate and his plots, hatched under the scrutiny of an all-seeing God, worthy only of divine and human scorn. He is, in brief, a fool to undertake opposition to the Almighty, and Milton's Christian readers may take comfort in the ridiculous figure he cuts in doing so.[6] As will be seen, however, he is not the inept bungler that such critics would have him; indeed he is all too successful in everything he undertakes after his challenge of omnipotence. It is perhaps time to dismiss the notion that Satan is ironically comic and Hell a huge joke. Milton's "Prince of Darkness" cannot be scorned simply because he lacks God's omniscience or the Christian reader's knowledge of his fate on the Final Day. Of course he will fail in the end; but meanwhile it is his successes that most concern Milton and his contemporaries, firm in their belief that when Hell is closed, that grave will hold the numberless tortured souls of those who fall under his sway.[7]

5. Hazlitt, "On Shakspeare and Milton," 63.

6. This reading owes much to Charles Williams, who in his introduction to *The English Poems of John Milton* drew attention to "the irrepressible laughter in Heaven" (xiii) and C. S. Lewis, who in his *Preface to Paradise Lost* described Satan as "the horrible co-existence of a subtle and incessant intellectual activity with an incapacity to understand anything" (99). John Tanner illustrates the continuing appeal of such a reading; he insists that Milton's God "laughs at the Satanic rebellion, for it is quite literally ridiculous. We, too, are meant to enjoy the parodic hilarity" (*Anxiety in Eden* 139). David Quint finds the account of Satan's voyage "slapstick comedy" (*Epic and Empire* 255). Marcia Landry does not find Satan funny, but does consider him "criminally delinquent" (" 'Bounds Prescrib'd' " 118).

7. Cf. 2:596-603. As Empson observes, "Satan was intended to strike terror into the reader, not to be a figure of farce" (*Milton's God* 98).

In an earlier work, I surveyed the spectrum of critical opinion on the figure of Satan (*CC* 167-73) and suggested that Milton created such an imposing figure, not to call down scorn on the power of evil but to warn his readers of the awesome forces ranged against their souls. Since the conclusions reached in that study have significant implications for an analysis of Milton's political imagery, it will be of value to summarize them briefly here. Satan, like God, is at once a theological abstraction and an active agent in a historical narrative, two roles not always logically or artistically compatible. Like God again, he appears to Milton's readers in different guises. As the Lord of Hell and eventually of Earth, he is the powerful antagonist of the Almighty in a cosmic struggle between the forces of good and evil; and after the disastrous war in Heaven, he has more victories than defeats to his credit. In his role as the Architect of Evil, the sire of Sin and Death, he illustrates the corrupting effect of wickedness upon the human soul. Within the narrative frame of *Paradise Lost* he is the only figure who offers Milton the opportunity to explore the consequences of sin. In his ambition, pain, and despair, he is far closer to the human experience than spotless Adam in his pristine Garden or the dazzling creatures of Heaven; so Milton, rather than create a monster, drew a figure who reflects the dilemmas of fallen Man. His gradual deterioration through the poem illustrates the effects of sin; and though his final defeat is foretold, more to the point, his history reveals with devastating irony that evil is ultimately self-defeating.

As the Father of Lies, he is devious in his dealings with both angels and men, and in this respect doubly dangerous, since he is able to confuse his victims, endangering their salvation by persuading them that what they had been told is evil is not at all, indeed can accrue to their good. It *is* difficult to distinguish the one from the other, a dilemma ably illustrated by the poet, who succeeds in making the Satan of *Paradise Lost* "look good" to his readers. Milton's figure of consummate evil, then, is a powerful and largely successful threat to salvation; he is vivid testimony to the self-defeating effects of sin upon the soul, though readers can take little comfort from that defect, subject as they are to the same corrupting influence; and he is deceptive in the skill with which he confuses our ability to distinguish between good and evil. In none of these qualities is he even remotely funny.

Heaven is a kingdom founded on the governing principle of divine love, Hell on consummate hatred. Love is expressed through creation, hatred through destruction; and in *Paradise Lost* both are worked out within a political frame. Critical commentary on the constitutional structure of the two realms has consistently proposed that each reflects its respective moral imperative. It is argued that Satan must, therefore, display all the qualities of the tyrant Milton deplored. Recent studies, for example, insist that he holds sway with all the absolute powers of an oriental despot, that his soldiers are "in a condition of helpless slavery," living in dread of their leader, whom they consider their "enemy," that they suffer under "the tight hand of autocratic domination,"[8] and that he "has assumed absolute dictatorship over them in hell."[9] If it had been Milton's purpose to testify to his political ideology in *Paradise Lost,* it would certainly have been more fitting to depict Satan's rule as tyrannically oppressive and his subjects terrorized slaves; but Milton's Hell is no such place. Indeed, it bears many marks, if not of a republic, at least of a government that is relatively open, allowing for a certain degree of representation, debate over issues, and decision by ballot. Although it cannot be said that "the people" determine public policy in Hell, neither is it a state where laws are proclaimed by irrevocable imperial decree, as in Heaven. God's rule is mysterious, far above Man's aspirations; indeed, in Milton's judgment kings who attempt to mirror it are damned as idolatrous. In *Paradise Lost* Milton is not stating a preference of one scheme of government over another by associating one with good and the other with evil. Neither the demonic nor the divine regimes are held up as model governments for Man; but it must be said that the politics of Hell, like Satan himself, is much closer to the human experience than the exalted rule of God.

Critical commentary on the figure of Satan has been based traditionally on a premise that, though nowhere stated, silently sets the parameters for discussion of Milton's political imagery: Since God is the font of all good and Satan the author of evil, it follows that the poem reflects Milton's moral judgment, even on his *sources* for the figures. One searches in vain for logical support for such a premise but it seems to be widely accepted, and without question. As we have seen, on this basis Malcolm Ross concludes that the poet was a closet monarchist all along, and William Empson that he made his God a king because he thought the Christian Deity "wicked."[10] As for Satan, the accommodations are even more inventive. William Blake, sensing Milton's sympathy for a revolutionary, suggested that he was "of the Devil's party

---

8. Davies, *Images of Kingship,* 58-59, 68.

9. Bennett, *Reviving Liberty,* 51. Hardin proposes that "Hell is a pattern for all the pseudo-divine states that will come into being on earth" (*Civil Idolatry* 177).

10. Ross, *Milton's Royalism,* 50; Empson, *Milton's God,* 10-11. As has been noted, Empson thinks Milton's God closely resembles Stalin (146).

without knowing it."[11] Wherever Satan has moments when he seems to demonstrate what might be characterized as "heroic" qualities, modern scholars are quick to brand the passage "ironic." Some find the figure laughable and picture an omniscient Deity chuckling at his pretensions;[12] others discover an implied criticism of the military ethic,[13] or of the epic tradition itself;[14] and still others find his every act a burlesque, unmasking, as one critic puts it, "the grotesque incongruities of existence and the tragic absurdity of the universe."[15] All make use of the same evidence, but each assumes that Milton must have modeled his God on sources he found admirable and Satan on those he condemned for one reason or another.

As we have seen, Milton drew on *both* Cromwell and King Charles in creating his Almighty, and, as will be argued below, his Devil as well. I shall stress the parallels between Satan and Cromwell, since Joan Bennett has so thoroughly explored the figure's resemblance to Charles. She equates that poetic figure, in imagery, characterization, and the exercise of power, with the poet's portrait of the king in *Eikonoklastes;* and though we may arrive at radically different conclusions about what the poet means by his Devil, she describes the influence of England's king on Milton's art so persuasively that any further comment on my part is unnecessary.[16]

The essence of politics is conflict, either in differences of opinion that are resolved in compromise or in clashing ambitions decided by the naked contest of force from which emerges a winner and a loser. The difficulty with demonstrating Satan's hatred politically is that after the war he is denied any outlet for direct action against Heaven. He cannot debate with God, nor can he assault him; and since he has no means to satisfy his desire for revenge

11. Blake, *Poetry and Prose,* 35.

12. Tanner finds that "God's laughter in *Paradise Lost* implicitly exposes to ridicule not simply the War in Heaven but *every* demonic enterprise (*Anxiety in Eden* 141).

13. Michael Wilding, "The Last of the Epics," 113.

14. Revard, *War in Heaven,* 197; T.J.B. Spencer, *"Paradise Lost:* The Anti-Epic," 93-98. In reply, Barbara Lewalski cautions that "Milton's intention is not to condemn classic epic or romance or tragedy; nor is it to exalt Satan as a hero" (*"Paradise Lost" and the Rhetoric of Literary Forms* 56).

15. Wooten, "Metaphysics," 259.

16. Bennett, *Reviving Liberty,* 33-58. If I question some of Bennett's conclusions, it is only to insist that since the influence of *both* Charles and Cromwell can be detected in Satan, the figure constitutes a most uncertain basis for any analysis of the poet's political allegiances. When confronted with these two influences, scholars feel obliged to choose between them. Quint, for example, rejects the notion that Satan represents "a kind of caricature Cromwell" and prefers to see him as a reflection of Milton's distaste for Charles I (*Epic and Empire* 269).

through direct confrontation with the Almighty, he is reduced to lesser goals. Because of the frustrations of his position, Satan is a very emotional figure: he is "rackt with deep despair" (1:106), and driven by "Ambition and Revenge" (9:168); he displays "Signs of remorse and passion" (1:605) and sheds "Tears such as Angels weep" (1:620). He can hope only to deprive God of delight in his creation or interrupt "his joy / In our Confusion" (2:371-72), strategies which, as he discovers, afford him no relief from his affliction. Deprived of the further use of force against the Almighty, he pursues his goals with all the art of a consummate politician and diplomat.

The Great Consult

Hell is the most fully developed government in *Paradise Lost* and Satan Milton's most complete representation of a political figure. In book 1 he is primarily a military commander, in book 2 a political leader; and as I have discussed the military figure at some length elsewhere, I shall focus here on him as a politician (*CC* 167-201). Satan's task in Hell is to bring political order out of chaos, in brief, to establish a state. The first step in this process is to reconstitute the power base of a government, in this case his army; the second is to convene a viable governing body empowered to maintain order within the body politic and shape national policy.

Critical commentary on "the great consult" in Hell has characterized it as an assembly firmly under Satan's dictatorial thumb. Stevie Davies, for example, dwells on the image of Satan as an oriental potentate with which book 2 opens; and disregarding the following five hundred lines, which describe free-wheeling debate and decision by vote, she discovers in the image evidence of "the tight hand of autocratic domination." She dismisses the entire passage in a brief phrase; it gives only "the appearance of 'free' debate."[17] Joan Bennett is no less perfunctory about the demonic assembly. For her "The great Seraphic Lords" are simply "no less slaves than the

17. Davies, *Images of Kingship,* 68, 103. Tanner is equally dismissive. Again, without a shred of evidence, he proclaims the assembly "to provide the illusion of parliamentary participation, but really little more than puppet politics" (*Anxiety in Eden* 139). Since they are all devils, so goes the notion, it could not be otherwise; and the wish is father to the thought. Buhler argues that it is "something rather less than an open parliamentary session" ("Kingly States" 62), apt perhaps if one has in mind a contentious sitting of the House of Commons, but certainly not if it is compared to a like assembly with the Almighty presiding.

masses"; and as oblique evidence she compares Belial and Mammon to "two royalist types that Salmasius" admired and Milton condemned.[18]

In fact, however, despite his claim of authority, in *Paradise Lost* Satan does not in any sense hold the absolute sway over his followers that some would claim for him; indeed, it may be questioned whether, within the narrative frame of the poem, he ever actually reigns in Hell at all, though that clearly is his ambition. With the army restored to its former discipline and vigor, the fallen angels meet in assembly to settle the government and plan for the future. As the governing body of Hell, this assembly deserves close attention. First, it is bicameral; and, second, one of its two houses is elective. The members of the larger body are selected on the basis of merit, "From every band and squared regiment / By place or choice the worthiest" (1:758-59). In the smaller and more important body sit "The great Seraphic Lords and Cherubim" (1:794), entitled by their hereditary position to do so. The larger, elected body, it should be noted, plays no part in the deliberations, which are conducted "In close recess and secret conclave" (1:795). Once the decision is made, "the great result" is simply announced to the entire populace, "By Herald's voice explain'd" (2:515-18).

The parallels between the regime in Hell and the governments of the English Republic suggest that Milton drew on his experience in public service to shape his vision of demonic rule. The two bodies meeting in Pandemonium immediately bring to mind the traditional structure of Parliament, a larger, elective House of Commons and a smaller, hereditary House of Lords.[19] "The great Seraphic Lords" of Hell differ from those at Westminster, however, in that demonic decisions are final; thus, "the great consult" exercises the authority of an executive body, in which regard it more closely resembles the Protectorate Council of State. The Council of the Commonwealth period was required to refer all important decisions to Commons, whereas the Protectorate Council was far more powerful, directing the course of government for long periods while Parliament was in recess. Its members sat perpetually and, in consultation with the Protector, it retained at least a voice in foreign affairs (*MG* 125-26). The decision to undertake the war with Spain in 1655, for example, was announced in much the same way as is "the great result" in Hell. It was simply declared as "The

18. Bennett, *Reviving Liberty*, 56.
19. For a short period at the end of the Interregnum, Parliament was composed of two houses. In January 1658 an "Upper" or "Other" house was reconstituted, consisting of sixty-odd members, "Oliver's Peers or Lords"; and it assumed some of the functions of the traditional House of Lords.

Lord-Protector's Manifesto, published with the consent and advice of his Council."[20] Parliament, the elected body, was not consulted, as it was not in session.

The "Stygian Council," then, is a perpetual body, in the most essential sense of the word, one over which Satan presides, but rather uneasily. A great deal has been made of the opening lines of book 2 of *Paradise Lost*, which picture Satan

> High on a Throne of Royal State, which far
> Outshone the wealth of *Ormus* and of *Ind*,
> Or where the gorgeous East with richest hand
> Show'rd on her Kings *Barbaric* Pearl and Gold.
>   (2:1-4)

The comparison of Satan's throne to those found in "the gorgeous East" suggests to some scholars, as we have seen, that he rules in Hell with the same absolute authority as an Oriental despot. The five hundred or so lines that follow, however, demonstrate that this is clearly not the case. Satan is "by merit rais'd / To that bad eminence" (2:21-20); but in the fluid political climate of the newly constituted state there is absolutely no assurance that he will keep his seat, since among the "great Seraphic Lords" are potential rivals to the throne. He had been their leader in Heaven, and is certainly the commander of the armies; but whether these credentials qualify him to assume control of the state remained to be seen.

There is an intriguing parallel between Satan's position in "the great consult" and Oliver Cromwell's on the Commonwealth Council of State. In September 1651, he returned from his victories over Ireland, Scotland, and the royalist forces of Charles II to resume his seat on the Council. Because of his enormous prestige and his position as Lord General, he sat on that body clearly as the first among equals, for the Council performed its executive functions as a committee and no single member could dictate policy. His status is comparable to Satan's in the company of his "Lords" in that neither is so powerful as to dictate terms or openly control deliberations, and each must endure debate and attempt to direct events within the limits imposed by the political system then in place (*MG* 125).

Satan's opening speech indirectly acknowledges how tenuous his position is, for he devotes the bulk of it to justifying his assumption of leadership

---

20. Masson, *Life of John Milton*, 5:46.

(2:11-42). He opens with the promise he had used to rally his despairing legions, "I give not Heav'n for lost," but it has the ring here of a plank in a campaign platform rather than a call to arms. He expands for the next twenty lines on his qualifications for his position, insisting first that he deserves it by "the fixt Laws of Heav'n," which would seem irrelevant at best, considering their fallen state. More to the point, he argues that he holds his station by virtue of his followers' "free choice." Because of what "in Counsel or in Fight, / Hath been achiev'd of merit," he claims, he occupies his position with their "full consent." There is no other evidence in the poem that he was elected to his office, but neither is there anything to cast doubt on his assertion that "the great Seraphic Lords" had indeed, by "free choice" raised him "To that bad eminence." There is no reason for him to lie about the process, since he is addressing the very body that presumably gave its "full consent," and he is after all the obvious choice. The selection of a political leader is a natural development in the establishment of a government, and there is precedent for such a figure in Milton's experience. The Commonwealth Council of State elected from its own numbers a president to preside over meetings and perform some of the administrative functions of a head of state, though the actual executive authority remained in Parliament. For two and a half years, before Parliament insisted that the position be rotated monthly, John Bradshaw held the post; and during the Protectorate, Council resumed the practice, selecting Henry Lawrence to preside over the body as its permanent "Lord President."

In his speech Satan further justifies his position by arguing subtly that no one else could possibly want it, that it is indeed a "safe unenvie'd Throne," since whoever sits on it must assume a "greatest share / Of endless pain" and not even the most "ambitious mind / Will covet more" suffering. He is openly disingenuous here, sounding like a modern chief executive who complains about how lonely it is "at the top" and then promptly declares himself a candidate for reelection. Satan's supposed reluctance is somewhat reminiscent of Cromwell's oft-stated contention that he neither sought nor enjoyed the burdens of head of state, declaring at one point that he "would have been glad . . . to have been living under a woodside, to have kept a flock of sheep, rather than to have undertaken such a place as this was."[21] In claiming that no "ambitious mind" would want the job, Satan is subtly implying that, as he casts his eye about the chamber, he can spy a seraph or two that covet it. He concludes by returning to his opening theme, the

21. Wilber C. Abbott, *The Writings and Speeches of Oliver Cromwell,* 4:705, 729.

promise that they will "return / To claim our just inheritance of old," and announcing the agenda, a debate to decide whether to do so by "open War or covert guile."

As it turns out, Satan has already decided on a course of action, a campaign of "covert guile" rather than "open War" to be undertaken, however, against Earth, not Heaven; but his political position is not so secure that he can simply dictate policy. In Hell critical issues such as war and peace are decided by the entire body of "Seraphic Lords," not by any single individual. Satan's ultimate goals at this point, however often he trumpets his intention to restore his followers to their blissful existence in Heaven, are not clear, for it is uncertain what he has learned from his defeat in the war. William Empson, something of a devil's advocate, insists that he is not yet convinced of God's omnipotence, and therefore his promises may be taken as sincere.[22] Empson argues that he does not fully realize the hopelessness of his cause until much later, when atop Niphrates "horror and doubt distract / His troubled thoughts" (4:18-19).[23] As Satan opens "the great consult," the narrative voice does indeed describe him as "insatiate to pursue / Vain War with Heav'n" since he has been "by success untaught" (2:8-9), the "success" here being God's victory; and he could well have thought of Earth as a base of operations for an assault on Heaven, as Beëlzebub later describes it (2:394-96). On the other hand, if the war in Heaven had taught him the meaning of omnipotence, his promises to his followers must be considered political rhetoric, designed to raise their spirits and retain their allegiance.[24] In this respect, he is no different from candidates for modern office who, though disastrously behind in the polls, persist in promising their advocates a victory.

Whatever Satan's attitude toward omnipotence may be, the debate immediately goes off in directions not to his liking, and he must sit through three long speeches, each of which proposes a course of action quite contrary to what he has in mind. The war god, Moloch, who has obviously learned nothing at all from his defeat, favors a direct assault on Heaven, engaging God's forces once more in battle. If this leads to their destruction, well, so be it; nothing could be worse, he urges, than the "pain of unextinguishable fire" that they suffer; and such an attack, even if it failed, would give them

---

22. Empson, *Milton's God,* 37.

23. Ibid., 62. Satan laments his claim that he "could subdue / Th' Omnipotent. Ay me, they little know / How dearly I abide that boast so vain" (4:85-87).

24. Tanner is of the opinion that from the outset "deep inside he knows his defiance is hopeless" (*Anxiety in Eden* 134).

the satisfaction of having alarmed God's "fatal Throne: / Which if not Victory is yet Revenge" (2:88, 104-5). Belial seems to have the surest grasp of their condition, arguing that nothing is to be gained by opposing God, who would only be further enraged by their resistance and retaliate by intensifying their punishment. "War therefore, open or conceal'd, alike / My voice dissuades," he advises, for to confront the Almighty openly would invite destruction, and guile would be fruitless against a Deity "whose eye / Views all things in one View," one who even at this moment "sees and derides" their debate. His advice is to do nothing. If they lie low, he argues, God will in time lose interest, leaving them to their own devices, and they will eventually grow accustomed to conditions in Hell: "This horror will grow mild, this darkness light" (2:189-91, 210-20). Despite the fact that just about everything he says is all too true, the narrative voice is curiously contemptuous of Belial, condemning him for his policy of "ignoble ease, and peaceful sloth, / Not peace" (2:227-28).

Mammon's counsel is essentially the same but he puts matters in a more positive light; and Milton gives him some stirring lines. He agrees that they cannot overpower the Almighty and argues that even if he should "relent / And publish Grace to all," to worship him again is unthinkable. The best course of action is simply to forget Heaven and build a new nation in the wilderness of Hell, one where they will be "Free, and to none accountable, preferring / Hard liberty before the easy yoke / Of servile Pomp" (2:237-38, 255-57). He sounds a bit like the early settlers of the New World, who spoke of founding cities free from the oppression of European monarchs. The fallen angels, who want nothing to do with Moloch's desperate plan, "for such another Field / They dreaded worse than Hell," and perhaps put off by Belial's pessimistic assessment of their condition, are swayed by Mammon's vision and "murmur" their approval (2:284-94).

But none of this is to Satan's purpose. The speakers have changed the agenda of the debate; rather than addressing the original question whether their opposition to God should be "open" or "covert," they have raised the issue whether they should oppose him at all. This is a critical moment for Satan, who must plot and maneuver to carry the day, since demonic decisions, it is clear, are arrived at by ballot. He is committed to action, which he senses is the only way to overcome despair, and he must quickly get the debate back on track before Mammon's position, which "pleas'd / Advising peace," gains too much support. An astute politician, Satan seems to have anticipated opposition to his design; but wishing to avoid the appearance of dictating terms, which might have angered the Lords and turned them against him, he stays above the debate, setting up a front man to argue his case.

Satan's position in the assembly suggests a posture often assumed by Cromwell, who, though he could act decisively at times, as in his dissolution of the Rump in April 1653, was at several critical junctures content to wait in the background, distancing himself from events, allowing them to unfold, positioning himself to step in and reap the benefits of others' actions at the crucial moment. Pride's Purge, for example, took place on the morning of 6 December 1648; and Cromwell, despite the urging of Lord Fairfax, delayed his journey to Westminster in order to arrive that evening.[25] A somewhat closer parallel was his behavior during deliberations leading to the founding of the Protectorate. *The Instrument of Government,* the first constitution of the Protectorate, was prepared by General John Lambert and a group of officers after the dissolution of the Barebones Parliament in December 1653. Cromwell remained aloof from the entire process, adopting a waiting posture on the edge of events and accepting the position of Lord Protector only when publicly urged to do so.[26]

After sitting through the dissenting speeches, Beëlzebub, Satan's front man, rises to give his own; and he is yet another demonic figure whom Milton endows, as he has Satan, with statesmanlike qualities:

> deep on his Front engraven
> Deliberation sat and public care;
> And Princely counsel in his face yet shone,
> Majestic though in ruin: sage he stood
> With *Atlantean* shoulders fit to bear
> The weight of mightiest Monarchies.
>
> (2:302-7)

It was in this same vein that Cromwell addressed Cardinal Mazarin in one of Milton's letters to France, praising him as a statesman "Renown to Govern Kingdoms, and manage the most important Affairs of the World" (W119, P155).

Beëlzebub delivers a masterful speech, first acknowledging that "the popular vote / Inclines" to Mammon's view but dismissing his proposal on the basis that they will never be able to "build up here / A growing Empire,"

---

25. Fraser, *Cromwell,* 268-69.
26. Ibid., 448.

since God rules over Hell as well as Heaven and will not permit it. Belial's plea for peace he discards with the peremptory "War hath determin'd us"; and, he argues, Moloch's "dangerous expedition to invade / Heav'n" will not be necessary. Beëlzebub's "devilish Counsel, first devis'd / By *Satan*" (2:379-80), is a model of compromise, satisfying the advocates of all parties to the debate. It appeases the militant Molochs of the assembly by calling them to action, it calms the fearful Belials by promising that they will not risk a direct assault on Heaven, it placates the materialistic Mammons by providing an opportunity to build a new kingdom, and it pleases all by offering a release from the torments of Hell. "With full assent / They vote" (2:379-89) and the plan is approved. Beëlzebub then asks who shall be appointed to find the Earth they are to conquer, setting up Satan for the final piece in his design, which he is confident will finally raise him "Above his fellows" (2:428) and show him worthy of Hell's throne.

Satan's speech, volunteering for the mission, may sound grandiose and self-serving; but it does not exaggerate the difficulties. "Long is the way / And hard, that out of Hell leads up to light," he begins, and then details the obstacles. He will first have to break through the "gates of burning Adamant" at the entrance to Hell and then traverse Chaos, "the void profound / Of unessential Night" whose terrors they have all recently experienced. Once he has met these challenges, who knows what more he will have to confront, "what remains him less / Than unknown dangers and as hard escape," among which may be God's legions, which, as Belial warns and Raphael confirms, "Scout far and wide into the Realm of night," (2:133; 8:229-40). During his absence, he directs, Hell's sentinels must be alert to "intermit no watch / Against a wakeful Foe" (2:430-66).

At the conclusion of his speech, Satan rises abruptly to end "the great consult," much as the Speaker of the House of Commons signals the close of a session by leaving his chair, and the assembled Lords rise as well. Satan's action here is cited on occasion as evidence of his tyrannical hold over his followers, who so fear him, it is argued, that none dare oppose his will; they "Dreaded not more th' adventure than his voice / Forbidding" (2:474-75).[27] Such readings make much of the word "Dreaded," ignoring the presence of "Rivals." It should be noted that in the parallel scene in book 3 the loyal angels are no more eager to volunteer. "Silence was in Heav'n" as each is reluctant to "upon his head draw / The deadly forfeiture" (3:218-21); but

27. Davies cites "Dreaded" as evidence of "the terror" Satan inspires in his followers (*Images of Kingship* 118), and Bennett of "the tyrant's full awareness of his subjects' servile character" (*Reviving Liberty* 56).

no one suggests that they stand in "terror" of God.[28] This preoccupation with "Dreaded" misses the consummate theatricality of the gesture, the instinctive act of a skilled politician maneuvering for advantage. His position, for all his bluster about accepting the "hazard as of honor, due alike / To him who Reigns" (2:453-54), is still tenuous; and he must outwit potential rivals for his power:

> Others among the chief might offer now
> (Certain to be refus'd) what erst they fear'd;
> And so refus'd might in opinion stand
> His Rivals, winning cheap the high repute
> Which he through hazard huge must earn.
>
> (2:469-73)

The point of Satan's sudden departure is that his throne is not so "unenvied" as he pretends; and so he stages his sudden departure to prevent those who "might in opinion stand / His Rivals" from diminishing the force of his dramatic gesture. Satan orchestrates the "consult" to enhance his image; in political terms he needs a triumph abroad to strengthen his position at home. God, whose power is genuinely "absolute," need not indulge in such theatrics.

Satan's offer has the desired affect of enhancing his authority over the fallen angels: "Toward him they bend / With awful reverence prone; and as a God / Extol him equal to the highest in Heav'n" (2:477-79), the first time we hear of him being honored with such high ceremony.

The challenges confronting Satan in book 1 and those facing the English Republic in its early months are so close as to invite comparison. The founders of the Republic, who called Milton to public service in March 1649, a short six weeks after the execution of Charles I, undertook the task, as does Satan, of establishing a new state; and the similarities between the two situations are striking. In both, the army formed the power base of the new regime. For both, the first meetings were devoted to debate over the prospects of further wars, the English faced by a multitude of enemies – Ireland, Scotland, France, Portugal – Hell but one, the kingdom of Heaven.[29] Oliver Cromwell, by virtue of his military position, was the most powerful man in England; Satan as commander of the rebel army and by what "in

28. Empson, *Milton's God,* 124.

29. Thomas Corns notes that at the early meetings of the Council of State Mondays and Fridays were reserved exclusively for consideration of Irish affairs (*Uncloistered Virtue* 201).

Counsel and in Fight / Hath been achieved of merit" (2:20-21) is a figure of comparable weight. Both were members of a governing body where they sat as the first among equals, Cromwell in Parliament and on the Commonwealth Council of State, Satan in the conclave of "great Seraphic Lords and Cherabim" (1:794); hence neither at the time could single-handedly dictate policy. Both gained in time all but absolute power by virtue of their achievements, Cromwell through his conquest of Ireland and Scotland, Satan through his conquest of the World.

There are, of course, marked differences between the two situations. In both instances, the military constituted the power base of the government, but the New Model Army was fully mobilized, the rebel angels a defeated and demoralized force. Cromwell's army was fresh from its victories in the civil wars; Satan had to reorganize and revitalize his forces after a devastating defeat. In setting up a governing body the revolutionary leaders reacted against the former regime, sweeping away many of the institutions of the monarchy and establishing the House of Commons as the unrivaled authority in England; in Hell, the demonic governing body is in effect but a restoration of the hierarchy in Heaven, with its titles and degrees intact. The jealous vigilance of Parliament prevented any single figure from assuming prominence during the early years of the Commonwealth; in contrast, Satan sat on the "Throne of Royal State," as he claimed, "through just right and the fixt Laws of Heav'n" (2:1, 18).

Here as elsewhere, the artists alters and omits elements of his source to suit the demands of his art, his intent to illuminate the difficulty of distinguishing good from evil. To that end he attributes recognizable human sentiments to Satan, who sheds "Tears such as angels weep" in compassion for the suffering of his followers; he after all shares the same pain. But the Devil proves adept in turning their distress to his own advantage by skillfully manipulating the consulting peers to fulfill his fierce desire to reign unopposed in Hell. It seems quite evident, therefore, that Milton is not passing judgment on the English government and its impetuous experiment with republicanism. Rather more to the point, he draws selectively on that experience, molding and shaping it to his purpose, to depict a conscience infected by evil. That Republic was not destined to last, nor is the one in Hell. Charles II would return from his wanderings to renew the monarchy and Satan from his voyage far more powerful than any *primus inter pares*.

The Voyage

The political imagery in *Paradise Lost* depicts the Fall as a conquest and occupation by one major power of a small colony or possession of another (*CC* 140-52). Though Satan, echoing Beëlzebub (2:358-70), characterizes his task as one of "conquering this new World" (4:391), he also describes it, ironically to be sure, as a diplomatic mission: "League with you I seek, / And mutual Amity" (4:375-76). As it turns out, the ironies are closer to the truth of the matter, for it is by persuasion, not force, that he achieves his end, enticing the rulers of this distant possession of Heaven to disobey their sovereign lord. He must call upon a wide range of diplomatic skills just to find the place, and once there employ all the arts of a wily ambassador to subvert Man's allegiance to God.

The obstacles to Satan's mission are formidable, and he stands much in need of help on his voyage. He arrives at the gates of Hell to find them locked, and guarded, moreover, by two grotesque but formidable figures, whose allegiance lies clearly with the enemy. Death, sounding like the Scourge of God, challenges him as "that Traitor Angel" and orders him "Back to thy punishment, / False fugitive" (2:689-700). Sin's revelation of the family relationship prevents a clash between the two, but the gates remain closed. The political allegiance of Sin and Death is curiously contradictory. Though Satan's offspring, they seem to guard the gates as servants of God, an impression enhanced by Death's condemnation of his father as one who "Conjur'd against the Highest" (2:693) and Sin's possession of the key, which she holds, as she tells him, "by command of Heav'n's all-powerful King" (2:851).

Satan needs to win them to his side; and, taking a quick measure of the situation, he "answer'd smooth" with an appeal first to the family relationship, reminding his "Dear Daughter" of the joys they had shared in Heaven, and referring to Death as "my fair Son." Satan never in so many words requests that Sin open the gates, though that is clearly his intent; he, rather, dwells on the importance of his mission and its advantage to them. He insists that he has not come as an enemy but as their potential deliverer, promising them access to a place where they "Shall dwell at ease" and, with an eye on Death, "be fed and fill'd / Immeasureably" (2:841-43). Sin arrives at the decision on her own, swayed less, it would seem, by the promise of gain than by the prospect of reunion with her father-husband, with whom she hopes to reign henceforth as "Thy daughter and thy darling" (2:870). Death, who maintains a sullen silence after his initial outburst, is mollified by the promise that he will "be fed." Though forbidden to do so, Sin produces the key, "Sad instrument of all our woe" (2:872) and unlocks the gates. The entire episode leaves the distinct impression that Satan has subverted the servants of God and drawn them to his side, enlisting to his cause powerful forces once loyal to the Almighty by persuading them adroitly that he is acting in their interest.

Satan steps through the gates and in a dramatic moment, marvelously captured by Gustave Doré's engraving,[30] "Stood on the brink of Hell and look'd a while, / Pondering his voyage" (2:918-19), as well he might, for the prospect is daunting. Milton once again depicts the Author of Evil in heroic proportions.

Satan has further need for help and must employ all his diplomatic skills to gain it when he comes on Chaos and his discordant court. Sensing hostility, he addresses that monarch, using some of the same devices of his speech to his offspring, there declaring "I come no enemy," here "I come no Spy," and appealing to their self-interest. He asks directions to the newly created World and promises Chaos that in return for his aid, once he has "expell'd" God's "usurpation" there, he will return the region to its "original darkness and your sway." He has no territorial ambitions, he insists; it's a personal thing with him, and once successful, "Yours be th' advantage all, mine the revenge" (2:968-84).

These are all lies, of course. He has no intention of keeping such promises; but he strikes a responsive chord in Chaos, who resents God's intrusion on his territories, "first Hell / Your dungeon stretching far and wide beneath; / Now lately Heaven and Earth, another World / Hung o'er my Realm" (2:1002-5), and so he readily renders Satan assistance. Satan is as successful here as he was at the infernal gates, though his purpose is quite different. He hints at a possible alliance but makes no effort to enlist the neutral Chaos to his cause, asking only for directions. An agreement is struck, and Chaos directs him to the new World.

Satan's appeal to Chaos resembles England's situation in 1650, when the Republic was engaged in an intense undeclared naval war with Portugal. That small country had secured its independence ten years earlier after several decades under the repressive rule of Spain, whose king, Philip IV, deeply resented the division. His indignation at the loss prompted him to assist the English, opening his ports to the fleets of Admirals Robert Blake and Edward Popham. Milton prepared a number of letters to both kingdoms

---

30. *Milton's Paradise Lost,* 21.

during and after the war, in which Parliament frequently expressed their gratitude for the assistance to their fleets, though there was no mention of an intent to return Portugal to Spanish control (*MG* 43-53). The poet may well have been impressed, however, by the image of a large and powerful kingdom deeply resentful over the loss of a substantial segment of its realm, and so drew on his memory of that time in explaining the readiness of Chaos to assist Satan.

On entering the World, Satan needs further aid, this time to locate Earth, but one of the myriads of stars that dot his way. Satan, having penetrated the universe, is now deep in enemy territory, where dangers await and quite different tactics are called for. Landing on the sun, he disguises himself as "a stripling Cherub" (3:636) and approaches the archangel Uriel deferentially, rendering him all the customary courtesies due a dignitary of higher rank. After eight lines of shameless flattery, he asks the way, confiding that he is curious to see all of God's "wondrous works, but chiefly Man," created since the Almighty had "justly ... driv'n out his Rebel Foes / To deepest Hell" (2:654-78). Uriel, though "The sharpest-sighted Spirit of all in Heav'n," is momentarily beguiled. He obliges Satan with a brief account of the Creation, which he had witnessed, and points the way, whereupon the deferential Cherub, after "bowing low [with] honor due and reverence" to the superior archangel, takes his leave and "Throws his steep flight" down to Nephrates (3:736-42). It is an impressive deception, with Satan's seemingly obsequious behavior toward Uriel no more or less objectionable than that of any English envoy sent on a mission to a potentially hostile court.

Up to this point Satan is entirely successful, even to the extent of infiltrating Eden as far as the bower of the sleeping Eve; but the vigilant angelic guards, alerted by Uriel, who finally penetrates the disguise, apprehend him and bring him before Gabriel. Here is a formidable obstacle indeed to Satan's cause; and no longer able to conceal his identity or his intent, he drops the diplomatic mask and resorts to the threat of force. He in

> all his might dilated stood,
> Like *Teneriff* or *Atlas* unremov'd:
> His stature reacht the Sky, and on his Crest
> Sat horror Plum'd; nor wanted in his grasp
> What seem'd both Spear and Shield.
>   (4:986-90)

The golden scales predict the outcome of any such encounter; and thwarted by the threat of greater force, he is compelled to retreat "murmuring" impotently to himself.

Not to be deterred, he insinuates himself back into Eden and finally comes before Eve in disguise as a serpent, where now he must draw on all his diplomatic skills, demonstrated during his encounters enroute, to persuade her to betray her lord. He opens his appeal with exuberant flattery, surpassing that he had employed with Uriel. He promises her greater sway, as he had Chaos, not however in territory but in knowledge and power: "ye shall be as Gods." And he appeals to personal concerns, as he had with Sin and Death, whom he had promised would be "fed and fill'd / Immeasureably." The race, he assures Eve, will lead a "happier life, [with] knowledge of Good and Evil" (9:697). Though Satan makes no mention of it, the narrative voice alludes to his judicious timing of the temptation, when "the hour of Noon drew on, and wak'd / An eager appetite" in Eve (9:739-40). His appeal, though unspoken, calls to mind his promise to sate Death's ravenous hunger. Satan succeeds and his success here as in all his encounters is based not on his appeal as a charismatic leader, which he had displayed in rallying his fallen legions, but as a skilled diplomat and politician, whose subtle art lies in the ability to persuade others that his own designs will be to their benefit as well.

Milton's entire account of the voyage, with its many encounters, may have been suggested to him by one of his duties as Secretary for Foreign Languages. When an envoy was sent on a mission requiring him to travel through a number of states, he was provided with a packet of letters, each individually addressed from his head of state to the ruling body of the several governments, requesting their hospitality and assistance enroute. Milton was responsible for preparing a number of these packets and included one group in the collection of state papers he intended for publication. In August 1657, Cromwell dispatched Colonel William Jephson on a mission to Charles X of Sweden, then encamped outside of Lübeck, preparing to invade Denmark; and Jephson's route took him through five cities and states, Hamburg, Bremen, Holstein, Brandenburg, and finally Lübeck itself, from each of which he required assistance, not necessarily to point the way but for accommodations and security (*MG* 166-68). The letters are all quite brief, the type of document that Milton prepared routinely during his years in office, hence very likely to have been composed by the poet himself. They all say pretty much the same thing, though with different wording. An excerpt from the letter to Lübeck illustrates the customary message:

> Collonel *William Jepson,* ... is to pass with the Character of a
> Publick Minister from your City to the King of *Sweden,* encamping
> not far from it. Wherefore we desire your Lordships, that if occasion
> require, upon the account of Friendship and Commerce between
> us, you will be Assistant to him in his Journey through your City,
> and the Territories under your Jurisdiction.
>
> (W97, P131)

Satan, like Jephson, needs assistance "in his Journey" and secures it with skill
and daring.

Unlike Satan, Jephson was not venturing into hostile territory, but Milton
had had occasion to prepare similar documents for those who were. An
envoy of the English Republic often had to serve in a dangerous European
capital, especially in the early years, when the crowned heads of Europe
responded predictably to the spectacle of one of their kind losing his, and
cities teemed with colonies of angry English royalists agitating openly against
the rebel government. Parliament's first tentative efforts to establish diplomatic relations resulted in the assassination of two of their envoys, Isaac
Dorislaus in The Hague and Anthony Ascham in Madrid. Milton does not
appear to have had any part in the Dorislaus mission, but he prepared the
packet that Ascham carried to Spain, and simultaneously that for Charles
Vane, the Republic's first envoy to Portugal, who had to flee home in fear of
his life after three months in Lisbon (*MG* 89-94). In this regard, Satan's
encounter with Gabriel is perhaps closer to Richard Bradshaw's mission to
Moscow in 1657. The czar was so adamantly opposed to the English Republic that he denied the envoy admission to the country (*MG* 166), even as the
archangel blocks Satan's entry into Eden. Milton prepared documents for
many such envoys, a task that may have inspired the hostile encounters Satan
experiences on his mission to Eden.

Satan's diplomatic achievements, then, are formidable. With the promise
of gain, he persuades hostile powers, Sin and Death, to ally themselves
to his cause, and with further promises, though this time specious, convinces a potentially hostile monarch, Chaos, to render him assistance. By
disguising his person he avoids detection by an enemy power, Uriel; and by
concealing his intent he secures the aid of that same power. Only when
both identity and intent are disclosed does he resort to the threat of
force, and then wisely abandons it when confronted by a superior force,
whereupon he devises other means entirely and succeeds in his mission.

Certainly, any ambitious head of state would welcome the services of such a diplomat.[31]

Of course, Satan's success depends in part upon lies and deceptions, and it is tempting to conclude that Milton is condemning such tactics by attributing them to the Devil. In dealing with Chaos and Uriel, Satan does not reveal his full intent, to be sure, but his reticence is well within accepted standards of diplomatic practice in Milton's day, or our own. One of the interesting aspects of the Republic's missions to Denmark and Sweden in 1657 was Cromwell's concealed intent. Both envoys traveled with a set of confidential instructions, revealing that while Philip Meadows had the difficult task of placating a wary king of Denmark, Jephson was engaged in negotiations designed to assist Sweden. One of his stops was Brandenburg, where Frederick William, the "Great Elector," was showing signs of entering the war on the side of Denmark; and it was Jephson's task to persuade him to remain neutral. At the same time, Jephson's instructions included the offer to Charles X of a substantial loan and the assistance of a fleet of warships on condition that the king cede the bishopric of Bremen to England. Cromwell, it seems, though genuinely disturbed by the war, was not above exploiting it to England's advantage. Neither design was successful, as it happened, since Charles rejected the offer and launched his invasion, whereupon Frederick William promptly declared war on Sweden.

Thus, Satan's tactics are no more or less reprehensible than those employed by the envoys Milton encountered during his decade of public service. Indeed, it can be argued that Milton's God is as little inclined to reveal his purposes as is his Devil. The Almighty does not lie, of course, but he sends his angels on missions whose ends he keeps hidden, missions, moreover, that he knows they cannot accomplish, Michael to battle in Heaven and Gabriel to guard over Eden. That the Almighty keeps his purposes to himself presents no problem for the loyal angels, however. During the days of Creation Raphael is sent with his forces "Squar'd in full Legion" on a military mission, "a voyage uncouth and obscure / ... toward the Gates of Hell" to ensure that no "spy / Or enemy" will venture forth to interrupt God in his work. Raphael knows full well that none "durst without his leave attempt"

---

31. David Quint sees these events in a different light. He argues that Milton was influenced by Camoëns's account of the exploration of Vasco da Gama in *The Lusiad* and Tasso's praise of Columbus. Since the poet recast these sources into a demonic journey, Quint concludes that he thought those historical voyages "the work of the devil," reflecting his anticolonial sentiments (*Epic and Empire* 254-55).

to do so, but nonetheless performs his mission without question, content with God's practice of assigning such tasks for undisclosed reasons of "state, as Sovran King, and to enure / Our prompt obedience" (8:229-40). Of course, God works for good, Satan for evil; but it is difficult to tell the virtuous from the wicked, Milton reminds us, and one cannot always distinguish between them on the evidence of their words or actions alone.

The account of Satan's return voyage seems more an exercise in fantasy than an image of political realities – a massive bridge over Chaos, his invisible ascendence of the throne and appearance to his followers in a "sudden blaze," and his final transfiguration to a monstrous serpent – but in some respects it rounds out the image of a consummate politician. He has conquered Earth and is in a position to fulfill his promise to Sin and Death. She is alert to his new status: "Thine now is all this World," she exults, "here thou shalt Monarch reign" and God must "henceforth Monarchy with thee divide / Of all things" (10:372-80). Satan, very full of himself, confirms that he has "made one Realm / Hell and this World, one Realm, one Continent"; and exercising his new authority, he designates Sin and Death his "Substitutes," creating them "Plenipotent on Earth, of matchless might / Issuing from mee," with power to exercise dominion "on the Earth" and "in the Air," but "Chiefly on Man, sole Lord of all declar'd" (10:391-405).[32] He is powerful enough as well to violate with impunity his agreement with Chaos, who rages against broken promises, furious at being "over-built": "And with rebounding surge the bars assail'd, / That scorn'd his indignation" (10:416-18).

Of all the figures in *Paradise Lost* Satan owes the most to Milton's personal and political experience. This should not be surprising, for he is the poem's fullest study of a fallen being in the social and political climate of a fallen world, the other figures in the narrative all being gods, angels, and

---

32. David Quint finds Satan's conquest topically linked "to the Stuart restoration," based on the account's "heavy dependence on Phineas Fletcher's *Appollyonists*" (*Epic and Empire* 269). Quint is entirely persuasive in tracing the "links" between the two works (273-78) but his conclusions are singularly forced. Fletcher's poem is, as he puts it, "a crude anti-Catholic work" (272) about the Gunpowder Plot; hence the parallels persuade Quint that *Paradise Lost* encodes a condemnation of the Catholic design to restore the monarchy. It is perfectly possible that a poem about a Catholic plot against a Stuart king may have influenced another about a Catholic plot in favor of a Stuart king; but the analogy is strained to its limits in the conjecture that Satan's success figures a Stuart success on the basis alone of a sequence of similar images. Certainly, Satan is evil and Milton had no love for Charles II, but to turn *Paradise Lost* into an anti-Royalist, anti-Catholic testament diminishes the poem. The parallels between Milton's great works and the thoroughly pedestrian, overtly political poems of the period are at times given more weight than they can reasonably bear, e.g., Wilding, "The Last of the Epics: The Rejection of the Heroic in *Paradise Lost* and *Hudibras.*"

perfect human beings. Adam and Eve do indeed fall and in consequence experience the despair, passion, and conflict the race is heir to; but they are in Eden until the last lines and leave consoled by their faith. Michael's narrative within a narrative offers an image of the world, to be sure, but the swiftly moving account does not pause to examine any of the figures in it. Satan alone reflects the psychological state of sinful Man who because of his stubborn opposition to God becomes enmeshed in a self-defeating web of anguish.

Thus, Milton employs this extended account of Satan's voyage, from its inception in the council chamber of Pandemonium to its end in Eden, to display the full range of Satan's parliamentary and diplomatic skills. It would be a mistake, however, to conclude that since this is the Devil in action, the poet considered the exercise of such talents inherently evil and all those so engaged wicked in the extreme. Satan, as has been observed, is Milton's image of fallen Man, the one figure in the poem who demonstrates the full effect of sin upon the sinner. Governments, the poet believed, are one of the most pervasive and visible effects of that first sin and those engaged in governing therefore reflect all the consequences of the Fall. Neither the simple, pastoral innocence of Adam and Eve in the Garden nor the perfect harmony of Heaven allow scope for the depiction of human governance. Satan, as a fallen being, is the only figure in *Paradise Lost* through whom Milton can display the full spectrum of the political art – Satan orchestrates assemblies, speaks with effect, declares himself devoted to the common good, conceals motives and intentions, shades the truth, and is adept at persuading others that his way, quite aside from the fact that it benefits him, is also best for them.

This survey of Satan's political activities offers ample evidence that the figure owes much to Milton's knowledge of the career of Oliver Cromwell.[33] It would be absurd to conclude, however, that Milton considered Cromwell an agent of evil, or even that the parallels imply a criticism of the historical figure. Cromwell was the most prominent statesman of Milton's time, a towering figure who dominated England's political life during the poet's decade of public service and for whom he labored loyally during his ascendency as Lord Protector. As Secretary for Foreign Languages, Milton was not responsible for making policy, but he played an important role in articulating it; and in that office he answered directly to the Secretary of State, John Thurloe, Cromwell's most intimate and trusted adviser. Thus Milton served

---

33. Milton provides a brief biography of Cromwell in the *Second Defence* (*Prose* 4:666-71).

but two administrative levels below the head of state. Cromwell could never have been far from his thoughts; indeed his name was doubtless on the poet's tongue every day of his service. It would be surprising indeed if Milton had not drawn on that experience to portray a figure he intended to represent this important dimension of Man's fallen nature.

We are often so anxious to have the Devil wrong as to insist that all his words are lies, all his actions wicked, and all his schemes futile. Milton, as we have seen, portrays a more complex figure than these rather common-place platitudes, which one may hear from any pulpit on any Sunday morning, would suggest. If Satan lies, he does so with the tongue of Macbeth's witches, who lie like truth.[34] Though he is to fail in the end, once in Hell he achieves everything he sets out to do. And although his motive is vengeance, he acts in a way appropriate to any successful political figure, driven by a less vindictive ambition.

To brand Satan a tyrant, however, simply because he is the Devil, is especially reductive and may cause a reader to miss the rich variety of political spectacle in *Paradise Lost.* His actions do not so much represent the sweeping exercise of tyrannical power as they do the calculated campaign of one intent on gaining that power, in which regard they probably owe more to the first ten chapters of Machiavelli's *Prince* than to the annals of imperial Rome. In the first two books of *Paradise Lost,* as we have seen, Satan has too little authority to conduct affairs in a manner that a tyrant would be condemned for. He is certainly engaged in a scheme to accumulate power, the unfolding of which is the source of our fascination with him, but he does not wield it as yet. He cannot govern by decree, but must employ political arts to attain his ends. Though certainly devious, he does not impose his will on others by threatening to retaliate should they refuse, as would a tyrant armed with the power to enforce his decrees. The source of his success, and of the reader's interest, is his ability to persuade others that his schemes will be to their benefit. He is, in brief, an accomplished politician, who to further his designs incites his followers to rebel against the Almighty; manipulates the demonic council into adopting his plan; wins potential foes, Sin and Death, to his cause; secures by deception the aid of a neutral power, Chaos, and an enemy, Uriel; eludes the angelic sentinels; and convinces Eve that she has "need of this fair Fruit." Some ends he achieves with ironic lies, some with ironic truths; it matters not, so long as he persuades.

34. *Macbeth* 5.5.44.

It was not to Milton's purpose to depict a Satan holding absolute sway over Man, who, were such the case, could justly plead that "the Devil *made* me do it." The Author of Evil can only persuade, and Man can reject; but in the art of persuasion the Devil is most adept, gifted with the skills of any of the effective political figures of Milton's experience, whether they persuaded for good or for ill.

4

HEAVEN AND HELL

As observed earlier, even those modern scholars most skeptical about our ability to discern an author's intent can agree that Milton expected his readers to contrast his Heaven and his Hell, and, we may safely assume, to prefer the former. It can perhaps be argued that if such had been his intent, he was not very successful, since he seems to have created in Hell a government closer in political structure to his own republican persuasion than is the absolute monarchy of Heaven. However, although Milton certainly drew heavily on his own political experience to depict both realms, he was not expressing his preference for one constitutional structure over another. The poet intended his readers to choose between the two, not on the surface impression of contrasting systems of government, but on the quality of spirit that shapes their political life.

Each of the several realms of *Paradise Lost* is informed by just such an abstract quality or "governing principle": Chaos by discord, Hell by hatred,

Heaven and Eden by divine love, and the fallen world by conflict. And with the possible exception of Chaos, each of the governing bodies assumes a shape appropriate to the expression of that quality.[1] To speak of structure in Chaos is, of course, to talk nonsense. It is a realm where discord reigns, a place wracked with "the noise / Of endless wars," where "four Champions fierce / Strive here for Maistry, and to Battle bring / Thir embryon Atoms," and where "*Chance* governs all" (2:896–910). Milton chose to depict that "dark / Illimitable Ocean" in political allegory, however, and, as we have seen, conceived a court of co-rulers, "Chaos and *ancient Night*" (2:970), with a retinue of eight attendants, reflecting the cosmic scheme of governance. Paradoxically, then, a realm whose governing principle is discord is ruled by a structured court that maintains itself by fomenting disorder. It is an uneasy allegory, to be sure, in which substance is imposed upon elements resolutely insubstantial; but the poet took the risk, using the occasion of Satan's voyage to develop the Devil further as an accomplished political figure.

The spiritual quality that best identifies Hell is hatred, to which may be added fear, from which it arises. It is the latter that prevails initially in the poem. Disorder reigns momentarily, for fear is a condition in which each individual, thinking only of his own safety, abandons the rational discipline necessary to the life of an ordered society (*CC* 174–78). The fallen angels "lay intrans't / Thick as Autumnal Leaves that strow the Brooks / In *Vallombrosa*," a shattered army like that of the "*Memphian* Chivalry, [whose] floating Carcasses / and broken Chariot Wheels" glutted the surface of the Red Sea (1:307–11). In addressing his fallen legions Satan capitalizes on their terror, inciting them with threats that God's armies, seeing their "abject posture," will seize the advantage and "descending tread us down / Thus drooping, or with linked Thunderbolts / Transfix us to the bottom of this Gulf" (1:327–29).

Part of Satan's imposing statue in the early books of *Paradise Lost* arises from his lack of fear. He challenges Death defiantly; and when confronted with the "wild Abyss" of Chaos, he only stands and looks "a while, / Pondering his Voyage" before he resolutely "spurns the ground" and soars into the "vast vacuity" (2:917–19, 929–32). Indeed, after his defeat in Heaven he shows no fear until he confronts the warrior angels once again, Gabriel and the celestial guards outside Eden, whom he "fled / Murmuring" (4:1014–15) and thereafter avoided, dreading their "vigilence" (9:157–58). The only other instance is the descent of the Son, come to judge Adam and

---

1. I discuss the qualities of Man's pre- and postlapsarian states in Chapter 5.

Eve, at the sight of whom he flees "terrifi'd" (10:338). In those early books, however, the terrors of the Almighty are so far overshadowed by Satan's obsessive "study of revenge, immortal hate" (1:107) that he is free of the paralysis that grips his legions, hence retains the will to act. Since fear is antithetical to the military order he seeks to reestablish, he sets out to work a similar displacement in the breasts of his followers; having called them to him, he "gently rais'd / Thir fainting courage, and dispell'd thir fears" and then excites their pride and anger, proclaiming dramatically that "War then, War / Open and understood, must be resolv'd" (1:661-62).[2]

Whatever unity prevails in Hell arises from a sense of common cause, an implacable hatred of the force that has condemned these former citizens of Heaven to the terrible punishment they share. Hate begets a compulsion to act, to set traps, hatch plots, and strike by night. In Satan's words, "only in destroying I find ease / To my relentless thoughts" (9:129-30). Hatred *demands* action; and its restless energy precipitates conflict, whether in debate over issues, the struggle for power, or the clash of arms, all readily represented in the imagery of the political arena.[3] If that action involves disobedience against authority, the rebel is immediately thrust into a political world and faced with choices between alternate ways to resist and replace that scorned authority. The political structure of Hell reflects that need to act and the consequent need to choose from among alternative courses of action. The fallen angels assemble a government that although it retains the traditional hierarchies of their former state, differs dramatically from the political order of Heaven. Denied the focus of a Godhead whose decrees had hitherto disposed their lives, they meet in a forum divided over the form of government to adopt and the direction of the new state. The political structure of Hell is determined, therefore, not by Milton's perception of good or evil governments, but by the needs of the poem at that juncture of the narrative – the poet sought to define the choices before the rebel angels, and the representative assembly is the most appropriate forum

2. Hardin is persuaded that "fear is the dominant chord in the first two books of *Paradise Lost*" (*Civil Idolatry* 179). This rather reductive reading of the fallen angels' mentality – and Hardin is not alone in his sentiments – may be morally satisfying but it is much too simple. To dismiss their reactions in this summary fashion is to miss the dramatic political interplay among them and, further, to reduce Milton's complex psychological study of the disease of evil to a single symptom. The political imagery certainly says otherwise. Moloch has no fear – he is enraged, and stupid perhaps, but not afraid – nor is Satan when faced with Death and Chaos. Milton is far more perceptive in his characterization of a fallen nature: fear gives way to hatred, which urges vengeance, which in turn demands action.

3. As Tanner puts it, "Milton's hell pulsates with erratic energy" (*Anxiety in Eden* 135).

for airing alternative courses of action. Their condition resembles closely that of the revolutionary leaders of England who, having deposed and executed the king in January 1649, replaced the rule of the monarch with that of "the Commons of England assembled in Parliament,"[4] and met to debate the shape of their new government and an appropriate response to the forces threatening the young republic (*MG* 25-26).

As we have seen, Satan ascends a throne that, however splendid, does not assure him absolute sway over his followers. He raises the constitutional question briefly, claiming his right to preside over the body by what "in Counsel and in Fight" he has achieved; but he quickly sidesteps the issue, tabling debate over who or what will rule in Hell by announcing a more pressing agenda item – how to work their vengeance on the Almighty. He urges that foreign affairs take precedence for the moment over domestic issues. It is a device that may have been on Cromwell's mind when, the Anglo-Dutch War having been successfully concluded, he proposed to challenge Spain in the Caribbean, over the vigorous objections of John Lambert, who argued that there were pressing matters to address at home (*MG* 129). It is a familiar debate, one that brings to mind Henry IV's deathbed advice to his son to "busy giddy minds / With foreign quarrels."[5]

Satan may have restored order among the fallen angels by providing a common cause in hatred of their conqueror but he has by no means dispelled fear of the Almighty in the breasts of all; and so a debate ensues, as each of the "Great Seraphic Lords and Cherubim" balances one passion against the other in his own mind. Moloch fears nothing, so possessed is he by hatred of his "Torturor" and a single-minded desire for revenge. Belial, although declaring himself "as not behind in hate" (2:120), fears that were they to assault "Th' Almighty Victor," he would "spend all his rage, / And that must end us" (2:144-45). Mammon lies between, rejecting submission and "worship paid / To whom we hate" (2:248-49) but advising that they dismiss "All thought of War" (2:283). But hatred must act; as Beëlzebub proclaims, "War hath determin'd us" and the only way open for them is to pursue "hostility and hate, / Untam'd reluctance, and revenge" (2:330-37).

It is not Milton's purpose to depict the forces of evil as so many puppets of a single diabolical will. Each of the fallen angels, later to lead men astray as false gods, is dangerous in his own right; and they retain the gift of reason,

4. The phrase appears repeatedly in the official records of the Republic. See, e.g., Samuel Rawson Gardiner, *The Constitutional Documents of the Puritan Revolution, 1625-1660,* 377, 386-87.

5. *Henry IV, Part 2* 4.5.212-13.

which they exercise in arriving at a solution. Hatred must act, to be sure, but once free to act, it must choose among alternatives; and if that choosing is depicted as political in nature, the decision is appropriately represented in the deliberations of a political body that allows for the same kind of debate over means that troubles the inner spirit of any being intent upon revenge – the where, when, and how to act.

Milton was familiar with such sentiments as they were articulated in public policy. The English Protestants hated the power of the papacy and engaged in endless debate over that same where, when, and how to act in opposing it. In the poet's State Letters, Cromwell urged a league of Protestant states united against the Catholic powers to the south; he exhorted Charles X of Sweden to attack the Austrians, attempted to rally those in the ranks of "Reformed Religion" to aid the massacred Piedmontese, and initiated the Western Design against Spain. He spelled out Protestant grievances and vented his anger in a number of Milton's letters, among them one to the king of Denmark:

> There's no necessity of calling to remembrance the Valleys of *Piemont* still besmear'd with the Blood and Slaughter of the miserable inhabitants; nor *Austria,* tormented at the same time with the Emperor's Decrees and Proscriptions, nor the impetuous Onsets of the Popish upon the Protestant *Switzers.* Who can be ignorant, that the Artifices and Machinations of the *Spaniards,* for some years last past, have fill'd all these places with the confus'd and blended havock of Fire and Sword?
>
> (W87, P119)[6]

The influence of Rome, of course, was as greatly feared as hated. During the Anarchy, Charles II was persistently rumored to be marching at the head a popish army preparing to invade England (*MG* 191).

As frequently as the word "hate" is to be found in the discourse and description of Hell, so often does the word "love" appear in Heaven. God's realm is a place where his will is immediately manifest as the will of the body politic, a phenomenon explainable only in terms of the love between the Deity and his creation. In this respect, Heaven doesn't really need a government. God speaks and the Heavenly Host concur, indeed join joyfully in celebrating his decrees.[7] They do so, not because they are puppets of

---

6. For others in a like vein, see W75, P109 and W79, P108.
7. As Laura Knoppers observes, "joy in *Paradise Lost* articulates obedience to a divine monarch" (*Historicizing Milton* 79; see also 75, 82).

the Almighty – they too can reason – but because of the mutual love between the king and his subjects; he acts, through the Son, and they burst into hymns of praise, perceiving in his actions the love he bears for his creation. His subjects return that love by "serving" him, a political metaphor for their devotion to the Godhead. This service has no stain of subservience on it, however; it is a sign of their desire to participate in the exchange of love with the Deity, as Raphael explains early in his discourse with Adam, "freely we serve / Because we freely love, as in our will / To love or not" (5:538-40).

For Milton, God is a singularity, he is "ONE" (*Prose* 6:146); and all creation is similarly "ONE" with him in the sense that everything that exists – Heaven and Hell, the angels, both loyal and rebel, the World with its light and darkness, sea and shore, birds and flowers, and finally Man – is part of him, that is, was created *ex Deo,* out of his substance.[8] In Milton's cosmology the warring elements of Chaos constitute the basic stuff of matter; it is the "Womb of nature" out of which all things are made. As such, it *is* God as well, representing all created things in potential; and the act of creation is thus a differentiation of the substance of the Deity into distinct entities. Chaos, the king, complains about the recent incursions on his realm, Hell and the World; and we may assume he is as unhappy about the earlier intrusion of Heaven itself (2:1002-5).[9] We are not given to see the making of Heaven and Hell but the process is presumably the same as that described at the creation of the World. There "His brooding wings the Spirit of God outspread" over the "vast profundity obscure" of Chaos, then but "Matter unform'd and void," until with "vital virtue infus'd, and vital warmth" the elements suspend their discord and converge to shape the Earth (7:229-36). Once formed, the Earth *is* the Deity, as much as any other cosmic realm, for as he proclaims, "I am who fill / Infinitude"; and though he may "put not forth [his] goodness," he cannot withdraw himself from substance that is himself (7:168-71).

The purpose of this systematic differentiation is obscure, but in *Paradise Lost* it makes possible the manifestation of that quality of the Godhead which in human tongue is called "love."[10] All things are made to demon-

---

8. Cf. *Christian Doctrine:* "It seems to me that, with the guidance of scripture, I have proved that God produced all things not out of nothing but out of himself" (*Prose* 6:310). See J. H. Adamson, "The Creation," 81-102.

9. For an intriguing alternative to this view of Chaos, see Regina M. Schwartz, *Remembering and Repeating.* Schwartz proposes "an evil chaos" (11), abandoned by God (19), one allied with Hell "in the common purpose of havoc, spoil, and ruin" (23).

10. The differentiation is discussed in greater detail on pp. 155-59.

strate that love, even the tortured regions of Hell, over whose gates the pilgrim Dante saw the puzzling inscription, "DIVINE POWER MADE ME AND . . . PRIMAL LOVE."[11] From the first moment of time, the initial tick of the cosmic clock, when God wills the differentiation of his sacred substance into Heaven and angels, politics becomes inevitable, that is, the representation of the consequent order of things demands political metaphor. Since all creation is part of God, and since the part is less than the whole, everything by definition is subordinate to him, subject to his rule; and the resultant order is comprehensible to human understanding only in terms of Man's experience with governing and being governed. In *Paradise Lost,* then, Milton employs the political metaphor to define both the relationship between the Deity and his creation as a whole, and the hierarchy among the various levels of beings within that creation as well. That he does so with such a lavish hand may be attributed to the richness of his own experience in public life, ten years of labor within the closest conclaves of the English government.

Divine love is the central principle of creation, the bond that makes it all work; but it must be reciprocated. It has no meaning unless God's creatures are free to return or withhold it, a principle that the Almighty defines somewhat imperiously: "Not free, what proof could they have giv'n sincere / Of true allegiance, constant Faith and Love" and "What pleasure I from such obedience paid" (3:103-7). The language – "proof," "allegiance," "obedience" – is judicial and political, perhaps appropriate to an occasion when God is justifying his judgment on Man; but it fails to convey the full dynamics of that mutual love, from which the Deity gains as much "pleasure" in the receiving as in the giving. Even God cannot love a puppet, so he endows his creatures with reason, empowering them to love him or not, and thereby prove themselves worthy of his in return. Choice, of course, presumes alternatives; and in *Paradise Lost* God provides occasions for his creatures to choose to love him or not, on some of which they prove themselves disappointingly deficient.

In *Paradise Lost,* disobedience is the political equivalent of divine love betrayed. The political framework defines the choice in Heaven when God disturbs the traditional hierarchy of Heaven by elevating the Son, offering the angels an occasion to exercise their reason in choosing to obey him or not, that is, to love him or not. Once Milton has established God in the image of an absolute king, the role must be played out in a manner befitting

11. *Divine Comedy* 1:47.

such a figure. Hence, it would be entirely indecorous for the mighty monarch to stand before his assembled subjects and proclaim, "*If you love me, bow down and accept my Son as your king*," though that in essence is the issue in any divine decree. John Rumrich describes the occasion as a shift from the natural to the moral law; but this is certainly not the first occasion the angels have been offered moral choice.[12] As it happens, it is the earliest known to the reader in the chronology of *Paradise Lost;* but if the angels return God's love through choice, they must be doing so continuously by frequenting his "high Temple... / With Ministries due and solemn Rites" (7:148-49). That this is the first occasion when some of them make the wrong choice and fail to return his love, does not mean that they have never before been confronted with such a decision. Heaven is a highly organized political state, established presumably by a series of divine decrees, which its subjects have been asked to obey. One can easily imagine the Almighty proclaiming at one point or another that the hierarchy of Heaven shall consist of eight orders of angels and three separate fiefdoms, each presided over by an archangel, and that a select seven, chosen by name, shall "nearest to his Throne / Stand ready to command" (3:649-50).[13] It must be admitted, however, that this latest decree proves the most difficult so far for those who may not embrace the Deity with that quality of complete love that inspires absolute obedience, in which the submission of their own will to his is not, once more, a mere act of thoughtless devotion, but the consequence of conscious choice.

Thus, the elevation of the Son is not an arbitrary act of a whimsical Deity; it is a trial of the very idea of endowing creatures with the power of reason, a test of whether a society of such beings can indeed survive under the rule of an omnipotent, omniscient, and omnipresent God. Reason is not a flaw in the divine plan, but a quality of created beings necessary, again, to the exchange of love God intends; but reason creates difficulties by inducing an awareness of individual identity with its own concerns and passions; and in consequence it introduces moral tension in beings confronted with absolute decrees. Reason, then, is both a blessing and a curse, rendering worship possible and at the same time troublesome. On its surface, such a design,

---

12. John Peter Rumrich, *Matter of Glory,* 161-62.

13. For example, when "th' Empyreal Host" gathers to hear God's proclamation about the Son, they carry "Standards and Gonfalons" on which "bear imblaz'd / Holy Memorials, acts of Zeal and Love / Recorded eminent" (5:589-94). The nature of these "acts" is left undefined; but they surely involved choices to be made, which to that time, it would appear, had all been the right ones. I am indebted to Diane McColley for this detail.

beings created with an individual identity which they are then asked to surrender to the divine identity, seems doomed to failure; it only makes sense if animated by an exchange of love. The external political fabric of Heaven reflects the inner tensions of the angels, whose submission as governed beings to the governing will of God depends on their ability to subordinate passion to reason. Subordination without reflects subordination within. Thus, the elevation of the Son in *Paradise Lost* is the inciting incident of a drama that all cosmic history will play out, testing whether God's plan will indeed work, that is, whether love is enough.

Milton's artistic problem arises from the fact that hatred is much easier to represent in political terms than is its opposite; hence the government of Hell is more vivid and immediate than that of Heaven. Since love is not a quality usually identified with political life, the demonic regime is closer to the poet's own experience, from which he drew most readily for the materials of his art. The politics of Hell allows for the representation of some of the common concerns of fallen Man – a desire to better his condition, find relief from pain, and live in freedom – as well as some of his less admirable qualities, such as overweening ambition, the drive of self-interest mindless of the cost to others, a compulsion for revenge, and unprincipled hatred; and Satan demonstrates all of these qualities at one time or another. Love, on the other hand, does not lend itself to expression in political metaphor, as any modern reader's response to the demand for *absolute* obedience will attest.

Hatred, as has been noted, is characterized by restless energy and the urge to act. Love, on the other hand, connotes rest, contentment, and a joyful acceptance of the bond that satisfies all yearning.[14] It has no counterpart in political life except in the image of the absolute monarch in perfect accord with his subjects, a bond which earthly monarchs fervently claimed for their kingdoms and which Milton with equal fervor condemned wherever claimed. The kings of Milton's time were fond of citing the reciprocal love they shared with their subjects and among their "cousins," the other crowned heads of nations, who were all related in one way or another.[15] Charles I, in the early years of his reign employed the traditional phrases in speech and correspondence, opening with such phrases as "Trusty and well

14. Tanner contrasts the two realms thus: "Milton's hell pulsates with erratic energy, while his heaven stands stately and serene" (*Anxiety in Eden* 135).

15. Charles II and Louis XIV, e.g., were first cousins, sons respectively of Henrietta Marie of England and her brother, Louis XIII of France.

beloved we greet you well" and referring frequently to "our loving subjects"; and they responded in like manner, "there was never a King more loving to his people."[16] Milton considered such monarchal posturing idolatrous, which helps explain why he avoided mention of love in his praise of Cromwell and the other leaders of the Republic in *A Second Defence*. In the Lord Protector's letters to heads of state, references to friendship, amity, union, and good-will abound; but the personal relationship is never said to go beyond "affection."

Divine love, then, though essential to the justification of God's ways, is difficult to represent in political terms. The angels sing of it and the Deity demonstrates it by surrendering his Son to death; but it lies outside human experience and defies description in the language of governance. Any effort to represent divine love politically invariably ends up as a resolution suspiciously circular – I love God because I am free, I am free because I love God. But that same love makes sense of the many paradoxes introduced by the political imagery, those which define the difference between the human and the divine experience: the perplexing contradictions – in absolute obedience lies absolute freedom, within the elaborate "Orders and Degrees" of Heaven all God's subjects are equal, and the Son's humiliation shall exalt him – to which may be added the oxymoron, "government of Heaven," itself. God may *sound* like a tyrant, but only because the rewards for allegiance to him are inexpressible in terms of the relationship between the governing and the governed. Though the politics of paradise, lost and regained, is a pervasive metaphor, it makes sense only in terms of the love that binds God's creatures to one another and him to his creation. Thus the harsh punishment for Adam's sin can only be justified once it is understood that obedience to God is, again, the political equivalent of that love returned and disobedience the political equivalent of that love betrayed.

Thus, Milton was confronted with the challenge of somehow expressing that "Inexpressible love" of the Deity for his creation, and for Man in particular, the latter in the face of evidence that would seem to call it into question. In *Christian Doctrine,* he lays little stress on divine love, perhaps because his purpose is to show that Scripture is accessible to human reason; hence, human emotion is little to the point. In his list of God's attributes, Milton comes no closer than to describe him as "SUPREMELY KIND" (*Prose* 6:150); and in his citations of the familiar lines from John 3:16, "God so

16. Gardiner, *Constitutional Documents,* 46, 83, 4.

loved the World ... " he is discussing other matters entirely.[17] It is an attribute of the Deity that cannot be ignored, however. Divine love is the central principle of all creation, the reciprocal bond that animates the cosmos, engaging its fallen and unfallen creatures in a celebration of existence; and although it may not lend itself to representation in a systematic theology devoted to forming "correct ideas about God guided by nature and reason" (*Prose* 6:132), it is a quality appropriate to expression in poetry, whose music touches an understanding above the merely rational. In *Christian Doctrine* Milton could only interpret God's ways; in *Paradise Lost* he sought to justify them, and does so in terms of God's love for Man.

Milton can *celebrate* divine love, of course, and in *Paradise Lost* he does so with soaring hymns, praising a God who created all things solely to express that quality of his nature through the person of the Son:

> in him all his Father shone
> Substantially express'd, and in his face
> Divine compassion visibly appear'd,
> Love without end, and without measure Grace;
>   (3:139-42)

and he gave his creatures the gift of reason so that they could respond in kind. When the Son offers himself for Man, "mee for him, life for life," God foresees the Incarnation as a victory by which "Heav'nly love shall outdo Hellish hate" (3:298), and the celestial choirs extol the sacrifice, "O unexampl'd love, / Love nowhere to be found less than Divine" (3:410-11).

But Milton had to do more than simply sing about God's love, he had to show it; and the means of doing so arise from his familiar definition from *Areopagitica:* "It was from out of the rind of one apple tasted, that the knowledge of good and evill as two twins cleaving together leapt forth into the World. And this is that doom which *Adam* fell into of knowing good and evill, that is to say of knowing good by evill" (2:514). In a striking series of parallels between Hell and Heaven, and between Satan and the Son of God, Milton defines love in terms of its opposite. His readers, who can only know good *by* evil, are presented with an image of celestial governance that

---

17. Michael Bauman, *A Scriptual Index to John Milton's "De doctrina christiana,"* 105. Bauman lists twelve citations in volume 6 of *Prose.* On 175 and 179 Milton discusses predestination; on 210, 226, and 247 he argues that the Son is not coeval with the Father; on 416, he points out that Mankind was redeemed prior to the Fall; and so on.

although beyond their comprehension, can be brought within the scope of human understanding when placed alongside the regime in Hell, whose political structure mirrors the governments of men and hence is all too familiar to them. The essential difference between the two realms can be grasped only through a vision of what they, like "two twins cleaving together," have in common. The parallels are close indeed, each almost a mirror of the other; and Milton draws them thus to underline the message that evil appears so often in the guise of good that one must peer beneath the surface acts and institutions to detect the difference (*CC* 168, 200-201, 228-29). Milton illustrates the difficulty of distinguishing between them in the figure of Abdiel, who, as he watches the rebel legions approach over the plains of Heaven, is perplexed by the spectacle and indignant at how closely they resemble the loyal armies awaiting them:

> O Heav'n! that such resemblance of the Highest
> Should yet remain, where faith and realty
> Remain not; wherefore should not strength and might
> There fail where Virtue fails, or weakest prove
> Where boldest?
>
> (6:114-18)

The parallel between the celestial and demonic trinities is frequently cited to illustrate Milton's intent to depict Hell as a parody of Heaven, that is, to underline the rather self-evident inferiority of one to the other.[18] The similarities between the trinities, however, the family relationships and the commitment of their members to a common goal, are designed to emphasize their disparate ends, the one motivated by hatred, the other by love. The purpose of such parallels is not to mock evil, but to define good.[19] For example, God's capacity to create the World out of the discordant elements of Chaos is matched by the power of Sin and Death, who construct a vast bridge out of the same materials. Whereas the Spirit of God brings the universe into existence by brooding over the abyss and infusing "vital warmth / Throughout the fluid Mass" (7:236-37), the infernal pair freeze the warring elements into place. Like the Spirit, they hover "upon the Waters," and separate the "raging Sea" into "Mountains of Ice," whereupon Death, "with his Mace petrific, cold and dry," hammers the bridge into being

18. Merritt Y. Hughes summarizes the scholarship up to his time in *John Milton, Complete Poems and Major Prose,* 177.

19. Again, for a parodic reading, see Tanner, *Anxiety in Eden,* 139.

(10:285-98). The contrast between the warmth of God's love and Hell's cold hate is accentuated by the parallels between the two creative acts.

The hierarchy of Hell mirrors that of Heaven, their conclaves are comparably splendid, and, after the "great consult," their subjects equally united in purpose.[20] The similarities serve to underscore the different purposes, the one to divide Man from God, the other to draw him closer. As we have seen, both Beëlzebub and God ask for volunteers for their separate missions and both are greeted with silence, as the two bodies ponder the consequences; in the one, none "could be found / So hardy as to proffer or accept / Alone the dreadful voyage" (2:424-26) and in the other, none "durst upon his own head draw / The deadly forfeiture, and ransom set" (3:220-21). When Satan and the Son offer to undertake the separate tasks, however, the two assemblies react in subtly different ways. The fallen angels' response to Satan's speech is relatively subdued: they "bend / With awful reverence prone; and as a God / Extol him equal to the highest in Heav'n" (2:477-79); in contrast, the Son's offer, once God has explained its significance, is greeted by "a shout / Loud as from numbers without number, sweet / As from blest voices, uttering joy" and the angels burst into a long hymn of praise (3:345-47, 372-415). The similarities here set up responses appropriate to the different motives of the two. Satan's personal ambition, his need to perform some exemplary act to prove himself worthy to reign in Hell, is greeted with begrudged admiration. The Son, with nothing to prove, having already demonstrated his right to the throne by his victory over the rebel angels, acts out of perfect love for Man, bringing joy to the Heavenly Host, who respond with exultant "sacred Song."

Both Satan and the Son embark on voyages to the World, the one to subvert Man, the other, in human form, to save him; and their missions have similar political consequences. Satan secures his right to reign in Hell, with his enhanced status defined by Sin. "Thine now is all this World," she declares, "here thou shalt Monarch reign" and God must "henceforth Monarchy with thee divide / Of all things" (10:372-80). He is anticipated in Hell as "thir Emperor" (10:429) and returns as "their great adventurer from the search / Of Foreign Worlds" (10:440-41). He enters Pandemonium invisible and suddenly appears "Star-bright" upon his throne. No longer bothered by potential "Rivals," he greets "the great consulting Peers," who "with joy / Congratulant approach'd him," now hailed as "Thir mighty Chief" (10:450-58).

20. Milton, indeed, finds Hell superior to Earth in this regard: "O shame to men! Devil with Devil damn'd / Firm accord holds, men only disagree / Of Creatures rational, though under hope / Of heavenly Grace" (2:496-99).

The Son is similarly confirmed as king of Heaven, for as the Father proclaims, on his return, "Here shalt thou sit incarnate, here shalt Reign / Both God and Man, Son both of God and Man / Anointed universal King" (3:315-17).

Both suffer humiliation on Earth, Satan's "foul descent" into the serpent, the Son's crucifixion; both triumph, Satan over Man, the Son over Death; both return in humble guise, Satan as a "Plebian Angel militant / Of lowest order" (10:442-43), the Son as Man; and both are greeted with animation, Satan to the loud acclaim and joy of the "Heav'n-banisht Host" and the Son, as Michael foresees, "exalted high / Above all names in Heav'n" (12:456). Satan silences his followers with a gesture, announces his victory, and directs them to "up and enter now into full bliss" (10:503). Rather than the hymns of praise that will greet the Son of God and Man, however, he hears only "A dismal universal hiss, the sound / Of public scorn" (10:508). The Son's "Humiliation shall exalt" him; but Satan's exaltation, in ironic contrast, only ends in further humiliation.[21]

The parallels between the two realms thus emphasize the different qualities of spirit that inform them. It is precisely because the hierarchy in Hell duplicates that of Heaven and trinities rule in both, because Satan seated "Star-bright" upon his "high Throne" reflects, though dimly, God's sun-burst glory in Heaven, and because the Devil's career resembles the Son's in so many ways, that we learn to look beneath the similarities, and come to know good *by* evil. And, again, the differences between the political structures of the two realms do not reflect Milton's preference for one over the other. He is not proposing that his readers favor the absolute monarchy of Heaven over the representative assembly of Hell; he is asking them to choose love over hate.

---

21. See Labriola, " 'Thy Humiliation Shall Exalt,' " 29-42, for an illuminating discussion of the paradox.

5

THE LORDS OF THE EARTH

There would seem to be little occasion for political life in Milton's Eden, since the poet assumed that prelapsarian Man, guided by natural law and the rule of reason, was disposed to act rightly, that is, in concert with God's will, and hence had no need for governments. As he observes in *Christian Doctrine,* "Man was made in the image of God, and the whole law of nature was so implanted and innate in him that he was in need of no command" (*Prose* 6:353). Paradise is not without its hierarchy, however, being in this respect no different from Heaven, Hell, and Chaos. Milton found it difficult to imagine any society, be it celestial, demonic, allegorical, or earthbound, without "Orders and Degrees." His public duties brought distinctions in political hierarchy to his attention with some regularity. Fully one-third of his State Letters make mention of an envoy's diplomatic rank, whether Agent, Resident, or Ambassador; and he learned that governments were punctilious in their observance of the dignities attached to each. Early in his public career he received an embarrassing lesson in the importance of such distinctions, on an occasion when he cited the wrong rank in Richard Bradshaw's credential letter to the city of Hamburg (W12, P16). The envoy was forced to return it to London for correction twice before Milton got it right (*MG* 38-41). Hence, the poet was well acquainted with the "Orders and Degrees" of diplomatic exchange, as well as their attendant privileges and protocols.

Prelapsarian Rule

Since the human population of Eden at no time numbered more than two, the politics of the earthly paradise inevitably involved a hierarchy of gender. Modern scholars find literary representations of the relationship between men and women heavily laden with the language of power, and they see Milton's Eve as a woman asserting her right to stand on equal footing with Adam. Whatever theological, biblical, cultural, or psychological readings of *Paradise Lost* may render on the question, the political frame would seem to confirm their equality, though Milton leaves unexplained Eve's motive for claiming the prerogative to work alone. A feminist scholar would doubtless observe that no explanation is necessary.

As we have seen, what imagery there is of governance in the Garden depicts Adam and Eve as "Lords" of the Earth, co-rulers of equal authority, a status modified by a family relationship that assigns them separate roles.[1] The two are distinguishable in many respects; and though the differences do not imply a scale of merit or value, there is a decided hierarchical distinction between them. The narrative bears out the dissimilarity, for in their daily round it is Adam who determines what they do, and when. It is he who signals the time to retire (4:610-12), who awakens Eve in the morning, urging that they not "lose the prime" (5:21), and who decides when to begin their "fresh imployments" (5:125).[2] When Raphael arrives, he bids her to "go with speed" (5:313) and prepare the refreshments that hospitality demands. He may not be said to give orders but it is clearly he who

---

1. See pp. 9-10. Suzanne Woods finds the family relationship at odds with individual freedom: "Milton's profound respect for human liberty has the ultimate effect of subverting his patriarchal assumptions" ("How Free Are Milton's Women?" 19).

2. It is perhaps significant that after the Fall, it is Eve who proposes that they resume work (11:171-76), though their expulsion precludes it.

arranges their daily round and sets the pace of their existence.[3] The elaborate language of address further marks their separate roles. Adam is by no means overbearing; the titles he ascribes to Eve highlight their equality more than anything else: she is his "Sole partner," "Fair Consort," and "Best Image of myself" (4:410, 610; 5:95). It is Eve who is most conscious of the hierarchy, addressing him as "my Guide / And my Head," "My Author and Disposer," and declaring,

> what thou bidd'st
> Unargu'd I obey; so God ordains,
> God is thy Law, thou mine: to know no more
> Is woman's happiest knowledge and her praise.
> (4:442-43, 635-38)

God's instructions to Raphael specify that the angel is to "Converse with Adam," that is, to "advise him," "warn him," "let him know," so that "All Justice" may be fulfilled (5:230-47). Eve is not mentioned. When the archangel arrives in Eden, he greets her respectfully as the "Mother of Mankind"; but she does not reply and utters not a word during his visit, leaving the entire conversation to Adam while "she sat retir'd in sight" (8:41); and Raphael takes no notice of her when he departs.[4] Indeed, the only time she speaks to God or his emissaries is in her brief confession, "The Serpent me beguil'd and I did eat," and this only when she is so commanded, "Say Woman, what is this thou hast done?" (10:158-62). The only other occasion when she speaks within an angel's hearing is her emotional outburst upon learning that they must leave Eden, uttered from "the place of her retire" (11:267), where she sits concealed, listening to the exchange between Michael and Adam. Though the angel answers her, it is not to him that she directs her involuntary exclamation. She addresses her Garden, to which she bids a plaintive farewell, "Must I thus leave thee Paradise?" lamenting the loss of its "Native Soil," "flow'rs," and, most sadly, her "nuptial Bower" (11:268-85).

Eve's proposal that the two work separately conveys the impression of a bid for equality, one that precipitates a political debate over status in the

---

3. The exception is their prayer, which they perform spontaneously, with "prompt eloquence" and with one voice "unanimous" (5:149; 4:736).

4. Milton leaves it uncertain whether or not she spoke when "A while discourse they held" (5:395); but in the narrative she never addresses the archangel directly, or indeed speaks at all in his presence.

Garden.[5] Milton gives no hint that she has been in any way dissatisfied with her position in the hierarchy, but she clearly wants to be free of the constant supervision of her "Head" and "Guide." Eve is not challenging the hierarchy of Eden but she does seem to find it a bit confining and, in modern terms, feels that she "needs her space." In broaching the subject, she is noticeably less effusive in her mode of address, calling her husband simply "Adam"; and although she later acknowledges him as "all Earth's Lord," it cannot escape notice that she omits any reference to him as *her* "Lord." This is clearly a political confrontation between one party intent on pursuing a course of action that another, vaguely identified as occupying a step above in the hierarchy, thinks ill-advised; and the point at issue, working conditions, is a traditional bone of contention between the governing and the governed in any society.[6]

Their dispute is doubly interesting in that it offers a model for the manner in which disagreements were to be resolved once the children start coming and the population expands.[7] Milton leaves largely unexplained the manner in which an unfallen state was to be governed, presumably since such a state never came into being and so would be irrelevant to the justification of God's ways. We are given only glimpses of the political future of unfallen Man, Raphael's prediction that their bodies "may at last turn all to spirit, / Improv'd by tract of time" (5:497-98) and Michael's suggestion that had Adam not sinned, Eden would have been

> Perhaps thy Capital Seat, from whence had spread
> All generations, and had hither come
> From all the ends of th' Earth, to celebrate
> And reverence thee thir great Progenitor.
>   (11:343-46)

Although the two destinies seem somewhat at odds, Milton is sufficiently vague on the matter to preclude all but the most determined criticism. It is unclear whether the population would "turn all to spirit" individually as each became worthy of translation, or all at once in a single metamorphosis

---

5. McColley, *Gust for Paradise*, 164.

6. It should be noted that after the Fall Eve promises Adam "never from thy side henceforth to stray" (11:176).

7. As Diane McColley observes, "The debate itself . . . is part of the prelapsarian process of working out the government of the human race" (*Gust for Paradise* 168).

of the entire race;[8] but in either case, Adam would have presided over his generations in some unspecified way during his indeterminate "tract of time." His reign would not have been free of controversy, however, as the dispute with Eve vividly illustrates; and in this respect it differs little from the other governments of *Paradise Lost*.

The debate between Adam and Eve arises from a disagreement between two unfallen beings, hence no taint of sin can attach to it. We are not told whether God approves of Eve's display of independence; but it will be recalled that earlier he had only praise for Adam's challenge of a divine arrangement that left him without a mate. On that occasion, he compliments Adam for expressing "well the spirit within thee free" and explains that the exchange on the subject was but a trial "To see how thou couldst judge of fit and meet" (8:440, 448).[9] If one can discount the consequences of the separation, it is easy to imagine the Father nodding his approval at her exercise of "the spirit within [her] free." Their dispute cannot be characterized as the first skirmish in the battle of the sexes; had the race not fallen, it is the sort of debate that would have occurred with some frequency quite irrespective of gender, when disagreements arose over issues well beyond the trimming of the Garden – issues of jurisdiction, authority, law, property, labor, and the like. Conflict would have been no less a problem on an unfallen Earth than it had been in Heaven; but in the progress of the debate between Adam and Eve can be seen the model for the resolution of differences. Man's desires will be weighed in balance with God's will and the dangers posed by Satan, and disputes will be resolved by consensus, since "unanimous" seems too grand a term for an electorate of two (though Milton does use the word in this sense: 4:736; 12:603). Again, disagreements are not evil in themselves, though evil may arise from them.

Thus, there is equality in Eden. As we have seen, it is modified, to be sure, by a family relationship that prescribes distinct roles for the two, markedly in the protocol observed in the reception of emissaries from a higher power; but insofar as Adam and Eve rule the Earth they do so as equals. As Diane McColley observes of the arrangement, "subordination is not inferiority," and in this regard their relationship mirrors that between the Father and Son

8. In *Christian Doctrine* Milton specifies that "the standard of judgment" for fallen Man will be "the individual conscience" and that each "will be judged according to the light which he has received" (*Prose* 6:623).

9. One cannot escape the impression of a God who, having endowed the race with reason and free will, visits Earth to satisfy himself that things have worked out as he intended.

in Heaven.[10] How this principle would have been applied to future generations in an unfallen world can only be a matter of conjecture – but conjecture can at times be illuminating. On the one hand, as we have seen,
prelapsarian Man needs no government, for "he was in need of no command."
In Michael's regretful vision of what might have been, there is nothing to
indicate that Adam would have "governed" the race. He would have been
the object of veneration, one to whom "all generations" would have come,
as on a pilgrimage, "to celebrate / And reverence thee thir great Progenitor"
(11:344-46); but it is questionable whether he would have called upon to
issue decrees or adjudicate disputes, since all humankind, guided by "the
whole law of nature," would have had the same capacity to reach consensus
as that demonstrated in Eden.

In effect, the race has a king already, one enthroned above, and the Earth
is but an outpost of Heaven, its affairs ordered by the same governing
principle that informs the celestial realm – divine love. In some respects, the
race is but a lower order of angels, one destined, "under long obedience
tri'd" (7:159), to eventually take its place in the angelic hierarchy. In this
sense it is already a part of the kingdom of Heaven and should need no other
government. On the other hand, it seems reasonable to assume that eventually the rule of Earth would come to mirror the other cosmic realms. The
race has already in place co-rulers and a trinity to include a female presence;
and an eight-order hierarchy might well follow, evidence of the hand of God
in his creation.[11] Again, as in Heaven, such a hierarchy would not compromise the equality of the citizens of Earth, who, walking in the full glow of
divine love, would represent the resolution of the political paradox: in a
kingdom of "Orders and Degrees," all are equal.

Thus love defines the prelapsarian state. God bestows the gift of life and
prepares a garden where it can prosper; Mankind responds with prayer at
evening (4:724-35) and at rising:

> These are thy glorious works, Parent of good,
> Almighty, thine this universal Frame,
> Thus wondrous fair; thyself how wondrous then!
>   (5:153-208)

In their response to divine love, Adam and Eve add a dimension to the
relationships in the cosmic drama not evident in the other realms – they

10. McColley, *Milton's Eve,* 35; Patrides, "Milton and Arianism," 71-77.
11. See pp. 14-16.

love each other. Hell is informed by hatred; but although we detect in the interaction between fallen angels varying degrees of ambition, envy, and self-interest, the hatred of God does not cause them to hate one another. In like manner, the love of God is not shown to induce a love of angel for angel, though, of course, it may be assumed to. Raphael answers Adam's rather forward question, confirming that "Spirits embrace" (8:626); but they are never seen so engaged. The angel does not elaborate, obviously preferring not to discuss the matter further, and promptly departs.

In contrast, the passages following the first appearance of Adam and Eve are suffused with images of their mutual love (4:300-775): "Hand in hand they pass'd, the loveliest pair / That ever since in love's imbraces met" (4:321-22). They exchange "endearing smiles . . . in happy nuptial League" (4:337-39), Adam presses "her Matron lip / With kisses pure" (4:501-2), and when they retire, it is to the "Rites / Mysterious of connubial Love" (4:742-43). Eve's love song is surely the most tender and gracious in the language (4:639-56), and Milton's epithalamion, though tinged with regret at what has been lost, among the most moving (4:750-75). For Milton, human love is a way to express a quality of the divine not elsewhere demonstrated – the love of God inspires love of others – and a way of describing the spiritual essence of Heaven in terms accessible to human understanding.

Postlapsarian Rule

If divine love is the spiritual quality that informs Eden, Milton's vision of the fallen world is a spectacle of incessant conflict. This quality is not to be confused with the discord of Chaos, for there is order in the World, but it is marked by the constant clash of contending factions. It begins immediately as the inner turmoil of the newly fallen pair:

> high Winds worse within
> Began to rise, high Passions, Anger, Hate,
> Mistrust, Suspicion, Discord, and shook sore
> Thir inward State of Mind,
>
> (9:1122-25)

distress that soon thereafter erupts into a bitter exchange. They evade the real cause of their misfortunes, however, preferring to accuse each other of failure to fulfill their civic responsibilities in the rule of Eden rather than admit to their own inadequacies. Adam upbraids Eve for not accepting his judgment: "Would thou hadst heark'n'd to my words, and stay'd / With me, as I besought thee" (9:1134-35). Eve flares back:

> why didst not thou the Head
> Command me absolutely not to go?
> . . . .
> Hadst thou been firm and fixt in thy dissent,
> Neither had I transgressed, nor thou with me.
> (9:1155-61)

Adam is incensed: "I warn'd thee, I admonish'd thee," he rages; and while admitting ironically to "overmuch admiring / What seem'd in thee so perfet," he turns his own weakness against her: "Thus it shall befall / Him who to worth of Woman overtrusting / Lets her Will rule" (9:1171-89). Milton seems acquainted with the unfolding of such arguments.

In a later encounter Adam is even more angry; "Out of my sight, thou Serpent," he rages and accuses Eve of collusion with the Devil, finally indicting her entire sex:

> O why did God,
> Creator wise, that peopl'd highest Heav'n
> With Spirits Masculine, create at last
> This novelty on Earth, this fair defect
> Of Nature, and not fill the World at once
> With Men as Angels without Feminine?
> (10:888-93)

Eve, in a tearful response, accepts all blame as the "sole cause to thee of all this woe" and softens his heart: "As one disarm'd, his anger all he lost, / And thus with peaceful words uprais'd her soon" (10:935, 945-46). Love survives the Fall, though conflict now becomes the mark of postlapsarian existence. Michael unfolds a spectacle of brother against brother, nation against nation, oppressor against oppressed, conflicts that will prevail until the end of time. But love survives the Fall.

Equality does not, however. The Fall works a dramatic change in the relative positions of Adam and Eve; rather than ruling as equals, one becomes the governor, the other the governed. Raphael had warned Adam that he should not jeopardize their equal status by permitting his love for Eve to subordinate his will to hers: her beauty is "worthy well / Thy cherishing, thy honoring, and thy love, / Not thy subjection" (8:568-70). This is precisely what happens, of course. The newly fallen Eve immediately begins to think like a politician, weighing alternative distributions of power, wondering whether she should keep what she imagines as "the odds of Knowledge" to herself so as to render her "more equal, and perhaps, / A thing not undesirable, sometime / Superior: for inferior who is free?" (9:820-25). Other considerations sway her, however, and she decides to forgo the opportunity to be "superior," insisting instead that Adam act, as an individual, against his better judgment: "Thou therefore also taste" (9:881). The issue is not what *they* should do as progenitors of the race, the question raised in their earlier discussion of working conditions, but what *he* should do as her husband. There is no debate. Her beauty reduces him to "subjection"; he simply submits to her will and "scrupl'd not to eat" (9:997).

There may be some question as to which of the two is the *moral* superior after the Fall; and Diane McColley observes that Eve is "the first to repent and seek reconciliation."[12] In *political* terms, however, once equality is upset and Man's fallen state requires the imposition of governments, there is no doubt who rules whom. God chides Adam, "Was shee thy God, that her thou didst obey / Before his voice" (10:145-46); and his harsh judgment on Eve is unequivocal, "to thy Husband's will / Thine shall submit, hee over thee shall rule" (10:195-96). Because she had imposed her will upon him, she must thereafter be subject to his.

That hierarchy is further defined when God sends a later envoy to Earth, and Adam identifies Michael as one "whom not to offend, / With reverence I must meet, and thou retire" (11:236-37). She withdraws obediently, in order not to "offend" Michael, and sleeps while Adam surveys the sorry future of the race. She awakens after having only "gentle Dreams... / Portending good" (12:595-96), those which, she says, are of "some great good / Presaging" (12:612-13). Eve has been spared, it would seem, the visions and accounts of savagery, murder, war, massacre, tyranny, catastrophe, and apocalypse with which Michael had plagued Adam. Therein lies the difference between their postlapsarian roles: she embodies the hope of the

12. McColley, *Milton's Eve,* 210. Wittreich has no doubts: "Before the Fall, Adam may seem to excel Eve, but after the Fall Eve excels Adam" (*Feminist Milton* 99). See also Jesse G. Small, Author-Functions and the Interpretation of Eve in *Paradise Lost.* "

race, "some great good" that will come to them, whereas he must contend with Man's hopeless depravity. The time frame of *Paradise Lost* does not permit the poet to develop the postlapsarian relationship further; but Michael's prophecy clearly reveals that their relative status will change once again when "the Woman's Seed," not man's, will produce a Messiah, whose sire is to be "The Power of the most High" (12:368–69). As the Mother of God, woman will be restored to her former dignity.

If governing was a challenge in an unfallen world, it presents enormous difficulties in one plagued by Sin and Death, as Adam learns in his long dialogue with the archangel. He is first presented with a panoramic view of the future, revealing the dizzying diversity of the governments of Man. He sees the empires of Asia and Africa, ruled over by Chinese kings, Indian moguls, Russian czars, Byzantine sultans, and the khans of Cathay. But strangely, on that visionary map Milton's own continent is all but blank; with but a fleeting glance at Europe and Rome (11:405), Adam's eyes sweep across the Western sea to the empires of Mexico and Peru. In his vision, Adam catches sight of Almansor, Tamerlane, and Montezuma, but not so much as a glimpse of Caesar, or Charlemagne, or Charles V; and one wonders why. Is Milton anxious about the licensers, fearful they might find such allusions too close to home? Does he omit some of these names because the Holy Roman Emperors were devoutly Catholic – Charles V was a contemporary of Montezuma, of course – or is it a matter of style, the list being long already, and the familiar names of Western history somewhat out of harmony with the exotic tone of his catalog? Or perhaps he already has in mind the long passage on Rome in *Paradise Regained* and is saving the material for a later work.

Michael's is more a moral than a political narrative, intended to "Dismiss them not disconsolate" (11:113), as God had charged him; so the archangel gives the bad news first – death, sickness, age, wars, and the flood. The biblical account opens with Cain and Abel and moves on to the righteous sons of Seth, who, seduced by the daughters of Cain, spawn a race devoted to war in a time when

> To overcome in Battle, and subdue
> Nations, and bring home spoils with infinite
> Man-slaughter, shall be held the highest pitch
> Of human Glory,
>
> (11:691–94)

all a consequence of "those ill-mated Marriages." The conquerors, their battles behind them, soon turn "To luxury and riot, feast and dance" (11:715), from which Adam learns "Peace to corrupt no less than War to waste" (11:784); and Michael explains why. It is not only the fault of rulers addicted to "Fame in the World, high titles, and rich prey," but blame must be shared by subjects who submit to them, those who "Shall with thir freedom lost all virtue lose" and be content "to live secure, / Worldly or dissolute, on what thir Lords / Shall leave them to enjoy" (11:793–804). Milton skirts close to an overt image of his countrymen in post-Restoration England, confident perhaps that in omitting European nations from his catalog of kingdoms, he will distract the licensers into assuming that he refers only to those who live under exotic despots, not Stuart monarchs.[13]

Milton's message throughout is that people receive the governments they deserve, and he returns to that theme as history repeats itself after the flood. Noah's descendents "spend thir days in joy unblam'd, and dwell / Long time by Families and Tribes / Under paternal rule" (12:22–24). They rule themselves, in brief, in small communities and have no need of kings and kingdoms, a political structure close in principle to the constitutional settlement he proposed in *The Readie and Easie Way,* where "every countie in the land were made a kinde of subordinate Commonalitie or Commonwealth" (*Prose* 7:458). These peaceful times pass, however, with the rise of rulers like Nimrod,

> Of proud ambitious heart, who not content
> With fair equality, fraternal state,
> Will arrogate Dominion undeserv'd
> Over his brethren, and quite disposses
> Concord and law of Nature from the Earth,

a despot who enslaves "With War and hostile snare such as refuse / Subjection to his Empire tyrannous" (12:25–32).

This world of oppressor and oppressed, Michael continues, will so displease the Almighty that he will finally turn his face from it and select "one peculiar Nation" as his own, to whom he will promise rule over their own

---

13. Perhaps, also, Milton is matching the caution of his prose, in which he consciously avoids reference to contemporary monarchs. See pages 31–32.

land.[14] They will have to struggle for their inheritance, however, though unlike the wars waged by the offspring of "those ill-mated Marriages" and the vainglorious depredations of Nimrod, theirs will be a just conflict. They must be hardened first, however, by their wandering in the wilderness, lest "War terrify them inexpert, and fear / Return them back to *Egypt,* choosing rather / Inglorious life with servitude" (12:217-20).

The fallen sons of Adam, then, though born naturally free, will have to be prepared for conflict to retain their liberty if they wished to avoid submission to a life of servitude. It is a theme that threads its way through all of Milton's mature works, from *Of Education,* where he urges that young Englishmen serve "out the rudiments of their Souldiership" in preparing to perform "all the offices both private and publike of peace and war" (*Prose* 2:411, 379), to *The Readie and Easie Way,* where he chides the English people for choosing wealth and luxury over liberty, preferring to put their "necks again under kingship, as was made use of by the *Jews* to returne back to *Egypt* and to worship of thir idol queen, because they falsely imagind that they then livd in more plentie and prosperitie" (*Prose* 7:462).

Michael concludes his chronicle with a swift account of the history of Israel, and then gives Adam the good news: from this "peculiar Nation" will come the Messiah, whose death and resurrection will "ransom" (12:424) the race and establish a rule "in whom shall trust / All Nations, and to Kings foretold, of Kings / The last, for of his reign shall be no end" (12:328-30).

Thus, in his major works Milton offers a graphic and varied array of the governments of Man; but it is not a hopeful history, as each nation inevitably succumbs to the inherent weakness of the fallen condition. As has been observed, central to his political philosophy is the conviction that people get the governments they deserve. The very concept of one man governing another had its origins in Adam's failure to govern his passion for Eve; thus fallen Man, having abandoned the rule of reason over his passions, must submit to the rule of others if he is to live in relative peace and order. Milton consistently traces a people's political status to its source in their moral and spiritual stature. It was the poet's conviction that freedom depends on the ability of individuals to order their inner lives; thus, the degree of authority others hold over them will be determined by the degree to which they can

14. Milton uses the word "peculiar" here in both its biblical (Deuteronomy 14:2) and its political sense, "of separate or distinct constitution; independent, particular, individual" (*OED* 2). In Canon Law, a peculiar was a district "not subject to the jurisdiction of the bishop of the diocese" (*OED* 5). Cf. a tasty Yorkshire ale, "Theakston's Old Peculiar."

impose the rule of reason on themselves. A weak, corrupt, and self-indulgent people can expect to suffer under tyrants; the strong and righteous will bear a lighter load. One who is a slave within will be a slave without; those whom passion rules, will be ruled by others.

Milton returns to this theme time and again, most extensively in Michael's reply to Adam's indignant reaction to the account of Nimrod's tyranny. Adam in his innocence finds it "execrable" that one man should assume authority over others, "from God not giv'n," and argues from his prelapsarian experience that God gave Man dominion over "Beast, Fish, Fowl . . . but Man over men / He made not Lord; such title to himself / Reserving, human left from human free" (12:67-71). It is Michael's sad task to reveal the changes that sin has wrought: "yet know withal, / Since thy original lapse, true Liberty / Is lost" with severe consequences for him. Once "upstart Passions catch the Government / From Reason," Man must submit to external government; and since he permits

> Within himself unworthy Powers to reign
> Over free reason, God in Judgment just
> Subjects him from without to violent Lords.
>   (12:82-93)

The same phenomena may be observed to enslave an entire people:

> Yet sometimes Nations will decline so low
> From virtue, which is reason, that no wrong,
> But Justice, and some fatal curse annext,
> Deprives them of thir liberty,
> Thir inward lost.
>   (12:97-101)

Thus, since Man is no longer ruled by reason, he will be ruled by others, some of whom will be tyrants, for, as Milton counsels in his peroration to *A Second Defence,* "a nation which cannot rule and govern itself, but has delivered itself into slavery to its own lusts, is enslaved also to other masters whom it does not choose." Man has it within his power to control his political destiny, however; and to those who desire freedom he advises, "If to be a slave is hard, and you do not wish it, learn to obey right reason, to master yourselves" (*Prose* 4:684).

Milton favored nations in their youth. Michael's chronicle of the fallen world alludes directly to a number, though Milton would appear to prefer the pastoral model where the absence of political life seems a blessing. The sons of Seth pursue a simple existence, herding their cattle and playing their instruments, until they venture, like the Piedmontese, "on the Plain" (11:580) and encounter the daughters of Cain.[15] After the flood, Noah's progeny are happy tending their herds, "Laboring the soil, and reaping plenteous crop" (12:18-20) until Nimrod arises, he "Of proud ambitious heart," to destroy their peace. The Israelites live well enough under the patriarchs, Abraham and Moses; and Michael describes God's delight when in the Wilderness they found "Thir government, and thir great Senate" from the twelve tribes and establish a rule "by Laws ordain'd" (12:222-27). The archangel speaks well of David's "Regal Throne" (12:323) as well; but his message is the same throughout: no matter how wisely they begin, the outcome is always the same, for, having lost inner liberty, the race sinks under the weight of corruption, sloth, and idolatry to inevitable tyranny, slavery, or destruction. These are only brief glimpses of the rule of Man, however, part of the sweeping spectacle of Adam's legacy; indeed, as we have seen, the most comprehensive description of human government in the poem is the regime of Hell itself.

The nations of the world seem unable to escape the cycle of growth and decay, freedom and enslavement; they begin well, but no matter how nobly conceived, end ill. Michael cites the Babylonian Captivity, when the "foul Idolatries" of the Israelites, as well as "other faults . . . will so incense / God, as to leave them, and expose thir Land . . . a scorn and prey / To that proud City" (12:337-42). When God relents and releases them from slavery, they "for a while / In mean estate live moderately, till grown / in wealth and multitude, factious they grow" (12:350-52), and weakened by dissension, become captive to yet another empire. Some nations fall out of innocence, reduced by forces that prey on their weakness. Michael shows Adam the Sons of Seth:

> Just men they seem'd, and all thir study bent
> To worship God aright, and know his works
> Not hid, nor those things last which might preserve
> Freedom and peace to men;
>
>   (11:577-80)

---

15. *MG* 140, 215-18. The Waldensians incurred the wrath of the duke of Savoy because over the years they had extended their holdings from their original mountain homeland into towns and villages on the Piedmont plain below.

but eventually they "yield up all thir virtue, all thir fame / Ignobly, to the train and to the smiles" of the Daughters of Cain (11:623-24). Others fall for no apparent reason, that is, they do "no wrong, / But Justice," as a consequence of their decline in virtue, deprives them of their liberty (12:99-100). The innocent sons of Noah live a virtuous, pastoral life, unburdened by government, spending "thir days in joy unblam'd," but yet they spawn a Nimrod, who "Will arrogate Dominion" over them (12:22-24). No nation, it seems, can evade the sin of Adam.

As mentioned, it is difficult to escape the impression that Milton's perception of governments was influenced by the failure of the one he served, which was rejected by the "perverse inhabitants" of England who chose "them a captain back for *Egypt*" (*Prose* 7:463). Whether his characterization of the decadent behavior of history's rulers reflects his observation of the court of Charles II must remain a question, however. During the years devoted to the composition of *Paradise Lost,* that court may not yet have displayed the full scale of corruption Milton envisions in the poem, the "sumptuous gluttonies," the "foul Idolatries," the "lust and rapine," the "riot, feast, and dance" of his doomed dynasties. The Restoration court was to become notorious for its decadence in time, of course; but the many products of the poet's "left hand" had schooled him well in the art of antimonarchal invective and he had little doubt that Charles II would eventually surpass the spectacle of his father's court (*Prose* 7:425-26). But the images of corruption probably owe less to Milton's immediate experience of the Restoration period than to the influence on his imagination of his works excoriating the court of Charles I.[16]

In the light of Milton's conviction that as a people grow great, they invariably grow corrupt, it is intriguing to consider just how much of his thinking on the rise and fall of nations derives from his experience in the governments of the English Republic. England did indeed grow great during the Interregnum and in the perorations of his two *Defences,* both addressed to his "fellow citizens," Milton draws attention to the potential dangers of that greatness. In the earlier tract he praises their sacrifices in the cause of liberty during the civil wars; but, he cautions, during time of peace they must show equal courage in the "fight against self-seeking, greed, luxury, and the seductions of success to which other peoples are subject. The bravery displayed in your fight against slavery must be equalled by your

16. In *Historicizing Milton,* Laura Knoppers sees the matter otherwise. She attributes much of the political imagery of the later poems to the poet's reaction against the Restoration regime, especially the royal court's employment of public display.

justice, restraint, and moderation in preserving your freedom." Should they falter, however, and "be as weak in peace" as they "have been strong in war," that is, should they fail to "fear God and love justice," he concludes dramatically, he will be forced to admit that the slanders of Salmasius are all too true (*Prose* 4:535-36).

Four years later, in the early months of the Protectorate, he is even more expressive in addressing his "fellow countrymen": Unless inner liberty, "sprung from piety, justice, temperance, in short, true virtue, has put down the deepest and most far-reaching roots in your souls," that which has been won by force of arms will be lost: "Unless you expel avarice, ambition, and luxury from your minds, yes, and extravagance from your families as well, you will find at home and within that tyrant who, you believed, was to be sought abroad and in the field – now even more stubborn" (*Prose* 4:680). Further, once enslaved they will be helpless to escape bondage; a decadent people "can perhaps change their servitude; [but] they cannot cast it off," witness "the ancient Romans, once they had been corrupted and dissipated by luxury" (*Prose* 4:683). The evidence of history makes it clear, he goes on, "that a nation which cannot rule and govern itself, but has delivered itself into slavery to its own lusts, is enslaved also to other masters whom it does not choose"; and again, "he who cannot control himself . . . should not be his own master, but like a ward be given over to the power of another," and he most decidedly should not "be put in charge of the affairs of other men, or of the state" (*Prose* 4:684).

Milton offers similar advice to the newly installed Lord Protector, urging him to demonstrate the "faith, justice, and moderation of soul which convince us that you have been raised by the power of God beyond all other men to this most exalted rank," and cautioning him "to yield to no allurements of pleasure, to flee from the pomp of wealth and power" (*Prose* 4:674). It has been suggested that this advice reflects an implied criticism of Cromwell, but this seems hardly the case.[17] The Lord Protector had only just assumed office as Milton penned the lines; and the poet is writing in a prophetic vein, as Louis Martz has demonstrated,[18] advising Cromwell as he does all those in positions of power.

Thus, the government of men will prove a constant trial for the Lords of the Earth, one moreover in which success is fleeting for nations caught up in the incessant cycle of growth and decay. But this is not the chief concern,

---

17. See, e.g., Don M. Wolfe, *Prose* 4:264; Hill, *Milton in the English Revolution,* 194; and Austin Woolrych, "Milton and Cromwell," 192-94.

18. Louis L. Martz, "Eden Restored."

Milton tells us; it is the inner conflict that decides the issue, the struggle set in motion the moment Adam's passions prevailed over his reason. Success in the struggle without is fruitless, unless the race of Man can achieve the victory within.

Fulfilled All Justice

Even though Michael makes it clear that all the strife Man is heir to – the incessant wars, the oppression of tyrants, the endless cycle of nations rising through virtue and falling through decadence – is his own doing, a consequence of moral weakness that flows from the Fall, the spectacle of suffering seems an unduly harsh judgment from a supposedly loving God. A poem whose avowed purpose is to "justify the ways of God to men" engages to accommodate the motives and actions of the Deity to Man's admittedly limited perception of justice. In the specific terms of Christian teaching, the poet undertakes the daunting task of representing all of this personal and political turmoil as "just" punishment for a single act of disobedience. The more to confound the task, the biblical account depicts a God who, not content that his creatures should suffer inner tumult, endless conflict, and death, sets out to make life physically miserable for them as well.[19] The sentence is stern: because Adam has eaten the forbidden fruit, "Curs'd is the ground" for him; he shall "eat Bread" in "the sweat" of his face (10:201, 205). Further, "The Poles of the Earth" will be turned so as "from the North to call / Decrepit Winter, from the South to bring / Solstilial summer's heat" (10:654-56). Can all this be "justified"? The love between Adam and Eve may survive the Fall, but can the same be said of their love of God? The Deity withdraws his person; no longer will they behold "His blessed count'nance," the sight of which was for Adam the "highth / Of happiness" (10:724-25); nor will he in the future "visit oft the dwellings of just men" (7:570), as had been promised. Can one love a father who inflicts torment on his children and then abandons them, or a king who exiles his subjects and leaves them to rot?

The Almighty's judgment on what is right and wrong need not conform to Man's, of course; but if God as the ruler of the universe wants to engage the allegiance of a being he has endowed with reason, he must present

19. Genesis 3:16-19.

himself as a just ruler insofar as Man is given to know what justice means. It is immaterial that he cannot fully comprehend the mind of God, however apparent that may be; but that mind must be accessible to human understanding of justice, else God will lose Man's devotion. Having endowed Man with reason, God must reason with him. As his sovereign, in brief, Milton's God must condemn Adam to death in such a way as to retain his love.

The argument for a just God proceeds on two levels: Within the narrative of the poem Adam must be persuaded of the justice of his punishment; and outside its lines, Milton's readers must be convinced as well. God leaves most of the labor of persuading Adam to his emissaries, Raphael and Michael. The Almighty demonstrates a nice awareness of the fine legal distinctions involved in the Fall. From the privileged position of omniscience, he is aware of what will happen and takes steps to ensure that Man will know where the fault lies once it does. He places guards about Eden, though this is more a ritual gesture of protection than anything else, since they cannot exclude a spirit; and he sends Raphael to warn Adam of the danger threatening him so that he will have no reason to claim he was unprepared for the event. These may seem ineffectual measures at best, since however alert the guards, they cannot prevent Satan from entering Eden, and however persuasive an envoy Raphael may be, he cannot prevent Adam from falling. These are measures taken, obviously, not for the purpose of staving off the inevitable. Raphael's role is to ensure Adam's future allegiance to his Deity, so that when it is all over, Man will continue to see God as just and to love him.

Michael's mission is more difficult. Adam has been condemned to a death he does not understand, has seen the inexplicable shift of the heavens, and sits in abject despair, convinced that his God has abandoned him. If his love for the Deity may not be entirely shattered, it is seriously undermined, and may in time fade completely under the weight of his suffering. God cannot leave his creatures thus, and sends the archangel to reveal "what shall come in future days" in order to "Dismiss them not disconsolate" (11:113-14). Michael's long chronicle of human misery does little to console Adam, but here and there arise to his sight just men such as Enoch and Noah (11:665, 719), figures who, faithful in the midst of misfortune, offer a visual paradigm for Adam's response to his own adversity. Michael concludes with an account of the Incarnation; and Adam's joyful response to the news, "O goodness infinite, goodness immense!" (12:469) can only be fully appreciated when compared to his former despair. He has not been abandoned, as it had seemed; his God will return one more time to visit again "the dwellings of just men"; and his love for Man, which Adam thought lost to him, is so profound that he will sacrifice his only son to redeem the race.

So Adam's love is retained and his hope restored, but can Milton's readers be satisfied with such a resolution? Our earlier analysis of the political structure of the cosmos, matters of which Adam is largely ignorant, provides some basis for satisfaction. If, as we have seen, the governing principle of all existence is divine love, the very survival of created beings depends on the exchange of devotion between them and their Maker. In *Paradise Lost* God creates his kingdoms to express that quality of his nature and receive it in return. Of Hell it may be said that the fallen angels demonstrate for Man the terror of existence deprived of that love; and, as the figure of Satan illustrates, in acting against God they punish themselves perpetually with the recurring memory of their loss. In a sense Mammon was right – forget Heaven, build here.

Obedience to the divine will is an outward sign of the love between God and his creation. Love is a state ideally defined as the perfect accord of two beings, in which the desire of the one becomes the instant wish of the other; and such indeed is the condition of Heaven, where the will of God manifests itself instantaneously as the will of his creation. Dante expresses it well in the *Paradiso,* when a shade in the circle of the moon explains to the pilgrim why the various spirits have no desire to advance in the hierarchy of Heaven:

> Nay, it is the very quality of this blessed state that we keep ourselves within the divine will, so that our wills are themselves made one; therefore our rank from height to height through this kingdom is pleasing to the whole kingdom, as to the King who wills us to His will. And in His will is our peace.[20]

But when love is defined within a narrative frame, time intrudes: the word must precede the act and the desire aroused before it can be satisfied. And in a political narrative, which represents the relationship as one that prevails between a sovereign and his subjects, the closest parallel is a king's decree joyfully fulfilled by his loyal citizens.

In *Paradise Lost* the mutual love between the Deity and his creation is often depicted as the absolute obedience of a subordinate to his military superior. During the war in Heaven the loyal angels follow God's orders without hesitation, even when it becomes apparent they cannot win; and Gabriel is a vigilant sentinel at the gates of Eden, even when he knows it is

---

20. *Divine Comedy* 3:53.

virtually impossible "to exclude / Spiritual substance with corporal bar" (4:584-85). When Gabriel confronts Satan in Eden, he admonishes him for his apostasy in just such terms: "Was this your discipline and faith ingag'd / Your military obedience?" (4:954-55).[21] In Milton's imagination, a subordinate's obligation to follow a superior's orders in battle is as close to absolute as any in human experience, since the consequences of failing to obey are so grave. Milton was well acquainted with such consequences. One of his letters to the duke of Tuscany (W37, P60) deals with a ship's captain in the English Mediterranean fleet during the Anglo-Dutch War, a man whose disregard for the express orders of the Council of State led ultimately to his capture and the loss of one-third of the fleet (*MG* 111-20).

Again, disobedience is the political equivalent of God's love betrayed. When Satan and Adam disobey, they strike at the very foundation of cosmic order, at the purpose for which all things were made and the pervasive spirit that makes them work, the mutual love between God and his creation. God is not, then, a haughty monarch who sees in rebellious subjects a threat to the authority of his throne, as doubtless Charles I viewed the Parliamentary forces ranged against him; he is rather a judge who in passing sentence for disobedience is protecting the law, without which a society sinks into anarchy. Deprived of love as a governing principle, all creation would revert to its original form, the warring elements of Chaos, "The Womb of nature and perhaps her Grave," there to be ruled once more by an "Anarch" who "embroils the fray / By which he Reigns" (2:908-11). The threat of such calamity brings to mind Othello's impassioned cry, "and when I love thee not, / Chaos is come again."[22]

In consequence, "Die he, or Justice must," the Deity proclaims, and take steps to retain the love of Man rather than abandon the race entirely. In his infinitely resourceful and merciful way, God devises a solution that salvages the original promise to Adam without compromising the law. It is still possible that Mankind "With Angels may participate," but no longer by mildly turning "all to spirit / Improv'd by tract of time" (5:494-97). Man may yet attain Heaven, but only through death, "His final remedy"; death then becomes a blessing that releases the race from the pain of eternal punishment, a fate that Adam fears and Satan suffers, and opens the gate to salvation. Having disobeyed once, however, Man will have to prove himself worthy to join the obedient ranks of the loyal angels; his will be a "Life /

---

21. For a more thorough discussion of this image, see *CC* 212-15 and 245-46.
22. *Othello* 3.3.91-92.

Tri'd in sharp tribulation, and refin'd / By Faith and faithful works" (11:62-64). God gives the race a second chance; but they must now demonstrate that they will not again place in jeopardy the design he has conceived to express his love.

The scales of justice may not be quite in balance, however, to the eye of human reason, since the rebel angels receive no such second chance; they are "cast out forever." God may make fine legal distinctions between those who disobey undeceived and those who are tricked into it; but the fact remains that the kingdom of Heaven is lost to the angels who disobey but could still be attained by a later race who commit the same sin. The firstborn of God are not given the same option as those who come after, that is, to die and be redeemed, a judgment troubling to a human sense of justice. To restore the balance and satisfy the faithful, the King of Heaven promises a sacrifice that although neither entirely rational nor strictly legal, would seem to quiet all doubts. He offers, in the person of the Son, to subject himself to human law, to suffer, and to die, accepting the same sentence divine law has imposed upon his subjects. Human reason must submit to the force of such a love and acknowledge this a just God. No earthly king could match him.

6

DIVIDED EMPIRE

For Mankind, the critical arena for the struggle between good and evil is the individual conscience, and the prize for the victor is the individual soul. To define that inner struggle, Milton employs the image of a vast military and political conflict between two great powers, a cosmic confrontation that has its beginnings on the plains of Heaven and shifts from thence to God's new world, where it will rage to the end of time. The first encounter in that conflict, the great war in Heaven, I have examined at some length elsewhere (*CC* 202-34), and need not review here, especially since the account seems to owe more to the library than to the life of a poet who never saw battle.[1]

After the civil conflicts of the 1640s, warfare did not intrude on the

1. Stella Revard surveys the sources of the war in Heaven in classic and Renaissance literature, particularly the works of Homer, Virgil, Hesiod, and Tasso (*War in Heaven* 148-52); and Barbara Lewalski discusses Milton's reliance on Homeric warfare (*"Paradise Lost" and the Rhetoric of Literary Forms* 60-62).

private life of John Milton, but it was a constant concern of the government he served. The English Republic was seldom at peace during his time in office. Cromwell's campaigns against Ireland and Scotland were followed by a royalist invasion, which ended in the defeat of Charles II's forces at Worcester in September 1651; and simultaneously, over this entire period, England was engaged in undeclared naval wars with Portugal and France. Their internal conflicts over, the leaders of the Republic were soon embroiled in a war with the United Netherlands, which lasted until 1654, and a year later another with Spain, which did not end until after the fall of the Protectorate. During Cromwell's entire reign, moreover, he was in danger of being drawn into the wars of Charles X of Sweden in northern Europe, conflicts deeply disturbing to the Lord Protector. It should not be surprising, then, that the poet conceived of the cosmic conflict between good and evil as the clash of two mighty powers in a struggle for supremacy, first as a civil war in Heaven and later as a contest for control of a third, smaller state.

Though Milton had no experience with the conduct of war, he was intimately aware of events leading up to the outbreak of hostilities – the precipitating controversies, the debate over blame, and the articulation of war aims. As Secretary for Foreign Languages, he assisted in the negotiations between the Council of State and a Portuguese envoy, which after three months of deliberations ended abruptly, with the result that the naval war with that nation was resumed (*MG* 46-49). His services were employed in the negotiations that led to the outbreak of the Anglo-Dutch War of 1652-54, during which the two sides wrangled for months over commercial issues, only to have their deliberations rendered meaningless by a sudden clash of opposing fleets in the Dover Downs. Ambassadors passed between capital cities, each adamant in his claims for the justice of his cause, until finally the English issued the *Declaration of the Parliament of the Commonwealth of England,* a document, partly in Milton's Latin, in which the Republic endeavored to justify to the nations of Europe a war with its Protestant neighbor and former close ally (*MG* 77-83). At the same time the poet was engaged in preparing documents exchanged in negotiations with Denmark, which culminated in that nation entering the war on the side of the Dutch (*MG* 101-9). And during the Protectorate he was responsible for the bulk of Cromwell's correspondence concerning the campaigns of Charles X in Poland and Denmark (*MG* 160-69). Thus Milton was well acquainted with the prelude to war, the preliminary posturing in protest of violated rights, both parties staking out a claim to the justice of their respective causes in anticipation of the outbreak of hostilities. It is this experience, rather than the wars themselves, that is most noticeably reflected in *Paradise Lost.*

Cosmic Conflict

The war in Heaven is, of course, a civil conflict; hence the preliminary posturing takes the form of a debate over internal grievances rather than controversies over trade, tariffs, and fishing rights. It is a debate, therefore, which probably owes more to Milton's prose defenses of the Republic than to his diplomatic duties; but the argument over just causes follows the pattern of events leading up to any war. The account in *Paradise Lost* opens with a familiar political act, the designation of the heir to a throne, an anointing that deserves particular attention, as Milton in his cosmic chronology traces the birth of evil to God's decree.

In the royal houses of Europe the designation of an heir was generally an occasion for celebration, for it promised a peaceful transfer of power and diminished the threat of internecine squabbles that erupted so frequently when the succession was in doubt. One of the king's obligations to his subjects was to produce an heir and invest him with the prospect of rule, so that powerful barons would not be tempted to covet the throne. The congratulatory phrases employed on the occasion of the birth of an heir are extravagant indeed. Milton prepared a letter for Cromwell on the occasion of the birth of a son to Charles X, the king of Sweden, which reads in part, "Certainly then, we have reason to rejoyce for the Birth of a young Prince Born to such an excellent King, and sent into the world to be Heir to his Father's Glory and Virtue" (W63, P89).

God's announcement of an heir is received with no great rejoicing, however; "All seem'd well pleas'd" is about as far as Milton goes in characterizing the occasion, adding, of course, the ominous "but were not all" (5:617). The angels turn quickly to their customary pleasures, entertaining themselves "In song and dance about the sacred Hill" (5:619), and enjoy a sumptuous feast provided by "th' all bounteous King" (5:640) before retiring for the night; but there is no celebration of the new heir, no hymns of praise or further speeches from either throne – indeed, it seems as if he is all but forgotten in the day's activities. By this subdued response to the announcement, Milton leaves the distinct impression that little is really changed in Heaven, except that Satan is "fraught / With envy against the Son of God" (5:661-62). The angels take the new order pretty much in stride; there is no discussion of the event and no show of enthusiasm or support for the new heir. The feeling seems to be that this anointing is all very well, but the Son will have to demonstrate himself worthy of the title somehow before anyone need get excited.

Satan is incensed, however, not so much by the proclamation of the Son as heir as by his simultaneous designation as "King anointed" as well. God demands that "to him shall bow / All knees in Heav'n, and shall confess him Lord," proclaiming that all shall be subject to "his great Vice-gerent Reign" (5:607-9). It is the elevation of another ruler, who will stand between God and his subjects that excites Satan's "sense of injur'd merit" (1:98). To that point none of the angels appear to have aspired to the throne of God; it is only when they see a second throne that they feel themselves diminished, "eclipst under the name / Of King anointed" (5:776-77), and begin to entertain thoughts of challenging the rule of Heaven.

William Empson finds evidence that there had been seditious talk among dissatisfied elements in Heaven prior to the proclamation, conjecture that aside from being questionable, is largely irrelevant. If we are to accept the maxim with which Adam comforts Eve, "Evil into the mind of God and Man / May come and go, so unapprov'd, and leave / No spot or blame behind" (5:117-19), the cosmos knew no evil until Satan committed an *act* of disobedience. According to the law of Man, evidence of intent alone is not sufficient to prove guilt; and so it seems in Heaven as well. On the day before battle, in Abdiel's mind at least, the rebels are not yet damned: "Cease this impious rage," he urges Satan, for "Pardon may be found in time besought" (5:845-48). When his advice is rejected, Abdiel dismisses them scornfully, predicting their defeat; but it is not until they actually march against God that he can say with assurance that it is "too late" (6:147). Their fate is signaled by the birth of Sin, who is conceived only after the first day of battle, appearing on the scene at an assembly, she reminds Satan, "Of all the Seraphim with thee combin'd / In bold conspiracy against Heav'n's King" (2:750-51). This timing is confirmed by Satan's experience of pain, which he "first knew" when struck by Michael's sword (6:327), and "knew" again thereafter when "miserable pain / Surprised" him at Sin's birth (2:752-53). The Almighty, then, may be seen as a just king, one who observes the law that a subject cannot be condemned simply for disloyal thoughts.

In response to God's proclamation, Satan at first takes care to conceal his intent to "leave / Unworshipt, unobey'd the Throne supreme" (5:669-70), proposing obscurely to Beëlzebub only that "new Minds in us may raise / In us who serve, new Counsels, to debate / What doubtful may ensue" (5:680-82). The only hint of dissatisfaction is his ironic insistence that they prepare entertainment for "The great *Messiah,*" who, he says, will shortly honor them with a visit, during which, he adds darkly, he will "give Laws" (5:691-93). In his speech from his "Royal seat" in the north he initially enunciates a policy similar to that adopted by Parliament in the early stages of the civil war. Deposing the king was far from the thoughts of the majority of members at the beginning of their resistance, nor did Milton propose such an extreme step in his tracts of 1641-42. Parliament insisted that their only goal was to remove the wicked counselors who were leading Charles astray.[2] Initially, Satan does not propose that they undertake a war against God, only that they "cast off this Yoke" and assert their rights as citizens of Heaven. The target of his protest is at first the Son as "King anointed," but he soon shifts his indictment subtly to condemn the entire regime.

The Devil argues a relationship between the governing and the governed that bears many similarities to one that Milton proposed repeatedly in condemning Charles I.[3] The "Sons of Heav'n" are everywhere equal, Satan declares, and "Equally free"; and though the governed may be "in power and splendor less" than their ruler, a monarch has no right to infringe upon their rights (5:790-96). The echo is striking between his protest that the angels are free beings, "ordain'd to govern, not to serve" (5:802) and Milton's position in *The Tenure of Kings and Magistrates:*

> No man who knows ought, can be so stupid to deny that all men naturally were borne free, being the image and resemblance of God himself, and were by privilege above all the creatures, born to command and not to obey.
>
> (*Prose* 3:198-99)

The echoes resonate through the entire debate with Abdiel. Satan questions God's prerogative, "can one introduce / Law and Edict on us, who without / Err not?" (5:797-99). Milton, of course, nowhere claims that men "Err not"; but his argument against the prerogatives of the king of England may be compared to Satan's against the King of Heaven. In *Eikonoklastes*

---

2. It was not until January 1645 that Marchamont Nedham, who published the *Mercurius Britanicus,* a semi-official periodical that supported the Parliamentary cause, shifted his position from the removal of "evil advisors" to a direct attack on the king (Joseph Frank, *Cromwell's Press Agent,* 23-24).

3. As Empson observes, a writer "who defended the regicide was ascribing to the devils the sentiments still firmly held by himself and his proscribed party" (*Milton's God* 82).

Milton charges the monarch with "contempt of all Laws" (*Prose* 3:214), and claims that since men are "free born to make our own laws," the king overstepped his authority when he began to "rule us forcibly by Laws to which we our selves did not consent" (*Prose* 3:573-75).

In intriguing contrast, Abdiel's reply sounds suspiciously like the excerpts from Salmasius's *Defensio Regia,* which Milton quotes and dismisses so scornfully in *A Defense of the English People.* The angel challenges Satan: "Shalt thou give Law to God, shalt thou dispute / With him the points of liberty? (5:823-24). Salmasius similarly challenges his opponents: "Let them bring forward any instance of a kingdom ruled by a single man where he has not been granted absolute power" (*Prose* 5:479). Abdiel again: "His Laws [are] our Laws" (5:844). And Salmasius: "The laws are called the king's" (*Prose* 5:482). Abdiel acknowledges that it is "unjust / That equal over equals Monarch Reign" (5:831-32), but goes on to argue that God existed before the angels, indeed created them, hence is above them and deserves their homage. In like manner Salmasius claims, rather grandly, that "Kings are coeval with the Sun's creation" (*Prose* 5:326). Satan's reply that "We know no time when we were not as now" (5:859) is the political equivalent of Milton's position that the people came first, kings and magistrates thereafter (*Prose* 3:199).

Thus, echoing Milton's charges against Charles, Satan claims that God has exceeded his rights, that he has improperly assumed "Monarchy over such as live by right / His equals," and that he has, therefore, abused their "Imperial Titles." Milton supported his challenge of the king's claim to superiority by calling on his considerable knowledge of Scripture, history, and literature. Satan argues epistemology. His "We know no time when we were not as now" questions God's claim that he created the angels. They were "self-begot," Satan insists, not made, hence by implication are God's equals. Abdiel finally goads him into revealing his true intent "to try / Who is our equal"; and the loyal angel will soon see, Satan goes on with heavy irony, whether they shall do so "Beseeching or besieging" (5:853-69).

Readers have been troubled by this apparent inversion of roles in the debate, since it runs afoul of our perception of Milton's political allegiances: the Devil argues against, and the loyal angel in favor of, submission to the royal will. But we should not conclude that when Milton puts his own arguments against Charles in the mouth of Satan and gives Abdiel lines from Salmasius, he is betraying the "good Old Cause"; nor need we go to extraordinary lengths to demonstrate the one is evil and the other good. The God of *Paradise Lost* is a king, and it is difficult to imagine how Abdiel could argue in his favor without sounding like a royalist.[4] At the same time, Satan is a rebel, and so reasons like a rebel. Milton was well acquainted with the case for both sides and was simply making good use of all the material at his disposal, drawing on a rich life in the political arena to create a credible conflict.

The account of the war in Heaven leaves little doubt that God orchestrates the battle to provide the Son with an occasion to prove himself worthy of both titles:

> For thee I have ordain'd it, and thus far
> Have suffer'd, that the Glory may be thine
> Of ending this great War, since none but Thou
> Can end it.

The war has been "govern'd thus, / To manifest thee worthiest to be Heir / Of all things, to be Heir and to be king" (6:700-708). This is not to say that the Almighty foreordains the conflict; but as an omniscient being he does foresee it, which is an enormous advantage in any political or military contest.[5] The principal effect of omniscience within the political frame of *Paradise Lost* is to provide God with prior knowledge of his opponent's actions and intentions. Knowing that Satan will rebel, he can manipulate the war to his larger purpose, which he does by limiting the angels' strength so that they will not tear up Heaven too badly (6:227-29) and by withholding one half of his forces so that the battle will be relatively even (6:49-50).[6] The only difference between the two sides is that the rebel angels sustain wounds and feel pain, though Milton nowhere attributes this effect to God, who implies that they are thus vulnerable because "sin hath impair'd" them (6:691). Two days of battle produce a stalemate, devised by God,

4. Zagorin's insight is again most apt: "In the civil war in heaven the rebel Milton had to be a royalist" (*Milton, Aristocrat and Rebel* 127). Abdiel's loyalty illustrates one of the paradoxes of celestial rule: in absolute obedience lies absolute freedom. As Danielson puts it, his "service to God is freedom's fulfillment" (*Milton's Good God* 117).

5. Cf. "if I foreknew, / Foreknowledge had no influence on their fault, / Which had no less prov'd certain unforeknown" (3:117-19). Danielson is satisfied with "Milton's presentation of divine prescience," that is, his narrative and dramatic presentation, his "literary solution" to the theodicy issue, is successful (*Milton's Good God* 163).

6. Cf. *Christian Doctrine,* where Milton, citing Revelation 12:7, 8, notes that "their respective forces were drawn up in battle array and separated after a fairly even fight" (*Prose* 6:347).

> That his great purpose he might so fulfil,
> To honor his Anointed Son aveng'd
> Upon his enemies, and to declare
> All power on him transferr'd.
>
>   (6:675-78)

The third day is the Son's and he returns from battle with his status greatly enhanced. Now the celebrations, so noticeably absent at his anointing, can more properly get under way:

> To meet him all his Saints, who silent stood
> Eye-witnesses of his Almighty Acts,
> With Jubilee advanc'd; and as they went
> Shaded with branching Palm, each order bright,
> Sung Triumph, and him sung Victorious King,
> Son, Heir, and Lord, to him Dominion giv'n,
> Worthiest to Reign.
>
>   (6:882-88)

The tradition of the heir to a throne proving himself worthy of the position is an ancient one, born of a time when a warrior king was the best deterrent to depredations by hostile neighbors. Though by the end of the seventeenth century it was less common for kings to ride into battle, they were still expected to exhibit martial qualities, if only symbolically.[7] The tradition survived in the practice of fitting out the king in an elaborate suit of medieval armor, which he was not actually expected to wear, of course, except perhaps to sit for his portrait.[8] In June 1641, Charles I marched his two young sons down to Finsbury Fields to enroll them in London's Honourable Artillery Company, though this was, again, but a symbolic enlistment (*CC* 46). The monarch was too valuable a figure to risk in combat; and kings fought their battles through surrogates, as does the Almighty in Heaven's war. Satan is in the thick of things, which, however

---

7. The seventeenth-century Swedish kings, Gustavus Adolphus, Charles X, and Charles XII, attest to the survival of the practice. Charles I did lead his army north in the Bishops' Wars but did not engage in battle. Charles II led a desperate sally at Worcester in an unsuccessful attempt to break out of the surrounded city (Fraser, *Cromwell,* 388), becoming perhaps the last English sovereign to risk his life in battle.

8. The armor of Charles I survives today in the Tower, as does, I recall, a smaller and equally elaborate suit for the young prince.

heroic, only emphasizes his subordinate status. The Son enters battle, of course, but he is armed with omnipotence, and in a single-handed display of God's power, defeats the rebels, thereby demonstrating his "Worthiness to reign" (6:888).

Milton knew of the tradition, of course, and was reminded of it in the spring of 1658. Louis XIV, still a youthful nineteen, joined his armies in Flanders in order to participate in the capture of Dunkirk; and Milton's letters to the young king on that occasion contain compliments that cast him in the light of one about to earn his spurs:

> So soon as the News was brought us, That your Majesty was arriv'd in your Camp, and was sate down with so considerable an Army before *Dunkirk* . . . we were greatly over-joy'd . . . that your Majesty, by your Military Prowess, will now take speedy Vengeance of the *Spanish* Frauds. (W116, P148)

The English Republic also went through a succession of sorts, when Oliver Cromwell's son, Richard, followed his father as Lord Protector; but despite inheriting the title, Richard remained but the heir to his father's greatness and survived for only eight months, never satisfactorily showing himself worthy of the position. So, too, the Son, though both heir and ruler, remains very much the former until he demonstrates, as Heaven's "Second Omnipotence" (6:684), that he can honorably bear the title of "*Messiah* King anointed."

Once the rebels are expelled, Heaven returns to the *status quo ante bellum,* impregnable to Satan's forces but with its population diminished by a third. God announces his policy: though there remain "Numbers sufficient to possess her Realms" and perform the necessary "Ministries due and solemn Rites," he plans to restore the angels to their former number, in order to deprive Satan of any satisfaction he may hope to derive from his rebellion, "lest his heart exalt him in the harm / Already done, to have dispeopl'd Heav'n" (7:147-51). The creation of Man has the desired effect; when Satan first views Adam and Eve, the sight infuriates him: "O Hell! what do my eyes with grief behold, / Into our room of bliss thus high advanc't / Creatures of other mould" (4:358-60).[9]

9. The irony of Satan's reaction to the sight of Adam and Eve, it will be observed, arises from his ignorance of God's designs for the race. Satan's indignation clouds his intellect; he sees them only as "Creatures of other mould," political pawns in his contest with the Deity. In *Paradise Regained* as well, he remains ignorant of God's designs, so intent is he on the political

With the defeated forces in Hell, all is despair; and certainly an important dimension of the heroic stature Satan achieves in the first two books is his resolution in mastering his grief. His armies are paralyzed by fear and a terrible sense of loss; but he is able to rally them to continue their opposition to the will of God, a policy he articulates in terms of continued warfare and foreign conquest. The sting of defeat will be salved by new action, and despair replaced by hope. Satan is equivocal about precisely what action is to be taken, for though at times he incites his despondent forces with rousing speeches promising a return to Heaven, it is doubtful that he believes it possible. Admittedly, as he lies "Chain'd on the burning lake" his first response to the horrors of his fate is a defiant resolve "once more / With rallied Arms to try what may be yet / Regain'd in Heaven" (1:268-70); but this is more likely an impulsive reaction to his defeat, or the hopeless rage of a new prisoner shaking the bars of his cell, or simply a device to raise the spirits of Beëlzebub.

In any event, Satan's initial resolve does not survive mature reflection. William Empson, something of a devil's advocate, finds him still uncertain about the powers of omnipotence in these books, hence quite sincere in his belief that they can "repossess thir native seat."[10] Empson argues that Satan is an entirely credible figure, and I certainly agree; but he also would have him an honorable man, free of deception, which is asking too much. Satan is an accomplished politician, quite skilled in deception, and he uses sound political strategy in rallying his supporters with fiery slogans while keeping a clear eye on what is within his power and what not. The display of God's omnipotence has not been lost on him; he knows he can never defeat such force in battle but suspects the Almighty may be vulnerable in other areas.

Satan's speech to his restored legions is a model of equivocation. He opens with a rhetorical flourish:

> For who can believe, though after loss,
> That all these puissant Legions, whose exile
> Hath emptied Heav'n, shall fail to re-ascend
> Self-rais'd, and repossess thir native seat,

and concludes that "this Infernal Pit shall never hold / Celestial Spirits in bondage"; but in between he advises that it would be wiser to use "fraud

---

consequences of the Incarnation. Milton takes no note of his response to the effect on Man's destiny of the Risen Christ, he who will lead his redeemed into "Heav'n long absent."

10. Empson, *Milton's God*, 37.

and guile" rather than force and that their efforts should be directed at God's "new Worlds" rather than Heaven itself. In any event, submission is despised and "War . . . must be resolv'd"; but he leaves unresolved whether it is to be "Open or understood" (1:632-62).

Later at the opening of "the great consult," he once more holds out the prospect that he and his followers may "return / To claim our just inheritance of old," but as before he offers alternatives, "open War or covert guile" (2:37-41); and from Beëlzebub's subsequent speech, "first devis'd / By Satan" (2:379-80), we learn that he has been quite realistically in favor of guile from the outset. The Devil is deceptive, to be sure, but not beyond the bounds of political practice.

Satan's political agenda for the citizens of Hell is the time-honored promise of a better way of life. Once the vote on his platform is taken, Beëlzebub delivers what amounts to an acceptance speech, outlining the campaign strategy; and he opens with the campaign slogan, "We may chance / Re-enter heav'n." But, he continues, should that not prove possible, at least they can live in "some mild Zone," able to "Purge off this gloom" in a place where "soft delicious Air / To heal the scar of these corrosive Fires / Shall breathe her balm" (2:397-402). Hell hurts. It is "A Dungeon horrible," filled with "sights of woe / regions of sorrow, doleful shades," where "torture without end / Still urges" (1:61-68); and although Milton prefers to stress the inner torment of the fallen angels, they are said to be in a perpetual state of pain. Moloch would rather risk destruction than remain in a place "Where pain of inextinguishable fire / Must exercise us without hope of end" (2:88-89). Beëlzebub's promise of a better life in "another World" wins over those who might have been drawn to Moloch's desperate gamble or Mammon's impossible proposal to forget Heaven.

Satan is the unrelenting adversary of God, who consistently couches his scheme for "Deliverance for us all" in terms of conquest. He promises Sin "a place where Thou and Death / Shall dwell at ease" (2:480-81) and Chaos that he will be able to "once more / Erect the Standard there of *ancient Night*" (2:985-86). He thinks throughout in political terms. On Nephrates he embraces evil as his "Good" because "at least / Divided Empire with Heav'n's King I hold / By thee, and more than half perhaps will reign" (4:110-12); and later in Eden he speaks of "conquering this new World" (4:391). Returning to Hell, he triumphs in his victory, exhorting his followers to "possess, / As Lords, a spacious World," urging them to "enter now into full bliss" (10:466-67, 503).

Milton's representation of the cosmic conflict between good and evil owes a debt to the spectacle of world affairs as it unfolded during his years in public office. In its broad outline it resembles the struggle between two great powers for control of a small possession of one of them. I have proposed elsewhere that the image may owe something to the mid-seventeenth-century struggle between France and Spain for control of the Spanish Netherlands (*CC* 140-48). England allied herself with France in 1655 and elements of the New Model Army participated in the culminating battle of the conflict, the capture of Dunkirk, a campaign that occasioned at least eight of Milton's State Letters.[11] The Devil's perception of the World resembles yet another of Cromwell's global initiatives of the time, his Western Design, a plan to seize Spain's possessions in the New World. Satan, in rallying his armies, holds out the hope that, as has been rumored, "Space may produce new Worlds" (1:650) accessible to them. Beëlzebub describes the Earth as a place where "may lie expos'd / The utmost border of his Kingdom, left / To their defense who hold it," one which, moreover, "may be achiev'd / By sudden onset" and occupied once they drive out its inhabitants "or if not drive, / Seduce them to our Party" (3:360-68).

Cromwell envisioned just such a conquest when in December 1654 he dispatched Admiral William Penn and General Robert Venables to the Caribbean with a force of some sixty ships and 9000 men, their mission to seize Spanish colonies there. As it happened, the expedition had only limited success, the two commanders failing to coordinate their efforts in an assault on Hispaniola; but they did occupy the comparatively defenseless island of Jamaica. The few Spanish soldiers stationed there fled, and Cromwell secured a possession that remained an English colony for the next three hundred years (*MG* 128-29).[12]

Satan's expedition enjoys more success than did Cromwell's, with his victory symbolized by the enormous bridge that Sin and Death construct over Chaos. Even as he embarks on his return voyage, they are securing Hell "to the Wall / Immoveable of this now fenceless World ... with Pins of Adamant" (10:302-5, 318), creating a "broad, / Smooth, easy, inoffensive" passage between the two realms. Milton compares it to Xerxes' famed

---

11. W113-16, P146-49; W118-19, P154-55; and W153-54, P156-57.

12. It is a pattern of warfare repeated frequently in modern history: the conflict between the United States and China for the Korean peninsula, between Greece and Turkey for the island of Cyprus, between India and Pakistan for the Kashmir, and, of course, the numerous clashes of European colonial powers over distant possessions during the eighteenth and nineteenth centuries. Perhaps the closest analogy in recent times is the conflict between England and Argentina for the Falkland Islands.

structure over the Hellespont, which "*Europe* and *Asia* joined" (10:304-10), justifying Satan's boast that he has made of "Hell and this World, one Realm, one Continent" (10:392). Although it may be said that in view of Xerxes' failure to subdue Greece, the simile foreshadows Satan's final defeat, the bridge will presumably remain in place until the Final Day, confirming his victory on Earth. It is substantial enough, for Sin and Death, as we have seen, possess a power akin to God's in their ability to form matter from the conflicting elements of Chaos. That unsuspecting kingdom, which had "Tamely endur'd" (2:1028) the early stages of the project, realizes too late that it has been deceived; and when Satan, in contrast to his perilous voyage to Earth, follows the "easy-thoroughfare" back to Hell, "Disparted *Chaos* overbuilt exclaim'd / And with rebounding surge the bars assail'd, / That scorn'd his indignation" (10:416-18). So much for treaties with the Devil.

The Missions to Earth

It must be said that from the perspective of Heaven the world does appear as a distant possession. The angels visit freely to admire God's handiwork, and Eden is guarded by a detail of imperial guards, the "Youth of Heav'n" (4:552), stationed there to ward off possible intrusion. Adam rules like some colonial governor-general; and God, as we have seen, takes great pains to ensure Man's continued loyalty to his reign, dispatching angels in the leading ranks of Heaven's hierarchy on diplomatic missions to clarify the political parameters of Man's authority. The two missions are markedly different, however, in purpose and composition. The angels are emissaries from the kingdom of Heaven to, first, the Lords of the Earth and, later, to an Adam and Eve sadly diminished in stature. Raphael's mission is to persuade Adam of the benefits that will continue to flow from Man's close alliance with God, Michael's to define new terms for that alliance and ensure that the race will remain loyal to the Almighty even while living under the rule of Satan.[13]

God instructs Raphael, the "sociable Spirit," to inform Adam that he is happy; that he is so because his will is free, though mutable; that he has an enemy, "Late fall'n himself from Heav'n," who will attempt to deprive him of

---

13. Kathleen Swaim contrasts the two missions in comprehensive detail, though not in political terms, as here (*Before and After the Fall* 3-25 and passim).

his happiness; and that he will do so through guile, since violence "shall be withstood" (5:233-43). Michael's mission is somewhat more complex, involving deeds as well as diplomacy. God charges him to expel Adam and Eve from the Garden, but as gently as possible: "all terror hide." In unfolding for Adam the future of the race, the archangel is to stress the advantages of continued allegiance with Heaven despite the trying times ahead, the rewards for which will be considerable, including ultimately the promise of God's "Cov'nant in the woman's seed renew'd." And, God instructs him further, he is to set up a watch at the entrance of Eden to frighten off any who might approach threatening to violate "all my Trees" (11:99-125).

As diplomatic missions, the visits of the two angels resemble in many respects a number of those with which Milton was associated during his years in public service. One of his many functions was to prepare the elaborate documentation that was required for a traveling envoy of the day, a packet containing his "letter of credentials" from the executive body of the Republic addressed to the head of state of the host nation, and at times an additional letter spelling out specific grievances or matters that the ambassador will place before them. He prepared as well letters of introduction to the governing bodies of states the envoy was called on to pass through enroute. Included also in these diplomatic packets was an involved set of instructions, defining the envoy's mission and setting limits to his authority during negotiations. Milton's published letters include one such set, that prepared for Richard Bradshaw on his mission to the duke of Moscovy in 1657 (W164, P123). The usual practice was to list in general terms the issues to be raised, then to rely on the skills of an envoy well trained in rhetoric to fashion a speech that would sway the hearer to the English position. Bradshaw's instructions on his address to the duke included such directives as:

> 1st. he must be sure to give him all his titles.
> 2. he shall assure that Great Duke, of the particular affection of his Highness toward him, both in behalfe of the nation which he governs . . . as [*sic*] also for the honor which he bears to his royall virtues, and puissance in war.

Since the purpose of Bradshaw's mission was to mediate a cessation of hostilities between Russia and Sweden, he was further instructed to inform the duke

3ly. that his Highness would count it a great hapynesse, if he could be any way instrumentall to make peace among Christian princes.

4. that hearing of an overture of peace made to him by the King of Sueden . . . his Highness could not but expresse his well wishing to so good a work and offer his mediation to the furdering therof.

Based on such instructions, the ambassador would then prepare his own speech, in Latin, for delivery at his audience. An exception to this practice was Samuel Morland's embassy to the duke of Savoy in 1655, dispatched to protest the Piedmont Massacre, when because of the importance of the occasion and the relative inexperience of the envoy, Milton prepared a speech for Morland to deliver (*MG* 149-50). The public records hold many such sets of instructions, a number of them carried by emissaries for whom Milton prepared credentials, suggesting that he may have contributed to more than just the one for Bradshaw.[14]

God's instructions to Raphael and Michael bring to mind Milton's labors with such documents. The Almighty defines in general terms what they are to impart to Adam and the tone to be adopted in the discussion: "such discourse bring on, / As may advise him of his happy state," "warn him to beware," "tell him withal / His danger," "all terror hide," "Dismiss them not disconsolate." It is left to the envoys to adapt their speech to fulfill God's will.

The two missions are very different in composition and tone. Raphael travels alone, passing by the celestial guardians of Eden, who respectfully "high in honor rise" at his approach (5:288). He interprets God's instructions rather broadly, readily answering Adam's questions about the creation of the World, since such knowledge will "glorify the Maker, and infer / Thee also happier" (7:116-17), but drawing the line at his curiosity about astronomy, advising him, somewhat unsociably, to "be lowly wise" (7:173). Michael's is a military mission, clearly an expedition into enemy territory. He ventures out as the commander of a "Cohort bright / Of watchful Cherubim," his "choice of flaming Warriors" (11:127-28, 101); and upon arrival on Earth, "The Princely Hierarch / In thir bright stand, there left his Powers to seize / Possession of the Garden" (11:220-22) while he goes in search of Adam and Eve. He is in full battle dress, wearing "over his lucid Arms / A military vest of purple," equipped with his "starry Helm" and "the Sword, / Satan's dire

14. For a list of envoys for whom Milton prepared documents, see *MG* 269.

dread, and in his hand the Spear" (11:240-48).[15] He follows God's instructions closely, digressing only to correct Adam's misconceptions about what he sees and hears.

There is a scriptural source for Michael's mission,[16] but Raphael's visit to Adam and Eve is Milton's invention entirely; and as a diplomatic mission warning of the dangers of disaffection, it has elements to be found in England's attempt to counter Spanish intrigues during the years 1656-58, which Cromwell saw as a deliberate design to disrupt his alliances with other Protestant states. At the time the ambitious Swedish king, Charles X, was creating turmoil in northern Europe. His conquest of Poland in 1656 was the first step in a campaign to transform the Baltic Sea into a Swedish lake; and other nations with important economic interests in the area, chiefly the United Netherlands and Denmark, were quick to oppose him. A hostile Dutch-Danish fleet soon faced the Swedish forces which had occupied the Hanseatic port of Danzig, and war threatened (*MG* 164-65). Cromwell saw the confrontation in religious terms, suspecting the Spanish of secretly fomenting discord among the Protestant nations of Europe to undermine their united opposition to Catholic powers; and, in letters prepared by Milton, he wrote to the contending nations, warning them of the dangers of Spanish subversion to the "Orthodox Religion."

Cromwell was particularly sharp with the Dutch, whom England had aided in their wars of liberation against Spain since the time of Elizabeth. The Spanish, offering "the false prospect of Advantage," as he puts it, seem to have persuaded the Dutch "to forsake your Ancient and most Faithful Friends the *English, French,* and *Danes,* and enter into a strict Confederacy with your old Enemy." Spain, "once your domineering Tyrant, now seemingly atton'd," is, he warns, "at present treacherously fawning to advance his own Design," that is, "Division and a Civil War among Protestants" (W75, P109). He warns Charles X that "the *Spaniards,* and the *Roman Pontiff*" are "inflam'd with inexorable revenge" against Protestant nations (W79, P108), and cautions Frederick III of Denmark to beware of "the Artifices and

---

15. As I have suggested in *CC* 145-47, Eden becomes a Heavenly foothold in a Satan-dominated world. Milton's decision to depict Michael's mission as a full-blown military expedition may have been influenced by Cromwell's persistent efforts to secure such a foothold on the continent of Europe as a base for the English fleet. He negotiated with the Swedish king, Charles X, to secure control of the duchy of Bremen, and failing that, he asked, in return for military assistance, for the Swedish port of Landskrona and the Elbe River city of Stadt, which the king was equally unwilling to part with (*MG* 153, 167n, 170). Cromwell finally acquired his "footing" on the Continent when he secured Dunkirk in 1658.

16. Genesis 3:24.

Machinations of the *Spaniards*" (W87, P119). He urges them all to maintain their allegiance to one another and stand firm in their common religion against the schemes of Rome. Later, Denmark declared war on Sweden, only to be soundly defeated by Charles X, whom Cromwell wrote again, congratulating him on his victory and, in a conciliatory gesture, suggesting that "the King of *Danemark* [was] made your enemy, not by his own will or interests, but by the arts of common foes," that is, the scheming Spanish again (W108, P143). Thus, Raphael's warning that Satan, "fraught / With envy" (5:661-62) will seek to undermine the alliance between Man and God has many of the marks of Cromwell's suspicions about Spanish subversion in northern Europe.[17]

The Conflict Within

Michael's mission seems a success; Adam and Eve depart "not disconsolate" and still loyal to their God. The archangel's chronicle of human history serves an additional purpose, however, the definition of terms under which the war will continue. There will be, apparently, more victories than defeats for Satan's side. The battleground is the World, ravaged by Sin and Death and, as the narrative voice had earlier foretold, occupied by the forces of evil, "wandering o'er the Earth" as false gods to corrupt "the greatest part / Of Mankind," provoking them to break allegiance and "forsake / God thir Creator" (1:365-69).

Michael's account confirms Satan's success, though it makes little mention of him. Adam is not offered a metaphysical spectacle of the Devil and his minions at work in the world, but, as Michael stresses, a chronicle of "Th' effects which thy original crime hath wrought" (11:424). Man's miseries are his own doing, the consequence of "envy," "ungovern'd appetite," "ill-mated Marriages," "wantonness and pride," and the loss of "true Liberty" within (11:456, 517, 684, 795; 12:83). These "effects" are indeed described as the "works" of Satan in the race (12:394-95); but Milton has no interest in depicting human sins as the result of devious manipulation by a secret conjuror tempting otherwise virtuous beings to do wrong. It may have been thus in the Garden; but Man is no longer innocent and the ills he is heir to

---

17. Raphael here echoes God's appraisal of Satan, "so bent he seems / On desperate revenge" (3:84-85), which again reflects Cromwell's assessment of Spain's role.

are of his own making. Satan is at work in the world, of course, and *Paradise Regained* gives dramatic evidence of his methods. He enjoys considerable success, if the political imagery of the work is to be credited; indeed he is said to rule over the affairs of humanity, proclaiming to Jesus in the wilderness, "The Kingdoms of the world to thee I give; / For giv'n to me, I give to whom I please" (*PR* 4:163-64).

There are setbacks for Satan, to be sure, in the ebb and flow of the war, the most serious of which is the Resurrection; and Milton explores the meaning of that mystery in political and military imagery that defines it as a major turning point in the conflict. Tradition identifies the event as the moment when, God and Man having finally been reconciled, the way to Heaven is once more open to the race, a doctrine confirmed by the Son who predicts that he then "shall rise Victorious" and "with the multitude of my redeem'd / Shall enter Heav'n long absent" (3:250-61). The mystery itself is defined in the imagery of battle. The risen Christ "through the ample Air in Triumph high / Shall lead Hell Captive maugre Hell" and ruin all his foes "Death last, and with his Carcass glut the Grave" (3:254-59). Further, as Michael prophesies to Adam:

> to the Heav'n of Heav'ns he shall ascend
> With victory, triumphing through the air
> Over his foes and thine; there shall surprise
> The Serpent, Prince of air, and drag in Chains
> Through all his Realm, and there confounded leave.
> (12:451-55)

"And there confounded leave" means, of course, that Satan, despite the indignities to which he has been subjected, will recover from this latest defeat as he had the first one, and the war will rage on with the kingdoms of the world still in thrall to him.

Thus, the race will be admitted to Heaven, and for that Adam rejoices; but he is curious about the consequences of the Resurrection for humankind in *this* life. Years earlier, in the *Nativity Ode,* Milton had described the birth of Christ as an event imposing limits on Satan's power:

> from this happy day
> Th'old Dragon under ground,
> In straiter limits bound,
> Not half so far casts his usurped sway.
> (167-70)

The political and military imagery of *Paradise Lost* does not quantify the victory in such specific terms; but the poem does address this mystery of faith, one of those Milton is reluctant to "tamper with" in *Christian Doctrine*. Adam is understandably concerned that when Christ ascends to Heaven, his progeny will be left without protection and suffer all the more from the forces of evil: "will they not deal / Worse with his followers than with him they dealt?" (12:483-84). Michael replies that God will send down the Holy Spirit to arm Mankind "With spiritual Armor, able to resist / *Satan's* assaults, and quench his fiery darts" and fulfill God's promise that thence-forth Mankind will have the spiritual resolve to suffer the cruelties of the enemy "so as shall amaze / Thir proudest persecutors" (12:485-97). The "just man," rather than submitting as a helpless victim to the forces of evil, will be empowered to enter the lists in the cosmic conflict as a combatant, opposing the enemy, as God had pledged: "Upheld by me, yet once more he shall stand / On even ground against his mortal foe" (3:178-79).[18]

Milton was convinced that the founding of the English Republic was yet another defeat for the forces of evil in the ebb and flow of the cosmic conflict. In 1649, "God and a good cause" were responsible for Parliament's victory over the king (*Prose* 3:192); and a decade later Milton welcomed the restoration of the Rump as "a new dawning of Gods miraculous providence among us" (*Prose* 7:274); but the "perverse inhabitants" of England proved unworthy in the end and evil reasserted its sway with the Restoration. The Commonwealth's initial letters to for-eign heads of state routinely opened with a pious statement justifying the establishment of the new government as a victory for the Almighty. In one of Milton's letters to the duke of Holstein, for example, the Council of State declares that "it has pleas'd the Most Wise God . . . to wage most just Wars in defence of our Liberty against Tyrannical Usurpation" (W38, P62). In another, to Hamburg, Parliament trusts that "God, with whose counte-nance and powerful aid we have conquered our tyrants in battle," will continue to "guide our counsels" (W151, P1). From the perspective of spiritual warfare the forces of good, embodied in an Army of Saints marching under the banners of the Almighty, prevail for a time in this corner of the battleground of Earth, only to falter in the end and be swept aside by

18. In his conception of Man's new role in the conflict, Milton may well have recalled that which England envisioned in 1658 for the inhabitants of the Spanish Netherlands, who, inspired by the Protestant presence in the recently acquired Dunkirk, it was hoped would be "induc'd to throw [off] the Spanish yoke" (Charles Harding Firth, *The Last Years of the Protectorate*, 2:219; *CC* 148-49).

resurgent evil in the form of Charles II, his stable of bishops, and his dissolute court.

Any rational being, when confronted with the tragedy of armed conflict, must puzzle over the folly of it. A war, when isolated from the events precipitating it and divorced from the consequences of victory and defeat, must appear absurd; and it is a simple matter to describe any single encounter in the conflict, so isolated and so divorced, in a way that opens the entire struggle to ridicule. In World War II, for example, the loss of innocent lives in the bombing of London, and of Hamburg, may be perceived as senseless human slaughter, as may any single encounter in a savage six-year war, when considered without reference to causes and consequences. In this respect Adam might well have asked why the forces of good and evil do not just cease hostilities, in keeping with the sentiments of a recent American statesman: "The way to end the war is to end the war." And he could have asked further, with some justification, why he had to be drawn into it, or, to continue the analogy to our own times, why a helpless Luxembourg had to suffer because of the antagonism between two powerful neighbors. Adam does not inquire in these terms, of course, but Milton's readers well may.

In *Paradise Lost* cosmic warfare conveys a spiritual message. The conflict without is an image of the conflict within; the "Arms on Armor clashing," the "madding Wheels / Of brazen Chariots," and the "ruinous assault" of Heaven's war (6:209-16) project the turbulence that possesses Adam and Eve after the Fall, when "Passions, Anger, Hate, / Mistrust, Suspicion, Discord . . . shook sore / Thir inward State of Mind" (9:1123-25). But however well the imagery of cosmic conflict reflects that turmoil within, the analogy falters when called on to convey the full sense of that "inward State of Mind" of the opposing forces that compels them to continue the war. It makes no sense to say that God fears for the safety of his throne, or that Satan, having achieved dominion over the Earth, must therefore continue to plague its inhabitants. As we have seen, Michael revives the military image momentarily when he tells Adam that the Holy Spirit will enable Man to quench Satan's "fiery darts" (12:490-92); but the image fails to explain satisfactorily why Satan is launching darts in the first place.

Political imagery, therefore, is effective up to a point; but it is inadequate in justifying the continuation of the war, since Satan is obviously driven by forces more profound than a naked lust for power and the Almighty is prompted by something more than a desire simply to maintain the *status quo.* There are any number of reasons a people will pursue a war once begun, the promise of victory, or fear of destruction, or blind loyalty to a cause; but none of these seem to apply to that waged between good and evil. The political analogy is entirely effective in attributing Satan's rebellion in Heaven to a sense of "injur'd merit" and his plot against Man to an abiding hatred of the Almighty – wars have been fought for such reasons. But when he announces his sweeping "Evil be thou my Good," even though he immediately reifies the thought as a conquest, "by thee at least / Divided Empire with Heav'n's King I hold" (4:110-11), we seem to have entered a region of spiritual and psychological abstraction where the analogy, if pursued further, does not serve so well – it ends up in a series of political paradoxes.

Satan, it seems, vows to continue the war because he must. The Devil is caught in the divine trap. As he eventually comes to realize, his ultimate motive for continued resistance to the Deity is the desire to find relief from pain, "For only in destroying I find ease / To my relentless thoughts" (9:129-30, 475-79). It is this compulsive need to destroy that dictates his goals from the outset:

> To do aught good never will be our task,
> But ever to do ill our sole delight.
> As being contrary to his high will
> Whom we resist.
>
> (1:159-63)

And he persists, paradoxically, knowing full well that his victories in the war will only intensify his suffering: "Revenge, at first though sweet, / Bitter ere long back on itself recoils" (9:171-72).[19]

God's motives are incomprehensible, but Milton insists that they can be understood within the scope of human reason. Michael's mission is to persuade Adam to continue the fight, much as a belligerent power might encourage a guerilla movement in a country occupied by its enemy; but as the archangel's account reveals, Man's resistance to the Devil will have no impact whatsoever on the outcome of the war. It matters not whether the race triumphs over evil in this world or establishes universal brotherhood or

---

19. One of the traditional motives attributed to Satan is a passion to persuade Man to hate God as much as he does. Milton says little of this, skirting close only in Satan's distortion of God's reasons for the forbidden fruit, by which he attempts to turn Eve against the Deity: "Why then was this forbid? Why but to awe, / Why but to keep ye low and ignorant, / His worshippers" (9:703-5).

governs itself according to this or that political scheme, for the end will be the same – Christ shall come again, in God's good time, to judge the living and the dead. From time to time in Christian history religious alarmists have arisen to prophesy that the race has become so vicious and corrupt – in other words, Satan seems to be winning – that the Almighty out of anger and disgust will precipitate the end prematurely; but Milton held no such belief. The war will go on to its destined end; but to pursue the political analogy to its logical conclusion would be to encounter a paradox of faith: in absolute obedience lies absolute freedom. Milton touches upon the matter in his argument against state control of the church, "who can enjoy anything in this world with contentment, who hath not liberty to serve God and save his own soul" (*Prose* 7:379); but in *Paradise Lost* he addresses the paradox directly. Only in unquestioned obedience to the will of the Almighty will Man be free to attain his promised reward. So he must continue to resist Satan's darts and fight on, even as Michael did in Heaven, knowing full well that his struggle will have no influence one way or the other on the final outcome. The prize to the victor in the war between good and evil is ever the individual soul.

God's incomprehensible intent can only be described, as we have seen, in terms of his love for all creation, a spiritual quality of the Deity that defies description in political terms. The imagery of *Paradise Lost* depicts a conflict waged in the endless reaches of the cosmos, but the real battleground is the intimate space of the human soul; and in the end each individual will be held responsible for the waging of his own battle, regardless of the larger war. That conflict continues so that love may triumph over hatred in the heart of Man, as it did in the angelic spirit on the plains of Heaven, and as it will with the Incarnation, which will confirm that "Heav'nly love shall outdo Hellish hate" (3:298). God continues the war so that he may fulfill his original promise to Man that he will in the end "turn all to spirit" and "See golden days, fruitful of golden deeds, / With Joy and Love triumphing, and fair Truth" (3:337-38). Adam comes to realize that in the struggle to come he will be called upon to remain steadfast in his allegiance to God so that love may triumph over hatred; and this is the "goodness infinite, goodness immense" at which he rejoices (12:469).

Evil, then, comes into existence as a consequence of Satan's act of disobedience against a divine decree; and though it cannot be said, therefore, that God is the cause of evil, he certainly provides the occasion for it. Once the political positions of the two sides have been clearly defined by Satan and Abdiel,[20] the armies clash; and the war between the forces of good and evil is joined, to rage without cease on the fields of Heaven, in the vast reaches of Chaos, beneath the floral bowers of Eden, and within the breast of fallen Man, until the end of time.

Such, then, is to be the cycle of human history: Satan works his evil out of good; from it God brings forth more good, which Satan in turn corrupts; and so it will go until the Final Day. And the political image of a divided empire, once again, serves as handmaid to spiritual truth.

20. Satan's two later confrontations, another with Abdiel (6:131-87) and the one with Michael (6:262-95), are largely in the tradition of epic warriors posturing on the battlefield and add little to the definition of war aims.

7

THE FINAL THINGS

"So shall the World go on, / To the good malignant, to bad men benign" until the very last day (12:573-38). A contemplation of Final Things may seem an unrewarding subject with which to conclude a discussion of the influence of Milton's political life on *Paradise Lost,* for at first glance it would seem that such far-off events can owe little to his temporal experience. This is not to say that the poet was unacquainted with the language of catastrophe. His letters on the Piedmont Massacre include passages of vivid detail depicting the desolation of the victims, who

> were assail'd by Armed Violence, that turn'd their Dwellings into Slaughter-houses, while others, without Number, were terrified into Banishment, where now Naked and Afflicted, without House or Home, or Covering from the Weather, and ready to perish through Hunger and Cold, they miserably wander through desert Mountains,

and depths of Snow, together with their Wives and Children.[1]
(W55, P76)

He concludes *The Readie and Easie Way* in a similar vein, urging his countrymen "to stay these ruinous proceedings; justly and timely fearing to what a precipice of destruction the deluge of this epidemic madness would hurrie us through the general defection of a misguided and abus'd multitude" (*Prose* 7:463).

There is a prophetic ring as well to some of Cromwell's letters to the Protestant rulers of northern Europe, in which he deplored their squabbles. He wrote to Charles X of Sweden, warning that because of his war with Denmark "of necessity the Protestant Religion must be in great jeopardy, if not on the brink of destruction" (W79, P108), and in a companion letter to Frederick III that should the conflict continue, "most certainly the Interests of the Protestants must go to ruine; and suffer a total and irrecoverable Eclipse" (W87, P119). One would not want to make too much of the common themes, however, since the prose seems pale beside the poetry, and since it is apparent that Milton's apocalyptic passages are obviously and chiefly indebted to Scripture; but, once again, Cromwell's vision of the consequences of discord among the nations may have influenced the political cast of the poetry.

The Trump of Doom

Though the details of Milton's various accounts of the Apocalypse owe much to his biblical sources, the event serves also as an essential episode in the broad political frame of the poem. It chronicles the outcome of the cosmic war between good and evil, which culminates in a cataclysmic act of violence, wherein the Son, with "one sling / Of [his] victorious Arm" (10:633-34), defeats Satan, Sin, and Death, after which "New Heav'n and Earth shall to the Ages rise" (10:647), heralding the end of politics itself, once God's creation will have achieved a state of existence that need no longer be defined in terms of the governing and the governed. The eschatology of *Paradise Lost* is complex indeed, as befits a vision of the end and purpose of all creation; but that end must appear as just to the eye of Man as

---

1. There is reason to believe that Milton was responsible for the composition of at least five of these letters (*MG* 215-19).

the beginning and the middle; indeed, it bears the burden of justifying all that comes before.[2]

Reducing *Paradise Lost* to a bare narrative outline, stripped of its metaphysical, moral, and psychological elements, does little credit to the poem; but it brings to light a puzzling aspect of Milton's chronology of cosmic history. The account constitutes a fairly plausible political scenario – until its very end: A kingdom ruled by an absolute monarch is torn by a civil war between loyal subjects and rebel elements that seek to dethrone him. The rebels are defeated and exiled to a prison colony, where they endure an unbearably painful existence. Their leader rallies them with a plan to break out of their prison and strike back at the monarch, not directly at his kingdom but at another of his colonies, a far more desirable place where the inhabitants enjoy a comfortable life in the midst of peaceful plenty, though, it would appear, they have yet to attain full citizenship in the kingdom. The rebels escape their painful prison and occupy this pleasant colony, whose inhabitants they subjugate. The king by various means is able to retain the loyalty of some of his former subjects during the occupation and eventually returns to liberate them, expel the rebels, and banish them once more to their prison, which he then secures in such a way that they can never again escape. He then establishes a tribunal to judge which of his subjects have been loyal to him and which not during the occupation; and he banishes the latter to the prison along with the original rebels. As a reward to those who remained loyal, he raises them to full citizenship in the kingdom – and he then destroys the colony.

That final destruction is perhaps the most perplexing of the Almighty's acts, hence the most difficult to justify. The Last Judgment seems in accord with a human sense of justice, but why demolish the World? It seems an unnecessarily willful deed, and is indeed a unique event in cosmic history, one in which the creator destroys an object of his own creation. The poet must submit to the authority of Scripture, of course, but he is able to accommodate other biblical passages satisfactorily through the medium of his art.[3] Apparently uncomfortable with the episode, in *Paradise Lost*

---

2. Both Michael Fixler ("The Apocalypse within *Paradise Lost*") and Austin C. Dobbins (*Milton and the Book of Revelation*) find the entire epic structured and informed by Revelation. As Fixler puts it, "Milton based *Paradise Lost* on an elaborate systematic transformation of the Apocalypse or Revelation of St. John" (131). He argues that the seven visions of the Apocalypse are matched by a comparable number in the poem (150-51). No such claim is made here, only that it is the culminating act in a narrative sequence of political events.

3. Milton lists the proof texts for the dissolution of the world in *Prose* 6:628.

Milton straddles some of the issues raised by tradition and offers readers several different versions of that last day.

As we have seen, in *Christian Doctrine* Milton urges caution when discussing the mysteries of the Christian faith: "We should let mysteries alone and not tamper with them. We should be afraid to pry into things further than we were meant." The faithful should rather "be satisfied with the simple truth," relying on "the most unambiguous" of biblical texts, which, he is confident, will be quite sufficient "for our salvation." "Nothing," he concludes, "would be more reasonable, or more adapted to the understanding even of the least intelligent" (*Prose* 6:421). Such caution may be appropriate to a systematic theology designed to interpret the Bible in the light of reason,[4] but these mysteries cannot be passed over in an epic poem intent on justifying God's ways, which must seem right not only to our rational understanding of the law but, perhaps more important, to our instinctive sense of justice. In *Paradise Lost,* then, Milton must confront these mysteries and "adapt" them, not just for the unquestioning Christian who accepts the revelations of biblical texts on faith, but to the satisfaction of his fit, though few, and far more demanding audience. He, therefore, accommodates the Final Things to human understanding, as he does other mysteries of the Christian faith, in terms of the political life of the fallen race of Man.

In *Christian Doctrine* Milton extracts his account of the end of things from various biblical passages, and a vivid tale it is: At a time to be determined by God, Christ will come again, a signal for the resurrection of the dead and the Last Judgment. This second coming inaugurates "the often-promised and glorious reign of Christ and his saints on this earth," for, as Milton explains, it will take some time for him to judge so many and to finally subdue all God's enemies (*Prose* 6:623-24). Christ's dominion "will really be a reign," Milton insists, "rather than a judicial session"; and it will last for a thousand years, at which time Satan will return to "besiege the church with huge forces" (*Prose* 6:625). He will be overcome finally and "condemned to everlasting punishment," after which will come the dissolution of the world, to be followed by "the renovation of, and our possession of, heaven and earth" (*Prose* 6:632). This last act will establish a new principle of rule, which Milton is content simply to define in the words of 1 Corinthians 15:28 – *"After everything has been made subject to him, then*

---

4. Here, as elsewhere, the language of logic is scattered through these pages: "Nothing would be more reasonable . . . ," "It follows that . . . ," "The following arguments may be used to prove that . . . ," and so on (*Prose* 6:421, 423, 428).

the Son himself will be made subject to him who subjected all things to him, so that God may be all in all" (*Prose* 6:626).

Thus Milton's theology, and thus the evidence of "the most unambiguous of texts," which are "adapted to the understanding even of the least intelligent," entirely sufficient "for our salvation." In *Paradise Lost,* however, the poet emphasizes certain of these events and omits others entirely. Nothing is said of the thousand years, and the second coming of Satan receives but one fleeting reference (4:3). The poem refers to Christ's reign in only the vaguest terms and is ambiguous as to whether it will occur before or after the dissolution of the World. Milton omits scriptural matters that although necessary as proof texts in the rational argument of a systematic theology, would only burden the poetry with doctrinal detail. The poet is more intent on arousing a sense of awe at the spectacle of those distant events, an effect that poetry has the power to excite; and, central to his purpose, he must validate the boundless joy with which Adam, though condemned to suffering and death, embraces God's ways on hearing of them. The political imagery prevails in the accounts but it is reserved for matters best designed to awaken that awe, the Son's victory over Satan and the glorious settlement at the very end, when politics itself shall pass away.

The impression conveyed by the apocalyptic passages is intensified by their close linkage in tone and imagery to other prophecies in *Paradise Lost,* two in particular, those that envision Man's future had he not sinned and those that foretell of the Resurrection. The political images of the accounts overlap in significant respects, producing what seems a conflation of the three prophecies. There are times when Raphael's description of the future of an unfallen Adam differs little from Michael's prediction of the fate of fallen Man. God's prelapsarian promise that in the end Earth will "be chang'd to Heav'n, and Heav'n to Earth, / One Kingdom, Joy and Union without end" (7:161) is echoed in his assurance that from the ashes of the fallen World will arise "New Heav'n and Earth, wherein the just shall dwell . . . / With Joy and Love triumphing, and fair Truth" (3:335-37), and in Michael's prediction that at the end "New Heav'ns, new Earth" will "bring forth fruits Joy and eternal Bliss" (12:549-51). The promise of inhabiting "One Kingdom" is open to both pre- and postlapsarian Man. In Raphael's words, if the sinless Adam remains obedient, once he has turned "all to spirit," he "may at choice / Here or in Heav'nly Paradises dwell" (5:496-500); and in Michael's, the fallen race will be received eventually into bliss "Whether in Heav'n or Earth, for then the Earth / Shall all be Paradise"

(12:463-64). In either case Man will finally stand equal to the angels as subjects of God: in the first instance "under long obedience tri'd" his body "may at last turn all to spirit" (5:497); in the second, he will achieve that same state, but having failed the test of obedience, he first must die.

There are comparable parallels between the apocalyptic passages and those predicting Christ's Resurrection. In both Death meets much the same fate. The last days will see his final defeat: "at one sling / Of thy victorious Arm, well-pleasing Son, / Both *Sin* and *Death*" will be "For ever" sealed in Hell (10:633-37). The Resurrection, of course, is itself heralded in Christian liturgy as a triumph over Death; and with the exception of "For ever," Milton's imagery here prefigures the same final victory. Christ's rising, Michael tells Adam, "Shall bruise the head of *Satan*, crush his strength / Defeating *Sin* and *Death*, his two main Arms" (12:429-31). In like terms the Son predicts that at his Resurrection, "Death his death's wound shall then receive, and stoop / Inglorious, of his mortal sting disarm'd," and as the Messiah he shall "ruin all [his] Foes / Death last" (3:252-59).

The allusion to Hell as a grave appears in both accounts. At the Apocalypse, "Hell, her numbers full, / Thenceforth shall be for ever shut" (3:332-33); the triumphant Son shall defeat "yawning *Grave*, . . . obstruct the mouth of Hell / For ever, and seal up his ravenous Jaws" (10:635-37). At the Resurrection again the "For ever" is omitted, but the image seems no less final: having defeated Death, the Son promises, he will "with his Carcass glut the Grave" (3:258-59).

These two victories of the spirit are depicted as physical triumphs, God's apocalyptic "one sling / Of thy victorious Arm (10:633-34) on the last day, and the Son's promise that at his Resurrection he "shall rise Victorious, and subdue / My vanquisher." He predicts further that he "through the Ample Air in Triumph / Shall lead Hell Captive maugre Hell" (3:250-55), an image that Michael later repeats more graphically: the risen Christ "shall surprise / The Serpent, Prince of Air, and drag in Chains / Through all his Realm" (12:453-55).

The three prophecies define the condition of the human race at the beginning, middle, and end of its history; but the common imagery fuses them into a single vision, so that the reader may see them through the timeless eye of God, for whom that history is but one event, a single tick of the cosmic clock. From the human perspective, however, they are episodes in a historical continuum that defines Man's relationship to the Deity at different stages in its progress. For John Milton and his readers in any era the most important stage in this chronicle is, of course, the present one; and the spectacle of human suffering prompts compelling questions: Who are we and what are we to do *now* in this post-Resurrection world? The first and last of the visions offer little in the way of answer. The brief glimpse of Adam's sinless future provides no guidance for moral action in a fallen world, however deeply it touches our nostalgia for a lost innocence; and the struggles of the race, as has been noted, will have no influence on the final outcome, a cataclysmic confrontation between the vast forces of good and evil, one in which Man's only role will be that of a defendant before a divine tribunal. The account of the Last Days may indeed arouse a sense of awe in Milton's readers, who can rejoice in the promise that good will eventually triumph; but it offers little in the way of guidance toward individual salvation. To that end, the most important of the three prophecies is the Resurrection; and the imagery that vision shares with the accounts of Mankind's lost past and destined future seems designed to clarify the present condition of the race, living out its numbered days under the divine dispensation of the risen Christ.

The Resurrection, as we have seen, represents a turning point in the cosmic conflict between good and evil. It is an event, however, with which Milton seems never to have been entirely comfortable. Early in his life he abandoned his series of poetic celebrations of Christian feasts when they brought him to Easter. In the Nativity Ode he cites "the bitter cross" but then, without so much as a glance at the Resurrection, moves immediately to the "trump of doom" heard at the Final Judgment. In "Upon the Circumcision" it is the bleeding, not the risen, Christ who renews "that great Cov'nant." In contemplating "The Passion," the eye of his imagination catches sight of "that sad Sepulchral rock / That was the Casket of Heav'n's richest store" (43-44); but his vision falters when it looks beyond that grave and he abruptly ends the poem. In *Christian Doctrine* the poet has little to say about the mystery. He cites Scripture to demonstrate that Christ died, rose again, and sits at the right hand of God (6:440-42), and that his sacrifice brought about "the reconciliation of God the Father and man" (6:449). The event itself, however, receives scant space, indeed but one brief paragraph, the opening sentences of which is worth citing to illustrate how perfunctory his treatment is:

> Resurrection, Matt., Mark etc. and I Cor. xv. 4, etc. Ascension into heaven, Mark xvi. 19; Luke xxiv. 51; John xiv. 12, etc.; Acts i. 9, etc.; Eph. iv. 8, 10: *he ascended far above all heavens.*

And that's it! The balance of the paragraph is devoted to proof texts confirming that Christ ended up at God's right hand (6:442).[5] The Resurrection is obviously one of those mysteries of faith that Milton advises the readers of *Christian Doctrine* to "leave alone and not tamper with," cautioning that "we should be afraid to pry into things further that we are meant" (6:421). Hence, in *Paradise Regained* he chose the temptation in the wilderness as the trial that regains lost Paradise. In brief, Milton found far more significance for Mankind in the life and death of Christ than in his miraculous resurrection.

The Resurrection could not be ignored in *Paradise Lost,* however, and in that obligation may be seen a purpose for linking the prophecies of Raphael and Michael with common imagery. The visions of the beginning and the end of the history of the human race cast light on its present spiritual state, one defined by Christ's promise of rebirth; and the political imagery carries the major burden of the spiritual message. Raphael's conditional prophecy that Adam's body "may at last turn all to spirit" and dwell thereafter "Here or in Heav'nly Paradises" (5:497-500) serves to define God's covenant with Man, that which is renewed by the Messiah; and the angel's promise that the unfallen race, if its "obedience holds," will live in "One Kingdom, Joy and Union without end" (7:161) is restored in Michael's prophecy that "new Heav'n, new Earth" shall rise from "the conflagrant mass," where the just shall live in "Joy and eternal Bliss" (12:548-91). The account of the victory of the risen Christ over Satan, Sin, and Death gains fuller meaning through the imagery it shares with the Son's triumph on the Final Day. The individual confrontation between Christ and Satan in which the Devil is dragged in chains "Through all his Realm" is a typological foreshadowing of the great clash of forces at the Apocalypse; and the fury of those last days reflects back upon the earlier triumph, enhancing its impact on the imagination.

Further, the differences between the two victories illustrate the fallen condition. Christ's early defeat of Satan will not crush him "for ever," nor will it usher in an era of "Joy and eternal Bliss." Satan will recover and the race remain embattled, still "Tri'd in sharp tribulation," but rearmed, now that the original covenant is renewed, by the hope of salvation. Michael's image of the Holy Spirit equipping Mankind with "spiritual Armor" is a military metaphor reifying that resurgent hope.

Thus, the shared imagery and the omission of differentiating detail that

5. Indeed, of the crucial biblical passages *Christian Doctrine* cites Matthew 28:6 but once, Luke 24:6 and Mark 16:6 not at all (Bauman, *A Scriptural Index*).

render the three accounts hardly distinguishable from one another in the imagination of the reader reaffirm God's promise that his love still shines upon Mankind, though fallen, and that those who return that love open the way to salvation, regardless of that first disobedience. But these similarities cannot entirely dispel the shadow over Adam, for whom sin has harsh consequences: rather than the slow, benign metamorphosis of body into spirit, he must submit to decaying age, wasting disease, and death.

These alternate routes to Heaven highlight the separate challenges that God's instructions put to Raphael and Michael, his two envoys to the race of Man. God's ambassadors, as we have seen, are charged with quite different missions: Raphael is to inform Adam of the past, Michael of his unfortunate future. They have the same end, however, to ensure his continued allegiance to God after the Fall. Raphael must enlighten Adam so that once he has sinned, he will not reject God as unjust, blaming the Almighty for his transgression rather than himself, a notion he considers momentarily in his long lament after the Fall: "Did I request thee, Maker, from my Clay / To mould me Man, did I solicit thee / From darkness to promote me?" (10:743-45). Later, Michael must reassure Adam that, despite the severity of the punishment, a compassionate God has not abandoned him and remains worthy of his love and allegiance.

Raphael's is perhaps the more awkward mission, however, for in carrying out God's charge he must not reveal anything to Adam of his coming Fall. The angel has the delicate task of warning him not to submit to his passion for Eve, knowing full well that he will; and he must inform him of the threat to his allegiance, knowing that Satan will indeed subvert it. There can be no doubt that Raphael knows what is to come. Milton, perhaps a bit uneasy with the angel's awkward position, attempts to provide him with a thin veil of deniability during the days of creation by sending him on "a voyage uncouth and obscure, / Far in excursion toward the Gates of Hell" (7:230-31); but the careful reader cannot fail to notice that when on a later occasion God predicts the Fall of Man and declares his punishment, "all the Sanctities of Heaven / Stood thick as Stars" in attendance (3:60-61), Raphael surely among them.

God does not explicitly instruct the archangel to conceal Adam's future from him, but his instructions pretty well cover the situation. Raphael is to tell him only of Satan's designs, "Lest wilfully transgressing, he pretend / Surprisal" (5:244-45) — not "When" but "Lest" he transgress, which we may read as "in the event of." God is relying on the angel's common sense, confident that the need for his silence on the matter goes without saying and that it is abundantly self-evident to him that any such disclosure would completely compromise the mission.[6] In practice English envoys who received instructions from their superiors were not given this degree of latitude; little went without saying in their written charges, which were frequently laden with anxious contingencies and prohibitions. When Cromwell, in August 1657, dispatched William Jephson to the court of Charles X of Sweden, more than half of the envoy's instructions concerned the Lord Protector's offer to exchange military aid for the bishopric of Bremen; but Jephson was cautioned, indeed cautioned twice, to maintain his silence about the offer unless the king himself first broached the subject (*MG* 167n). Raphael, to his discomfort, encounters an unexpectedly inquisitive Adam, curious about what angels eat and how they love, why nature is so "superfluous" and the heavens so full, and other matters "above his World" (5:455), questions which have at their core an unspoken desire to know the purpose of it all, including how it will end. Raphael finds that he must do more than simply tell Adam that he is happy; and so he touches on Man's future.

Angels don't lie, of course, but Raphael, like any accomplished diplomat, is not above shading the truth. On the two occasions when he alludes to the future of the race, the first is crowded with qualifications: The "time *may* come when men / With Angels *may* participate" and "perhaps" their bodies "*may* at last turn all to spirit" but only *if* they "be found obedient" (5:493–501; italics mine). So intent is Adam on the last qualification that the others escape his notice. The second occasion is Raphael's account of God's speech prior to the creation; and here there are no ambiguities: the race of Man, the Deity predicts, will dwell on Earth "till by degrees of merit rais'd / They open to themselves at length the way / Up hither," again "under long obedience tri'd" (7:155–59) – no "if" or "may" about it. In this passage, however, Raphael is simply repeating the words of God on that occasion,

---

6. This constraint on Raphael's mission makes extremely unlikely Dennis Danielson's contention that Adam knew of Christ's messianic role before the Fall (*Milton's Good God* 222, cited by Diane McColley, *Gust for Paradise*, 174). Certainly the Son is referred to frequently as the "Messiah" on books 5 and 6; but the word there has its original Hebraic meaning, "anointed" (*OED;* see 5:664, 6:718). In the war in Heaven he is cast as the "deliverer" of the loyal angels, but not the human soul, which had yet to be created. Christian readers will see the Son's triumph in Heaven as a foreshadowing of his victory on Earth, but Adam must remain ignorant of his future role. Such a revelation would have raised a question in Adam's inquisitive mind: "Why will I need a Messiah?" Milton would not have introduced such a contradiction in his lines.

presumably leaving nothing out; and if the Deity chose to withhold the revelation of the Fall until a later time (3:92-95), that was certainly within the divine prerogative. Thus Raphael, though not entirely forthcoming with Adam, follows God's instructions closely, perhaps stretching their limits just a bit in discussing Man's future.

In one respect, God's ambassador, in failing to reveal his sovereign's full intent, is well within accepted standards of diplomatic practice, as Milton would surely have understood. In September 1654 he prepared a letter for Cromwell's signature addressed to the Spanish prime minister, one in which the Lord Protector assured that dignitary of his "cordial Inclinations toward the King of *Spain,* and ready propensity to hold Friendship with that Kingdom" (W47, P69). What the letter failed to say was that Cromwell had been busily engaged for months fitting out a force of ships and men intended for an expedition against the Spanish possessions in the Caribbean; the fleet sailed in December.[7]

Michael's mission is not burdened with the need for such equivocations, though it has its own challenges, not the least of which is to tell the fallen pair of their fate in such a way as to "send them forth, though sorrowing, yet at peace" (11:117). His brief glimpse of Adam's role in the governance of Earth had he not fallen is an account of lost opportunities. Eden, the angel remarks, would have been

> Perhaps thy Capital Seat, from whence had spread
> All generations, and had hither come
> From all the ends of th'Earth, to celebrate
> And reverence thee thir great Progenitor.

Adam would have enjoyed a prominence on Earth comparable to God's in Heaven were it not for his sin; but sadly he has been "brought down / To dwell on even ground now with [his] Sons" (11:343-48).

The Apocalypse is the final act, of course, when the World will be dissolved; but even here Milton is ambiguous concerning the means. Michael concludes his account of human history with three long speeches (12:285-372, 386-465, 485-551), summarizing the lessons of his chronicle, predicting Christ's mission, and describing the Final Things, in order to dismiss Adam and Eve "not disconsolate," as he had been instructed. Both of his last two

---

7. *MG* 129; for a more complete account of preparations for the expedition, see Fraser, *Cromwell,* 523-26.

speeches conclude with a vision of the final cataclysm and its aftermath, a prophecy that Milton finds worth repeating, for scarcely eighty lines separate the apocalyptic passages. The accounts are essentially the same, with one significant exception. The earlier one places the second coming indeterminately at a time "When this world's dissolution shall be ripe" (12:459) with no mention of how or when the end will come; the second is more specific, revealing that the "Saviour and Lord" will "dissolve" the world into a "conflagrant mass" (12:544-48). God himself is ambiguous about how it all will end, predicting at one point that "The World shall burn" (3:334), at another that it will simply be "renew'd" (10:638). Milton is deliberately vague here, for Scripture is not clear. He gives the issue some attention in *Christian Doctrine,* where he concludes that there will be a "conflagration" but is impatiently dismissive of the whole controversy: "Whether this end means the actual abolition of the world's substance, or only a change in its qualities, is uncertain, and does not really concern us. But we are told as much as is useful for us to know about the end of the world and the conflagration" (6:627-28).

His attitude toward the end of the world seems to echo his assessment of the significance of conjecture about events prior to the Creation: whoever asks about such matters is a fool, "and who answers him is not much wiser" (*Prose* 6:299). In a theoretical treatise, Milton may well dismiss the outcome as "uncertain" on the basis of insufficient evidence; but a historical narrative requires a beginning, a middle, and especially an end, and God's determination of the final state of creation is surely one of his ways that demands attention. Thus Michael concludes with a vision of the condition of Man after the world's end, however it may occur. He promises that then "the Earth / Shall be all Paradise," (12:463-64) a prediction he repeats: there will be "New Heav'ns, new Earth, Ages of endless date, / Founded in righteousness and peace and love, / To bring forth fruits Joy and eternal Bliss" (12:549-51). It is this prophecy that inspires Adam's exultant response, "O goodness infinite, goodness immense!" (12:469), a confirmation of Michael's success in his mission. A sinful Adam, thrust into a world of suffering and death, goes forth confident of God's eternal love, secure in the belief that should he not fail to return that love, he will receive the rich reward originally intended him.

All in All

There is yet another phase in this chronicle of cosmic history, however, the last act of the Final Things, recorded in 1 Corinthians 15:24-28, which, as noted, Milton quotes in *Christian Doctrine*. It reads in part:

> *Then will come the end, when [the Son] shall hand over the kingdom to God the Father, after annihilating all domination, authority and power. . . . And after everything has been made subject to him, then the Son himself will be made subject to him who subjected all things to him, so that God may be all in all.*
>
> (*Prose* 6:626)

In keeping with his judgment that "we should let mysteries alone and not tamper with them" (*Prose* 6:421) Milton makes no effort to explain this enigmatic *"all in all"* in *Christian Doctrine*. He limits his discussion to the resolution of the apparent conflict between the passage and Luke 1:33, "There will be no end to his kingdom." On that matter he concludes, somewhat opaquely, "Thus his kingdom will not *pass away,* like something ineffectual, nor will it be *destroyed.* Its end will not be one of dissolution but of perfection and consummation" (*Prose* 6:627), and lets it go at that. This is all very well, but it fails to explain what is to *happen* at this point in history, a metamorphosis that Christopher Hill has compared to Marx's concept of "the withering away of the state." Hill's analogy may seem somewhat singular but it is quite apt in its recognition that Milton defines this final phase in political metaphor.[8]

The phrase appears twice in *Paradise Lost,* the first in the chronology of events occurring when the Son prepares to engage the rebel angels and assert his right to the title of king:

> Sceptre and Power, thy giving, I assume
> And gladlier shall resign, when in the end
> Thou shalt be All in All, and I in thee
> For ever, and in me all whom thou lov'st.
>
> (6:730-33)

8. Hill, *Milton and the English Revolution,* 304. Empson also finds the image political, concluding that God plans to "abdicate," giving him a "democratic appeal," the author goes on, which makes him "just tolerable" (*Milton's God* 137). As will be seen, this reading is somewhat wide of the mark.

The second, from the mouth of God himself, comes at the close of his long speech praising the Son for his act of love, the fullest account in the poem of the Final Things. Though the Almighty had only just proclaimed that the Son's reign would last "for ever," in the sweep of eternity even "for ever" seems to have its limits. God prophesies that at the end of time "Orders and Degrees" will be superfluous; indeed all distinctions, political or otherwise, will lose their meaning, even the title, "Christ the King": "Then thou thy regal Scepter shalt lay by, / For regal Sceptre then no more shall need, / God shall be All in All" (3:339-41). But what, again, is this enigmatic state of "All in All," when men, angels, and even the Son himself, it seems, shall join in the nature of the Godhead and no longer stand in need of hierarchies, kings, kingdoms, scepters, or indeed of power itself, when the struggle between good and evil having come to an end, the political structure of all creation will no longer serve a purpose and so shall pass away?

Whatever the theological implications of the phrase, the political metaphor points to it as the culmination of a cycle of divine events, the first phase of which, discussed earlier, involves a systematic differentiation of the substance of God in a series of creative acts by which all the cosmic realms and their subjects are brought into being. The political imagery associated with the notion that God shall finally be "All in All" strongly implies that once the purpose of created things has been accomplished, they will be reintegrated back into the divine substance, with the single exception of Hell. It is a spiritual phenomenon defined in Raphael's description of the relationship between the Deity and his creation: "O *Adam,* one Almighty is, from whom / All things proceed, and up to him return, / If not deprav'd from good" (5:469-71). In the phrase, "All things proceed, and up to him return," Raphael explains the dynamics of that relationship at any moment in time. But the words also describe the entire historical process as it unfolds from the beginning to the end of time. All things – Heaven, Hell, Earth, angels, humans, and perhaps those "other Worlds" that Satan "stay'd not to enquire" of (3:566-71) – all proceed from the substance of the Deity and then, with the exception of Hell, are finally reunited with him.

This is the way the war ends. At some point in time God determines to dissolve these cosmic divisions and reintegrate the various disparate parts of himself back into the unity of his being. The differentiation phase ends with the Last Judgment, the final division of God's creatures into two groups, the saved and the damned. The reintegration begins when the Almighty destroys Adam's World and from its ashes raises a "New Heaven and Earth," uniting the two realms into one kingdom and their subjects into one body politic.

Thus the destruction of the World may be acknowledged as a just act, merely the initial event in a continuing process that will end when all creation is once more united in the "All in All" of the Deity. Hell is closed, a part of God unworthy of rejoining the divine nature, and shut within it is the antagonist whose opposition had shaped the political dynamics of the cosmos. With conflict ended, the political model with its "Orders and Degrees" no longer represents the spiritual state of existence; once the inner tension between passion and reason is resolved, there is no further need for the external political structure that mirrors it. In the final act of reintegration the Son can resign the "Sceptre and Power" he assumed when God "begot" him to the angels, the initiating event in this chronicle, for "regal Sceptre then no more shall need" in a society once more united in the Godhead, the "All in All" of his nature as it was prior to his embarking on a career of creation.

The Deity engages in this cyclic pattern of creation and destruction (which bears some resemblance to modern theories of the expansion and contraction of the universe) so as to express that quality of his nature which we identify as divine love. It is perhaps too much to say that the Almighty *needs* to so express himself; it is sufficient to observe simply that he does. When God, in conversation with Adam in the Garden, protests that he is "alone / From all Eternity" (8:405-6), he is somewhat disingenuous. In this "trial" of Adam's ability to "judge of fit and meet" (8:447-48), the Deity may be merely accommodating the divine condition to human understanding; but he is something less than candid here, for *Paradise Lost* depicts him participating in an exchange of mutual love, either directly or through the Son, with his entire creation, or at least with that part of it which chooses to respond in kind. Adam acknowledges that "All human thoughts come short" of comprehending God and then demonstrates his limitations by getting the point only partially: "No need that thou / Shouldst propagate, already infinite; / And through all numbers absolute, though One" (8:419-21). God reveals a "need" to "propagate" by the very act of creating Adam, which he has done by dividing himself, though remaining "One"; and the whole history of his interchange with those of his making is an expression of the divine equivalent of the "Collateral love, and dearest amity" that Adam seeks (8:426). So God differentiates his substance in creating Adam out of the dust which is himself in order to make possible an exchange of love, and repeats the process by creating Eve out of Adam to the same purpose.

The Final Things, then, signal the end of the war between good and evil, and of the "Divided Empire" that reifies it. The Last Judgment represents the final division of God's creation, this time into the saved and the damned; but we are still left with that puzzling dissolution of the World. There can be little doubt of the Almighty's motives as taught by Scripture and interpreted by Milton. In *Christian Doctrine* the poet finds him destroying the World because it is "foul and polluted" (*Prose* 6:625), a reading reflected in one account of the final appearance of the Son, who comes "to dissolve / *Satan* and his perverted World" (12:546-47); but the poem provides for an alternate reading, one that Michael repeats at the close of two consecutive speeches, as if to underline its significance (12:458-64, 544-51). The poet softens considerably, indeed all but dismisses, the image of a vengeful God venting his wrath upon a wayward World. He is rather a loving Deity who out of that dissolution creates a united kingdom where his creatures shall live "Whether in Heav'n or Earth, for then the Earth / Shall all be Paradise" (12:463-64); out of the "conflagrant mass" will emerge "New Heav'ns, new Earth," where the faithful will live "in righteousness and peace and love" (12:549-50). Whatever the traditional interpretation of the dissolution of the World, then, Milton turns it to his own poetic purpose, the final union of the contending realms of that tragically "Divided Empire" into a single kingdom "To bring forth fruits of Joy and eternal Bliss" (12:552).

Further, that union fits the poem's broader vision of the divine intent, God's election to differentiate his substance into separate realms in order to manifest his love. At a certain point in cosmic time, and for reasons beyond Man's understanding, the Almighty determines that his purpose has been fulfilled; and he initiates the process of reintegrating all created things back into his divine substance. The conflagration of the world is a turning point in the recorded history of God's progress through time, for it results in the union of Heaven and Earth, the first rejoining of separate elements of the divine being, hence the initial step in that mysterious process, which will be complete when all divisions are erased and God is once more the "All in All" of existence.

And in this vision, again, we can see the purpose of the striking parallels in Milton's description of Adam's prelapsarian destiny, the Resurrection, and the Apocalypse, that duplication of imagery which conflates time, depicting the beginning, middle, and end of Mankind's history as one, single glorious event.[9] God's promise to Adam in the Garden, delivered by his envoy

9. C. A. Patrides examines Milton's tendency to conflate time typologically in adapting apocalyptic passages to his purpose. Patrides observes, for example, that the poet transfers the war of the Apocalypse (Revelation 20:8-9) to a time before the Creation ("Something Like Prophetic Strain" 228-30), though Milton is obviously drawing more heavily on classical than

Raphael, will after all be fulfilled. As a consequence of the Son's sacrifice, God's Covenant is renewed; Man will indeed turn "all to spirit," and the Earth "chang'd to Heav'n, and Heav'n to Earth."[10] Sin has altered only the means by which God achieves his end. Man will turn to spirit, but because of his disobedience, to achieve that final unity with God he first must die; and the Earth will be changed into Heaven, but since it too "felt the wound," it first must burn.

If the political imagery of *Paradise Lost* seems at times to depict the Deity as the source of the divisions that plague creation, it also justifies his acts as measures taken to make himself known to his creatures, who can only comprehend the scale of his goodness in terms of its opposite. In this sense the political life of Man, the very essence of which is conflict and confrontation, offers a ready image for the revelation of the divine nature in a poem designed to accommodate God's ways to human understanding; and the purging of those political divisions, the dismissal "Of Hierarchies, of Orders, and Degrees" (5:591), of kings and kingdoms, of governing and governed, at a time when the Son shall lay by his "Regal Sceptre," is an equally ready image for the ultimate state of that same divine nature.

---

biblical sources here. Bernard Capp surveys the persistent strain of millenarianism in the sixteenth and seventeenth centuries ("The Political Dimension of Apocalyptic Thought").

10. Michael Fixler touches on the poet's concept of the final state of Man: "Milton apparently regarded the condition of the beginning and the end as essentially identical, with history cyclically returning upon itself, so to speak, once man was to be absolutely restored to beautitude" (*Milton and the Kingdoms of God* 227). Such an ending confirms that "the justice of God [is] made manifest as love" (228).

8

EMBATTLED HUMANITY

God's promise will be fulfilled, then, but before the human race can enter into that glory, it must endure an existence of Hobbesian brutishness, beset by forces determined that the sufferings of this life will prevail in the next. In his later years Milton composed two works relating how God's cosmic design plays out in human life. The poet turned his gaze from the reaches of space to the surface of the Earth and his thoughts from spirits to ordinary beings, offering in the Jesus of *Paradise Regained* and the tormented Samson patterns for those struggling to avoid the devices of the Devil and triumph over the frailties of their human nature. In these figures, further, Milton fashioned a model for human action, the individual spirit entering the lists in the war between good and evil as combatants in the conflict rather than helpless victims in the cosmic clash of gigantic forces.

Paradise Regained

These later works display a spectrum of the historical governments of Man not to be found in *Paradise Lost*. Milton is more descriptive in *Paradise Regained,* especially in the case of Parthia and Rome, empires all but ignored in Adam's panoramic vision of the nations of the world in *Paradise Lost*. Again, it is an intriguing notion that the poet, in composing the longer epic, already had the later work in mind and omitted mention of those states for which he had future use.

The brief epic, like its longer companion, is crowded with armies on the march, councils in session, empires, kingdoms, tribes, monarchs, dictators, senators, ambassadors about their trade, and human beings bearing the burden of a conflict-plagued world. As in *Paradise Lost,* the most finely drawn of these political figures is Satan himself, the seasoned diplomat negotiating with Jesus "By parle, or composition, truce, or league," as he puts it, "To win him, or win from him what I can" (4:529-30).

In obedience to Satan's command to "up and enter now into full bliss," the forces of Hell have occupied the Earth and seem in full control of human affairs. In the appearance of Jesus, however, they detect a threat to their hegemony. Satan, having heard the voice of God expressing pleasure in his "Son" at Jesus's baptism, calls a council, now in "mid-air" rather than Pandaemonium, to consider their options. These councils in *Paradise Regained* differ from the earlier "great consult," however, in important respects. The political imagery duplicates the pattern of the earlier epic, linking the two in a single narrative of the cyclic rise, fall, then rise and fall again, of demonic power; but it is obvious that the scope of Satan's authority has been much enlarged. In the first of the meetings (1:39-118) Satan, now "their great Dictator" (1:113), does all the talking, as he simply informs his subjects of what he intends to do; and his speech, like that of God following it (1:130-67), echoes with the imagery of conflict. Though they have long since escaped from Hell, their former "hated habitation," and now rule "In manner at our will th' affairs of Earth," a man has appeared, he warns, who threatens their dominion over "this fair Empire won of Earth and Air" (1:47, 63). His followers react anxiously to the news; the "Regents and Potentates, and Kings, yea gods / Of many a pleasant Realm and Province wide" fear that the Son of God has come to end their "Reign on Earth so long enjoy'd" (1:117-25). But they are uncertain "Who this is" and Satan announces his intention to discover if this frail human is indeed the same "Son" whose "fierce thunder drove us to the deep" (1:90-91).

At the second meeting, held again in "the middle Region of thick Air" (2:117), Satan, having taken the measure of Jesus, confirms his earlier fears that "an Enemy / Is ris'n to invade us, who no less / Threat'ns than our expulsion down to Hell" (1:126-28); and he asks his followers "with hand / Or counsel to assist" him in countering the threat (1:145). Belial is still there, and he is still talking; but this time Satan can scornfully dismiss his proposal. Though he had, with hollow courtesy, asked for any assistance of "hand / Or Counsel," he obviously dislikes debate and feels no need to hide his impatience. He no longer has to endure the ramblings of that "dissolutest Spirit," nor to plot and maneuver through a front man to have his way, but can silence opposition now with a "quick answer" (2:172). He has convened the council, it would appear, not to ask advice, but simply to inform them, again, of his intent and enlist a "chosen band / Of Spirits" (2:235-36) to assist in his design. The enhancement of Satan's political status after the Fall, as noted earlier, may be compared to the waxing of Cromwell's powers after the establishment of the Protectorate. Satan's new authority over his "gloomy Consistory" (1:42) is analogous to Cromwell's over his "Privy Council." Both the "great Dictator" and the Lord Protector consult when it suits them, but such is their power that they need not consider themselves bound by the advice they receive (*MG* 127-30).

I have discussed at some length elsewhere the figure of Satan as a consummate politician and diplomat during the encounter in the wilderness, outwardly generous in his offer of assistance, disguising his true intent under the mask of a potential ally, and tendering aid to an apparently resourceless Jesus, whom he hopes in the end to suborn (*CC* 192-98).[1] In brief, the Devil is a skilled negotiator and saves his best offer until last. He first extends vague inducements in the form of power and wealth but soon gets down to serious bargaining. He recommends that Jesus accept specific kingdoms, first the throne of David, next Parthia, then the empire of Rome, raising the bid each time until in exasperation he finally offers all "The Kingdoms of the world" (4:163). Jesus will have none of it, of course, for reasons both personal and political: he does not like the "giver" (2:322); and since, as has been prophesied, his kingdom is to last forever, he finds little to recommend the transitory crowns that Satan tenders.

Until the very end of the poem, Milton's Jesus is very much a human being, one whose state of knowledge is no different than that of any other

---

1. Of particular interest are the parallels between Satan's temptations and Cromwell's position during the Anglo-Dutch negotiations of 1653 (*CC* 189-99; *MG* 84-86).

human; he has learned what he does know from his mother's account of his birth and from studying Scripture. The political imagery of the poem clarifies the scope of his knowledge. In his youth, as he recalls, "victorious deeds / Flam'd in my heart, heroic acts"; he dreamed of freeing "*Israel* from the *Roman* yoke" and ridding the world of violence and tyranny until "truth were freed, and equity restor'd" (1:215-20). His mother tells him of the angel's prophecy that he would indeed sit on David's throne and that of his "Kingdom there should be no end"; but from Scripture he learns that the way to that throne will be hard, "even to the death / Ere I the promis'd Kingdom can attain" (1:240-41, 263-64). But this is all Jesus does know, except for the single episode at his baptism, when a voice from the cloud declared him "his beloved Son" (1:285). He seems unaware of the nature of the promised realm, only that, as his mother has revealed and as he repeatedly tells Satan, it will be everlasting (2:442; 3:185, 199; 4:151). Satan ignores the remarks and it is not entirely clear that Jesus comprehends the full significance of the prophecy himself. Although he knows that he is intended for David's throne, which he likens to a tree that will overshadow all kingdoms and a stone "that shall to pieces dash / All monarchies," and that it will have no end (4:146-51), it does not appear that at this stage of his life he conceives of it as a spiritual kingdom. He at no time claims that his "kingdom is not of this world," nor does it appear that he knows how he will attain it.[2] In brief, he is unaware of how truly he speaks when he says that his rule will "dash / All monarchies."[3]

The political frame of *Paradise Lost* is carried over into the later poem more or less intact, though the metaphysical is somewhat less evident. God speaks but once, and then only to explain to Gabriel the significance of the encounter between Jesus and Satan. He issues no decrees, nor does he intercede in any way to influence the outcome. The imagery of conflict, so prominent in the earlier poem, prevails in his speech, however; the Son will drive "Satan back to Hell, / Winning by Conquest what the first Man lost," a victory for which the encounter in the desert is but a preparation:

2. John 18:36. Jesus's statement comes later, of course, when he appears before Pilate, and Luke's account of the temptation in the wilderness makes no mention of it (4:1-13); thus Milton is correct in assuming that Jesus is not yet aware of the nature of his "kingdom."

3. In *Christian Doctrine* Milton argues that "it is not for us to ask whether he retained a two-fold intellect or a two-fold will, for the Bible says nothing of these things" (*Prose* 6:425). Until the very end of *Paradise Regained,* however, Jesus clearly is not conscious of his divinity.

> There he shall first lay down the rudiments
> Of his great warfare, ere I send him forth
> To conquer Sin and Death the two grand foes.
> (1:153-59)

The angelic chorus is heard on but two occasions, in the first quite briefly (1:173-81), in the other at somewhat greater length (4:596-635); and both hymns are relatively muted when compared to earlier paeans.

Thus, whereas Satan's powers are enlarged in *Paradise Regained,* the Son's are much diminished. He is shorn of the supernatural powers of his former existence and has no memory of that former "Son." Milton depicts him as a man, one, moreover, who is deprived of food, shelter, and fellowship, and who, as we have seen, knows of his divinity only through his mother's stories, the study of Scripture, and that voice from the cloud.[4] Satan is uncertain whether this "Son of God" is the same one who struck terror into the rebel host on the third day of the war in Heaven or just another extraordinary man; and the poem is an account of his efforts to prod Jesus into speaking or acting in a manner that would reveal his nature one way or the other. The poem reflects none of the ambiguities about the origins of the Son that mark the longer work, not until, that is, the climactic moment when Satan has his answer and Jesus comes to a full awareness of who he is: "Tempt not the Lord thy God" (4:561). In this sense, his balancing act on the temple's golden spire is as much a revelation to him as it is to Satan, for until that epiphany God and the vast forces at his disposal remain aloof from the contest. This is a battle that Man must win on his own.

The battle once won, however, Heaven is free to intervene. As if to punctuate Jesus's sudden awareness of his divinity, "a fiery Globe / Of Angels" appears to succor him – since Earth remains in the hands of the enemy, it is a military formation – and he is refreshed with "Celestial Food" and "Ambrosial drink" while the angelic choir celebrates his victory (4:581-95). Their hymn identifies that victory with the three great triumphs of the Son over Satan. It is likened to the first, when "him long of old / Thou didst debel, and down from Heav'n cast / With all his Army" (4:604-6). Milton appropriates the traditional imagery of the Resurrection to celebrate the victory, in lines recalling Michael's account to Adam: Jesus "by vanquishing / Temptation, hast regain'd lost Paradise, / And frustrated the conquest

---

4. As Mary Ann Radzinowicz observes, "What he knows of himself is what has been revealed in the Old Testament" ("How Milton Read the Bible" 210).

fraudulent"; he is "A Savior come down to reinstall" Mankind who hence-forth "shall dwell secure" when assailed by the "Tempter's" wiles (4:607-17). The choir predicts an apocalyptic end for Satan: "thou, Infernal Serpent, shalt not long / Rule in the Clouds," but in time shall receive a "last and deadliest wound" when the Son "Shall chase thee with the terror of his voice / From thy Demonic holds, possession foul, / Thee and thy Legions" (4:618-29). The political and military imagery of the hymn once again fuses past, present, and future into a timeless vision of triumphant good, and elevates the victory over temptation in the desert to a level of importance comparable to the Son's more celebrated triumphs.

Though Jesus' resistance to temptation is indeed an altogether human victory, the Christian reader will be conscious throughout the encounter that it is the "Son of God" who dismisses political power, a Deity who is little concerned with the manner in which men govern themselves. Jesus has come to preach the salvation of the individual soul; and as one whose kingdom, as he is later to declare, "is not of this world,"[5] he has no need of governments in such a task. Thus, though during his debate with Satan Jesus is not conscious of his metaphysical identity, his responses to the temptation of the kingdoms define human government from the perspective of the divine. He rejects the offer of David's throne because the time is not ripe and he is not yet tempered in his role: "who best / Can suffer, best can do; best reign, who / Well hath obey'd" (3:194-96). The display of Parthia's power he rejects as so much "cumbersome / Luggage of war, . . . argument / Of human weakness rather than of strength," and, again, because his time "is not yet come" (3:400-402, 397).

Satan, though unsure if this is "the Son," takes no chances, seizing every opportunity to distract Jesus from his prophesied role. One of the Devil's devices in proposing the Parthian crown is to advise that Jesus, once so installed, will be able to seek out and liberate the ten lost tribes of Israel, who still live in servitude somewhere in that kingdom, and thereby harvest the "full glory" of the throne (3:374-83). Jesus is characteristically disdainful of such a wild goose chase, dismissing the tribes as better off lost: "No, let them serve / Thir enemies, who serve Idols" (3:431-32).

Satan's tactics recall a similar design of Cromwell's, mentioned earlier in a different context. In 1657 he sent Richard Bradshaw on a mission to Moscow to prevail upon the czar to abandon his military opposition to the campaign of Sweden's Charles X in Poland (*MG* 166); and Milton was

---

5. John 18:36.

responsible for Bradshaw's letter of credential to the czar (W91, P124) as well as the Cromwell's set of instructions for the envoy (W164, P123).[6] Those instructions directed him, among other things, to propose that the czar undertake a crusade against the Turks, "thereby to win him selfe honour throughout Europe as cheif defender of Christiandome." It was an obvious device, indeed too blatantly obvious, to distract the czar from his concern about Charles's occupation of Poland by luring him into a crusade to liberate the lands lost to Islam. Needless to say, Cromwell was no more successful than is Satan with the device.

The display of Rome's glories draws Jesus' most detailed, and damning, political analysis. He rejects Satan's characterization of the empire as that "great and glorious *Rome,* Queen of the Earth / So far renown'd, and with spoils enricht / of Nations," famed for its "ample Territory, wealth, and power, / Civility of Manners, Arts, and Arms" (4:45-47, 82-83). Beneath the "grandeur and majestic show / Of luxury," Jesus detects the stink of corruption, "sumptuous gluttonies and gorgeous feasts." He sees for what it is Satan's public-spirited proposal that he replace the emperor in order to "A victor people free from servile yoke" (4:102). His reply has a sting: rather than displace this "brutish monster," why not better "Expel the Devil who first made him such" (4:129). The animated diplomatic bustle, the "Praetors, Proconsuls to thir Provinces / Hasting or on return, in robes of State" (4:63-64), he dismisses as a waste of time for those who must "sit and hear / So many hollow compliments and lies, / Outlandish flatteries" (4:123-25). Milton's long experience with the stilted protocol of diplomatic exchange and the insincere hyperbole that custom required of international correspondence can be felt in such lines (*MG* 106, 152-53).

Paradise Regained echoes many of the themes developed in the longer poem. Jesus favors nations in their youth. He rejects wealth as a necessity for rule and praises those early figures who rose from humble means to govern righteously, the biblical Gideon, Jephtha, and David and the Roman *"Quintius, Fabricius, Curius, Regulus"* (2:446). He approves of the early Romans, who at first were "just, / Frugal, and mild, and temperate" (4:133-34). A people in their youth and vigor are pleasing to God, but inevitably, Milton laments, as they grow great, they grow corrupt. As Jesus observes, the Romans, who

6. Some time later, Milton prepared a letter to the duke of Courland (the modern Baltic states) thanking him for his courteous reception of Bradshaw. Courland was as far as the envoy got, for the czar was so unsympathetic with the English Republic that he refused to permit Bradshaw to cross the border, though apparently Cromwell's letter to the czar was delivered (*MG* 166).

"conquer'd well," now "govern ill the Nations under yoke, / Peeling thir Provinces, exhausted all / By lust and rapine" (4:134-37). He dismisses the great empires, the Parthian as empty beneath its "ostentation vain of fleshly arm / And fragile Arms" (3:387-88), and the Roman, grown to little more than a shallow "majestic show" (4:110).

Jesus echoes Michael's judgment that a people get the government they deserve. Of Satan's rule on Earth, he observes that "God hath justly giv'n the Nations up / To thy Delusions; justly, since they fell / Idolatrous" (1:442-44). Of the ten lost tribes, he says, "themselves were they / Who wrought their own captivity" (3:414-15). When Satan proposes that Jesus liberate the Roman people from the rule of their oppressive emperors, he dismisses them scornfully as a "people victor once, now vile and base, / Deservedly made vassal," and asks,

> What wise and valiant man would seek to free
> These thus degenerate, by themselves enslav'd,
> Or could of inward slaves make outward free?
>   (4:143-45)

Jesus confirms Milton's oft-repeated conviction that true liberty lies within, and that only those who are masters of themselves are fit to rule others:

> Yet he who reigns within himself, and rules
> Passions, Desires, and Fears, is more a King;
> Which every wise and virtuous man attains:
> And who attains not, ill aspires to rule
> Cities of men, or headstrong Multitudes,
> Subject to Anarchy within.[7]
>   (2:466-71)

As has been noted, it has seemed to some curious that Milton should have conceived of the temptation in the wilderness as the occasion of Man's redemption. The traditional time of triumph is the day of Resurrection, the moment of victory when the Son defeats Death and drags Satan through the air in chains. That is the day, it is said, that regains Paradise for the race, when, as the Son promises in *Paradise Lost,* he "with the multitude of [his]

---

7. To use Barbara Lewalski's phrase, Jesus represents a "Kingship over the Self" (*Milton's Brief Epic* 219-55).

redeem'd / Shall enter Heav'n long absent" (3:260-61).[8] But the "Paradise Regained" of the later poem is the inner one. Jesus is a pattern for Man's resistance to temptation, his life an inspiration that will rearm the race spiritually. Thus when he defeats Satan yet a second time, he must do so armed with only such resources as will be available to human beings in future encounters with evil, the confidence in God's love and faith in his kingdom to come. This earlier victory in the wilderness, where Jesus lays "down the rudiments / Of his great warfare" makes the triumph of the Resurrection possible; and it is as a man that he wins.

Samson Agonistes

In the figure of Samson Milton's readers encounter, finally, a fallen being, not a celestial spirit responding to the word of God with unhesitating obedience, or a spotless human, or an incarnate god impervious to the wiles of Satan, but a sinful man beset by all the sad consequences of his state, subject to anger, obsession, and remorse, one who, however, despite his frailties strives to serve his God. And we catch a glimpse of fallen nations as well, whose conflicts reflect the clash of metaphysical realms and the struggle within the human heart. Politics is built into *Samson Agonistes* from its opening lines when the chief figure appears, not only a captive, but a slave, at the lowest rung of the civic ladder.

The political imagery of *Samson Agonistes* defines the role Mankind plays in the cosmic struggle between good and evil, portrayed in the drama as a contest between God and Dagon. Metaphysics, however, enters little into the action of the work; it is limited indeed to a single instance, Samson's notice of the "rousing motions" that "dispose to something extraordinary" his thoughts.[9] Recent commentary would even deny that event a supernatural origin, attributing those motions not to God but to Samson's essential brutality and deep desire to be revenged upon his enemies.[10] For

---

8. Shawcross cites early critics who found the poem incomplete because it "did not accomplish the regaining of Paradise, for this would occur only with the Crucifixion" (*"Paradise Regained"* 133).

9. Two other instances, the angel's annunciation to Samson's parents (23-29, 1431-35) and his marriage to the woman of Timna that "motioned was of God" (222), are mentioned in retrospect.

10. Joseph Wittreich, in *Interpreting "Samson Agonistes,"* contends that Samson kills "of

reasons that will become apparent, the present study proceeds on the more convincing premise that Samson, although he is by no means pacific in temperament and has little love for the Philistines, is moved by an inner voice from God, who finds in him, precisely because of his nature and his captivity, a fit instrument for his divine purpose.

Samson and the Israelites illustrate those qualities of fallen beings that prevent even the most righteous among them from joining effectively in the struggle, he because of "foul effeminacy," "shameful garrulity," and pride (412, 491, 532), and they through timidity and overriding self-concern, or in spiritual terms, a lack of faith. Samson's indictment of his countrymen's failure echoes many of the themes repeated time and again in Milton's prose and epics: A people are ruled by the government they deserve: "servile mind / Rewarded well with servile punishment" (412-13) and,

> what more oft in Nations grown corrupt,
> And by thir vices brought to servitude,
> Than to love Bondage more than Liberty,
> Bondage with ease than strenuous liberty.
> (268-71)[11]

Again, those unable to assert mastery over themselves are unfit to lead others: Samson is a Judge, a leader of his people, who it was promised would "*Israel* from *Philistian* yoke deliver"; yet because of his submission to Dalila he now lies languishing, "Eyeless in Gaza" (39-41).[12]

Milton further links the tragedy with *Paradise Lost* by characterizing Samson's sin as disobedience, thereby identifying him closely with Adam. Though there is no mention of a divine prohibition in the biblical account,[13] the drama repeats time and again that Samson was forbidden to reveal the source of his strength. He is under a divine injunction, a "Seal of silence," "a sacred trust," charged with "a holy secret"; and his sin was a violation of that trust: he "profan'd / The mystery of God giv'n [him] under pledge / Of vow" (49, 428, 496, 378-79; see also 201, 1001).

---

his own accord" (1643); it is "an act never coming from God" (355). Wittreich bases his argument on this single phrase, Samson's remark to the assembled Philistine lords after he has performed according to their commands, contending that the impulse for his destruction of the temple has a personal rather than a divine origin. It is a weak reed, indeed, upon which to lean a case against divine direction, missing entirely the irony of the allusion.

11. Cf., e.g., *Paradise Lost* 11:797-804.

12. Cf., e.g., *Paradise Regained* 2:464-72.

13. Judges 13-16.

We do not see much of governments in *Samson Agonistes* but we hear a great deal about them. The play begins and ends with one nation enslaved to another, and in its middle we discover why the captive people still "serve." Samson complains of his betrayal by "*Israel's* Governors, and Heads of Tribes" (242), who surrendered him bound to the Philistines; and he recalls his feats that day, breaking his bonds and slaying "the choicest youth" of their oppressor "with a trivial weapon." Had the men of Judah joined him in the battle at the time, he chides the Chorus, they would have "lorded over them whom now they serve" (263-67); but they had become so timid and accustomed to their "servitude" (269) that they were reluctant to seize the opportunity.

Later events bear out his evaluation of his countrymen, for their response to his final act is far from militant, confirming what may be called the slave mentality of the tribes of Israel and their leaders at this juncture in their history. On hearing the sound of the temple crumbling, they cower in fear, "Best keep together here, lest, running hither, / We unawares run into danger's mouth" (1521-22); and on hearing of the destruction of their oppressors, they are content simply to philosophize that God works in strange ways. Milton leaves open the consequences of Samson's deed, that is, whether the Israelites seize the opportunity to liberate their nation, per-haps because it would detract from the dramatic impact of his sacri-fice, and because it is somewhat beside the point.[14] The inclusion of subsequent history would transgress the strict limits of Aristotelean unity of action, to which Milton declared himself bound.[15] More to the point, the destruction of the temple is not a crucial event in the long his-tory of Israel's cycle of enslavement and liberation from a sequence of oppressors. It is, however, important in the continuing conflict between the

14. It has been observed that Samson's sacrifice failed to free the Israelites (most recently by Laura Knoppers, *Historicizing Milton,* 61). The Book of Judges, however, has nothing to say on the matter, stating only that they were "delivered into the hands of the Philistines forty years" (13:1) and that Samson judged for twenty (16:31). The chapters following record the story of Micah, in which it is stated only that "In those days there was no king in Israel, but every man did that which was right in his own eyes" (17:6, repeated in 21:25). Joseph Wittreich, who finds Samson wanting in most respects, considers his death fruitless (*Interpreting "Samson Agonistes"* 97-99). Wittreich's contention that Samson was "the last of the judges, the judge also who made kingship necessary" (103) must be questioned in the light of 1 Samuel 8: 1-6. Samuel appointed his sons judges and it was their corruption that prompted the elders to demand "a king to judge us."

15. In Milton's introduction to the work he cautions that in a tragedy "it suffices if the whole Drama be found not produc't beyond the fifth Act." In like manner at the end of *Oedipus Rex,* the blind king is led off the stage, his fate undecided.

Almighty and his innumerable imitators, in this case " 'Twixt God and *Dagon*" (462).

Of the Philistine rulers we see little. If Harapha is representative, they may be assumed arrogant masters and cowardly braggarts; and their treatment of Samson seems excessively cruel, though perhaps not by the standards of the time. On the other hand, the Public Officer seems a reasonable man, and Manoa confides hopefully that some Philistine lords are favorably disposed to release his son, since they feel he poses no further threat (481-86). Their chief fault seems to be their worship of the wrong god, though, as Milton reminds us, that in itself can be the cause of corruption and decline. Unlike the sober Israelites, the Philistines honor Dagon with feasts and games, wine and debauchery, customs which their god demands of them and which lead to their destruction. As Samson observes, "Lords are Lordliest in thir wine; / ... / No less the people on thir Holy-days / Impetuous, insolent, unquenchable" (1418-22).

To achieve his destiny, Samson has to set aside some of his most valued allegiances. The drama incarnates issues that could be addressed only in the abstract in the epics: the relative value of the scale of obligations within the body politic, those to the individual, family, nation, and God. The responsibility of the individual is a matter Milton broaches frequently in his political tracts, though for the most part from a different perspective, a subject's release from civic obligation when ruled by a government grown corrupt, oppressive, and unlawful.

Manoa values the family over the individual; he is prepared to sacrifice himself, to surrender all his "Patrimony" and live the poorest of [his] Tribe," if necessary, to ransom his son (1476-84). Dalila places her nation above family. There is no evidence in the drama that the Philistine government has grown oppressive to its own people, hence her allegiance to it is not entirely unjustified:

> the Magistrates
> And Princes of my country came in person,
> Solicited, commanded, threat'n'd, urg'd,
> Adjur'd by all the bonds of civil Duty
> And of Religion,
>
> (850-54)

until she submits, persuaded in the end that "to the public good / Private respects must yield" (867-68). Samson argues that her marriage to him dissolves the obligation to her country. In forcing her to betray her husband, the Philistine "Magistrates / And Princes" violated "the law of nature, law of nations," he declares (888-90). Further, since they had enslaved the Israelites and since in marrying him she had become an Israelite, they were "Not therefore to be obey'd" (891-95). Lastly, Harapha places the obligation to himself above all other allegiances, concerned only that his knightly reputation would be tarnished were he to enter into combat with "A Man condemn'd, a Slave enroll'd" (1224).

Samson ultimately places his obligation to God above all other considerations, nation, family, and self. Prior to his final commitment, however, he declares himself loyal to the allegiances of this world. At what may be considered, in the Aristotelean paradigm, a moment of "peripeteia" in the drama, that is, his sensing of the "rousing motions," he undergoes a sharp reversal in his scale of values. As noted earlier, some modern scholars question whether those "motions" represent a divine imperative, finding it rather a surge of Samson's anger against his tormentors.[16] Several factors argue for the traditional reading. Admittedly, to attribute the impulse to a divine origin one must first acknowledge Milton's conviction that God *can* move the human spirit to act; but this would seem a reasonable interpretation of the poet's beliefs.[17] There is even precedent for it in the drama, Samson's assertion that his decision to marry the woman of Timna, which, he avows, "motioned was of God," and which he knew to be right "From intimate impulse" (221-23), a passage faithful to the biblical source.[18]

Further, these motions prompt him to do something repulsive to every fiber of his being, an act that he takes pains to rationalize to the Israelites before he leaves. The contrast between his statement of allegiances before and after the "motions" is striking. When asked to participate in the festival of Dagon, he rejects the order three times (1321, 1332, 1342), despite the veiled threat of retaliation. And yet he finally agrees! As he departs, he promises his countrymen that he will do "Nothing dishonorable, impure, unworthy / Our God, our Law, my Nation, or myself"; but surely he does violence to the latter three. By participating in the festivities he certainly

---

16. Wittreich insists that Samson is motivated solely by "the spirit of revenge" (*Interpreting "Samson Agonistes,"* 253, 256). As he puts it, "The same code of vengeance is shared by Samson and the Philistines" (231).

17. Cf., e.g., *Christian Doctrine* 6:638: "GOOD WORKS are those which WE DO WHEN THE SPIRIT OF GOD WORKS WITHIN US, THROUGH TRUE FAITH, TO GOD'S GLORY."

18. Judges 14:4: "it was of the LORD." The marriage to Dalila was not divinely directed, however; Samson simply "thought it lawful from my former act" (231).

violates the Law, which he had just moments before declared "forbids at thir Religious Rites / My presence" (1320-21). To display his strength "in a place abominable," he protests, would be "prostituting holy things to Idols," a thing "vile, contemptible, ridiculous . . . execrably unclean, [and] profane" (1358-63). Indeed, it is the possibility of sacrilege that makes him most uneasy; before leaving he assures his countrymen three times that he will do nothing "that may dishonor / Our Law" (1385-86, 1409, 1425), perhaps sensing that he might have to.

Further, Samson demeans his nation by submitting to the will of its captors. He who had only just defied the "*Philistian* Lords," declaring that their "Commands are no constraints" (1371-72), now meekly admits that "Masters' commands come with a power resistless / To such as owe them absolute obedience" (1405-6). As for "myself," he agrees to suffer the humiliation of performing circus tricks before a heathen congregation on the feast day of their false god, an act he had denounced as "The worst of all indignities" (1341). And, of course, in taking his own life he does the ultimate violence to self. He obeys the "rousing motions" without thought and with no plan, there being no way the blind Samson could have known of the significance of the temple pillars, even as he stood between them. Trusting God, he knows only that he will do something, but has no idea what (1388-89, 1426). Samson's allegiance is to the Almighty alone, that loyalty overshadowing all other obligations; and he obeys the divine command, doing violence to all temporal levels of the body politic, depriving his nation of a leader, his family of a son, and himself of life.

Where does the obligation lie, and which act is a betrayal? In defending the English Revolution, Milton found it necessary to redefine the status of a rebel. Since the king, he argued, had overstepped the limits of his constitutional powers, he was the true enemy of the state, and the republicans the real defenders of the ancient liberties of the people; hence, the king was the rebel, his opponents the guardians of traditional freedom. When in 1649-50 Prince Rupert commanded a royalist fleet that preyed on English shipping in nearby waters (*MG* 43-46), Milton prepared a number of letters condemning their depredations, labeling Rupert and his followers, "Pyrates and Revolters (*defectores*)" (W6, P7; W158, P18). Thus, those who fought to put down a revolt become in turn, by a shift of history, the "Revolters" themselves. Of course, in *Samson Agonistes,* none of these questions are resolved satisfactorily. It is a drama, one in which acceptance or rejection of a political position depends largely on a personal response to the character articulating it. If one is sympathetic with Dalila, her arguments have a certain convincing force.[19] If one is sympathetic with Harapha – well, that must give one pause.[20] Milton, like any great dramatist, strives to give arguments of weight to both sides, much as he does to Satan and Abdiel in *Paradise Lost.*

In the end, all of Samson's violations of temporal obligations are justified by his final act, the destruction of the "Lords, Ladies, Captains, Counsellors, [and] Priests" of his nation's idolatrous oppressors (1653), and the demonstration that the God of Israel is more powerful than the Philistine Dagon, or any like him. This is Samson's destined end, and he is ennobled by his obedience to God: "he heroicly hath finish'd / A life Heroic" (1710-11). Joan Bennett's lucid and scholarly discussion of Milton's antinomian sentiments as they appear in *Samson Agonistes* removes the need to discuss the matter further here.[21] Nor need I rehearse my arguments elsewhere that Samson responds to the word of God with an obedience as absolute as that demonstrated by Michael in battle on the plains of Heaven or Gabriel at the gates of Eden, parallels which confirm that Mankind may participate, as the spirits do, in the war under way (*CC* 245-48). Like them, Samson through perfect obedience finds perfect freedom and is able to act. *Samson Agonistes* confirms Milton's conviction that the human race, for all the frailties of its fallen state, need not be mere slaves of Satan, but in obedience to the word of the Almighty may take part in the cosmic conflict between good and evil, in Samson's case "'Twixt God and *Dagon*" (462).

It is difficult to ignore the autobiographical echoes in the work.[22] Milton, like Samson, was betrayed by his first wife, who deserted him to rejoin her royalist family in Oxford and returned years later to beg forgiveness. The poet was blind and, as a renowned defender of the English Republic, imprisoned briefly after the Restoration while Parliament debated whether he would live or not. The English people, like the Israelites, rejected his

19. John Ulreich proposes a Dalila who "is sincere in her profession of loving concern for Samson"; she is a woman "therefore more deserving of compassion than condemnation" ("Incident to All Our Sex" 186). Empson finds her "a deeply wronged wife" (*Milton's God* 211).

20. Don Cameron Allen, for one, is persuaded that Harapha's first speech at least is "that of a genuinely valorous man" who speaks "honestly and generously" (*The Harmonious Vision* 91-92).

21. Bennett, *Reviving Liberty,* 117-60.

22. The autobiographical analogy raises the question of dating the work, some scholars arguing for composition as early as the 1640s. Despite some cogent elements of their argument, I accept the traditional date of composition as sometime in the 1660s. Parker surveys opinion in "The Date of *Samson Agonistes* Again." See also Radzinowicz, *Toward "Samson Agonistes,"* 387-407.

efforts and submitted to the rule of royalists who enslaved them, as Milton saw it, by imposing an oppressive and idolatrous court on the nation, one given to riotous feasts, corruption, cruelty, and decadence.[23] There are differences, of course. There is no evidence that Milton attributed his imprisonment and subsequent silencing to any weakness of his own; and he certainly never blamed his blindness on himself, declaring, rather, that he had lost his sight "overplied / In liberty's defense" (Sonnet 22). Further, he accepted Mary Powell when she appeared again, rather than returning her to her people, and he did not hold her responsible for his later blindness and servitude.

To catalog the similarities and differences thus illustrates an artistic imagination shaping material to its own ends. Milton, as we have seen, alters, omits, and adds to elements of his sources to meet the needs of his art, casting epic tradition and scriptural accounts into shapes that suit his poetic purposes. In *Samson Agonistes* he omits mention of the burning foxtails, the fate of the woman of Timna, and the subsequent slaughter,[24] perhaps because they duplicate accounts of betrayal and physical prowess portrayed elsewhere. He brings Manoa to life,[25] makes Dalila wife to Samson, and raises the secret of his strength to the sanctity of a sacred vow, in order, as has been suggested, to dramatize the imperatives of the human condition and illustrate the relative merit of an individual's obligation to family, state, and God. In similar manner he draws on his own life experiences as a source for his art, altering events and shaping historical figures, not to pass judgment on them, but to enrich his lines. Dalila is not Mary Powell. Samson rejects his wife; but Milton restored his to her place in his home. Certainly Milton called on the memory of his ten-year marriage, but to the purpose of dramatizing the biblical figure, not to deliver a farewell blast at his long-dead wife. Samson is not Milton, but who can fail to hear in the cries of the enslaved Nazarite the voice of the blind poet, lamenting the loss of his eyes, "O dark, dark, dark, amid the blaze of noon" (80).

The poet's trials and triumphs resonate in the lines, as do his sorrows; but it should not be concluded, therefore, that *Samson Agonistes* represents a judgment on his life, any more than Satan is a condemnation of Charles I, or Oliver Cromwell, or the Israelites a denunciation of the English people for their backsliding. Milton's experience surely informed his art but he shaped

---

23. Joan Bennett notes the similarity between a Samson abandoned by the Israelites and a Milton by the English people ("A Reading of *Samson Agonistes*" 228).

24. Judges 14:20–15:8.

25. Samson is interred "in the buryingplace of Manoah his father" (Judges 16:31).

it to a larger purpose, the spectacle of Mankind entering the lists in the struggle between good and evil. And he drew on all the resources at his disposal, including his own most intimate afflictions, to create a vivid image of one man who, thinking himself denied such service, found a way in the end to overcome his own weaknesses so that he could strike a blow for his God.

In the eyes of the Chorus and poor Manoa, Samson's sacrifice is justified by the destruction of the Philistine nobility; but both prove unreliable judges of motives and events in the drama. They may at the end be satisfied, calm of mind and all their passion spent; but the reader will recognize that the ultimate justification for Samson's extraordinary act lies in his perform-ance of it in obedience to the will of God, which, as we have seen, is the political equivalent of the eternal love between the Almighty and his creation.

Readers at times hear in Jesus' rejection of the kingdoms and dismissal of classical learning, and in Samson's despair, the voice of a disillusioned old man turning his back on the world, denying the value of his years of service to the English Republic, indeed of all political action, and in disappointment at the failure of the Revolution withdrawing into a life of reclusive quietism.[26] And, indeed, if one is listening for such a voice, it can be heard in these later works of the aging poet. It would not have been an unusual response for one subject to his fate, blind, imprisoned, cut off from public life, he who had been the trumpet of the Revolution now silenced. But however vehemently Milton's Jesus and Samson reject the things of this world, in the end they answer the call to act in it. And thus it was with the poet himself, who, though surely valuing the inner life, remained to his last days convinced that individual liberty depended on a willingness to bear the burden of public service.[27] Milton was ever the advocate of action in this world, from the

26. E.M.W. Tillyard, for example, finds Christ's rejection of the kingdoms a "bitter confes-sion from Milton that at last he understood the futility of his own share in the defense of the Parliamentary cause" (*Milton* 505-6). More recently, Arnold Stein hears a Milton declaring "the business of the world bankrupt" (*Heroic Knowledge* 131); and Hugh Richmond reads *Paradise Lost* as "the most comprehensive, vivid, and memorable discussion of causes, conditions, and consequences of failure that has ever been written" (*The Christian Revolutionary* 140).

27. Those of this mind include Merritt Y. Hughes who takes exception to readers who see in the Christ of *Paradise Regained* "the self-portrait of a defeated old man," and in his *contemptus mundi* a reflection of Milton's own disappointment with the English Revolution ("The Christ of *Paradise Regained* and the Renaissance Heroic Tradition" 254-55). Hughes is especially short with Tillyard. More recently, Christopher Hill has rejected any such image of the poet in either *Paradise Regained* or *Samson Agonistes:* "There is no evidence that Milton ever adopted the post-1661 Quaker position of pacifism and abstention from politics" (*The*

time when he dismissed the "cloistered virtue" that shuns "the dust and heat" of the race; and although those who "stand and wait" are as blessed as any other, it was his firm conviction that those who are called to "serve" must answer the summons and enter the arena.

Those who detect that note of denial in Milton's lines interpret it as a judgment on his times, the poet uttering a plague on both houses, royalist and republican; but the message of his art goes well beyond such momentary concerns. He envisioned an Almighty who orders things so that Man can act to save his soul, whatever the temporal consequences; and though he surely drew on the experience of defeat to enrich his lines, he was not simply airing his disappointment at the failure of his hopes. Success or failure in the public sphere is beside the point; it makes no difference whether one sets up this or that government, amasses a fortune, or converts a nation. What matters is the willingness to follow the dictates of right reason, which Milton considered a spark of divinity possessed by every human being, a particle of the infinite mind of God, with whose guidance each could direct a life in accordance with his will. In doing so, one may fail in the world; that path does not always lead to success and often results in suffering and death. Indeed, failure can be as salutary as success in a design that requires that each be "Tri'd in sharp tribulation, and refin'd / By Faith and faithful works" (11:63-64) in order to be worthy of divine approval and numbered among the just on the Final Day. This is the message of Job among the ashes, Samson at the wheel, and Jesus in the desert, or so it surely seemed to Milton in his prison.

Adam and Eve and the entire race of Man are called to play a part in the cosmic conflict between good and evil, one first joined well before their making in a distant, almost unimaginable place, to then spread until it engulfed their peaceful arbors and innocent lives, a conflict, moreover, upon whose outcome their success or failure will not have the slightest influence. But they must engage God's enemies, as Jesus does the Devil in the desert

---

Experience of Defeat 315). Perez Zagorin confirms that the Restoration "did not cause him to subside into an apolitical quietism or indifference" (*Milton, Aristocrat and Rebel* 132). John T. Shawcross confirms that Milton remained to the end of his days convinced that individual liberty depended on a willingness to undertake "employment in public service" (*Paradise Regained* 126). Shawcross finds in *Samson Agonistes* Milton's conviction "that the way to true peace and ease and 'the blissful seat' is to act in this world, certainly not simply await and certainly not simply lead the cloistered life" (120). Peter Lindenbaum finds in the activities of Adam and Eve in the Garden evidence of "Milton's favouring of the active life over the contemplative" ("John Milton and the Republican Mode of Literary Production" 105). See also Radzinowicz, *Toward "Samson Agonistes,"* 116, and *CC* 236-37.

and Samson the worshipers of Dagon, for this is the design of a loving God, "whom to love is to obey" (8:634). This is Milton's "higher argument," enriched surely by the experience of defeat, but a vision surpassing any momentary disappointment at the failure of the English Revolution.

In the closing lines of each of Milton's final great works, the last we see of God's servants is their departure to embark upon their destined role in that conflict, Adam and Eve, "with wand'ring steps and slow" (12:648) to conceive the human race in whose breasts the struggle will be played out, Jesus returning "Home to his Mother's house" (4:639) to found a kingdom "that shall dash to pieces / All monarchies" of the Earth, and Samson striding off to "begin *Israel's* Deliverance" in a display of the miraculous power of the Almighty in Man. The political imagery defines Mankind's role in the spiritual struggle between good and evil in terms all too familiar to Milton's readers, who labor daily under the weight of demands imposed by the governing on the governed, terms that arose readily in the imagination of the poet, who drew on a decade of public service to shape his vision of the spiritual forces contending for the human soul as vast powers struggling for supremacy within a "Divided Empire."

Works Cited

Abbott, Wilbur Cortez, ed. *The Writings and Speeches of Oliver Cromwell.* 4 vols. Cambridge: Harvard University Press, 1937-47.

Adamson, J. H. "The Creation." In *Bright Essence: Studies in Milton's Theology,* 81-102. Salt Lake City: University of Utah Press, 1973.

———. "Milton's 'Arianism.' " In *Bright Essence: Studies in Milton's Theology,* 53-62. Salt Lake City: University of Utah Press, 1973.

Addison, Joseph. *The Spectator,* no. 315 (1 March 1712). Published in *Notes Upon the Twelve Books of "Paradise Lost."* London, 1719.

Allen, Don C. *The Harmonious Vision: Studies in Milton's Poetry.* Baltimore: Johns Hopkins University Press, 1954.

Barker, Arthur. *Milton and the Puritan Dilemma, 1641-1660.* Toronto: University of Toronto Press, 1942.

Bauman, Michael. *A Scriptual Index to John Milton's "De doctrina christiana."* Binghamton, N.Y.: Medieval and Renaissance Texts and Studies, 1989.

Bennett, Joan S. "A Reading of *Samson Agonistes.*" In *The Cambridge Companion to Milton,* ed. Dennis Danielson, 225-41. Cambridge: Cambridge University Press, 1989.

———. *Reviving Liberty: Radical Christian Humanism in Milton's Great Poems.* Cambridge: Harvard University Press, 1989.

Blake, William. *The Poetry and Prose of William Blake,* ed. David V. Erdman. Garden City, N.Y.: Doubleday, 1965.

Buhler, Stephen M. "Kingly States: The Politics of *Paradise Lost.*" In *Milton Studies XXVIII,* ed. James D. Simmons, 49-69. Pittsburgh: Pittsburgh University Press, 1992.

Campbell, Gordon. "The Authorship of *De Doctrina Christiana.*" *Milton Quarterly* 26 (1992): 129-30.

Capp, Bernard. "The Political Dimension of Apocalyptic Thought." In *The Apocalypse in English Renaissance Thought and Literature: Patterns, Antecedents, and Repercussions,* ed. C. A. Patrides and Joseph Wittreich, 93-104. Manchester: Manchester University Press, 1984.

Cohen, Kitty. "Milton's God in Council and War." In *Milton Studies III,* ed. James D. Simmons, 159-84. Pittsburgh: Pittsburgh University Press, 1971.

Corns, Thomas N. *Uncloistered Virtue: English Political Literature.* Oxford: Clarendon Press, 1992.

Danielson, Dennis Richard. *Milton's Good God: A Study in Literary Theodicy.* Cambridge: Cambridge University Press, 1982.

Dante. *The Divine Comedy of Dante Alighieri.* Trans. John D. Sinclair. 3 vols. New York: Oxford University Press, 1961.

Davies, Stevie. *Images of Kingship in "Paradise Lost": Milton's Politics and Christian Liberty.* Columbia: University of Missouri Press, 1983.

Dobbins, Austin C. *Milton and the Book of Revelation: The Heavenly Cycle.* University: University of Alabama Press, 1975.

Empson, William. *Milton's God.* Norfolk, Conn.: New Directions, 1961.

Erlanger, Philipe. *Louis XIV,* trans. Stephen Cox. New York: Praeger, 1970.

Fallon, Robert Thomas. *Captain or Colonel: The Soldier in Milton's Life and Art.* Columbia: University of Missouri Press, 1984.

——. *Milton in Government.* University Park: Pennsylvania State University Press, 1993.

Firth, Charles Harding. *The Last Years of the Protectorate, 1656-1658.* 2 vols. 1909. Reprint, New York: Russell and Russell, 1964.

Fish, Stanley. *Surprised by Sin: The Reader in "Paradise Lost."* New York: St. Martin's Press, 1967.

Fixler, Michael. "The Apocalypse within *Paradise Lost.*" In *New Essays on "Paradise Lost,"* ed. Thomas Kranidas, ch. 7. Berkeley and Los Angeles: University of California Press, 1969.

——. *Milton and the Kingdoms of God.* London: Faber and Faber, 1964.

Frank, Joseph. *Cromwell's Press Agent: A Critical Biography of Marchamont Nedham, 1620-1678.* Lanham, Md.: University Press of America, 1980.

Fraser, Antonia. *Cromwell, the Lord Protector.* New York: Knopf, 1974.

——. *Royal Charles: Charles II and the Restoration.* New York: Knopf, 1979.

Frye, Roland M. *Milton's Imagery and the Visual Arts: Iconographic Tradition in the Epic Poems.* Princeton: Princeton University Press, 1978.

Gardiner, Samuel Rawson. *The Constitutional Documents of the Puritan Revolution, 1625-1660.* Third edition, revised. Oxford: Clarendon Press, 1962.

Gaxotte, Pierre. *The Age of Louis XIV.* New York: Macmillan, 1970.

Goldberg, Jonathan. "Dating Milton." In *Soliciting Interpretation: Literary Theory and Seventeenth-Century Poetry,* ed. Elizabeth D. Harvey and Katharine E. Maus, 199-222. Chicago: University of Chicago Press, 1990.

Hardin, Richard F. *Civil Idolatry: Desacralizing and Monarchy in Spenser, Shakespeare, and Milton.* Newark: University of Delaware Press, 1992.

Hazlitt, William. "On Shakspeare and Milton." In *Lectures on English Poets: The Spirit of the Age,* ed. Ernest Rhys, 44-67. Reprint, New York: Dutton, 1934.

Helgerson, Richard. *Self-Crowned Laureates: Spenser, Jonson, Milton, and the Literary System.* Berkeley and Los Angeles: University of California Press, 1983.

Hill, Christopher. *The Experience of Defeat: Milton and Some Contemporaries.* New York: Viking, 1984.

———. *Milton and the English Revolution.* New York: Viking, 1977.

———. "Professor William B. Hunter, Bishop Burgess, and John Milton." *Studies in English Literature* 34 (Winter 1994): 165-93.

Hughes, Merritt Y. "The Christ of *Paradise Regained* and the Renaissance Heroic Tradition." *Studies in Philology* 35 (1938): 257-77.

———. *John Milton, Complete Poems and Major Prose.* New York: Odyssey, 1957.

Hunter, William B. "Animadversions upon the Remonstrants' Defenses Against Burgess and Hunter." *Studies in English Literature* 34 (Winter 1994): 195-203.

———. "Milton's Arianism Reconsidered." In *Bright Essence: Studies in Milton's Theology,* 29-52. Salt Lake City: University of Utah Press, 1973.

———. "The Provenance of the *Christian Doctrine.*" *Studies in English Literature* 32 (1992): 129-66.

———. "The Provenance of the *Christian Doctrine:* Addenda from the Bishop of Salisbury." *Studies in English Literature* 33 (1993): 191-207.

Hunter, William B., and Stevie Davies. "Milton's Urania: 'The Meaning, Not the Name I Call.'" In *The Descent of Urania: Studies in Milton, 1946-1988,* ed. William B. Hunter. Lewisburg, Pa.: Bucknell University Press, 1989.

Kelley, Maurice. "The Provenance of John Milton's *Christian Doctrine:* A Reply to William B. Hunter." *Studies in English Literature* 34 (Winter 1994): 153-63.

———. *This Great Argument: A Study of Milton's "De Doctrina Christiana" as a Gloss upon "Paradise Lost."* Gloucester, Mass.: Peter Smith, 1962.

Kleinman, Ruth. *Anne of Austria, Queen of France.* Columbus: Ohio State University Press, 1985.

Knoppers, Laura Lunger. *Historicizing Milton: Spectacle, Power, and Poetry in Restoration England.* Athens: University of Georgia Press, 1994.

Labriola, Albert C. "'Thy Humiliation Shall Exalt': The Christology of Paradise Lost." In *Milton Studies XV,* ed. James D. Simmons, 29-42. Pittsburgh: Pittsburgh University Press, 1981.

Landry, Marcia. "'Bounds Prescrib'd': Milton's Satan and the Politics of Deviance." In *Milton Studies XIV,* ed. James D. Simmons, 117-34. Pittsburgh: Pittsburgh University Press, 1980.

Lewalski, Barbara Kiefer. *Milton's Brief Epic: The Genre, Meaning, and Art of "Paradise Regained."* Providence: Brown University Press, 1966.

———. *"Paradise Lost" and the Rhetoric of Literary Forms.* Princeton: Princeton University Press, 1985.

Lewis, C. S. *Preface to "Paradise Lost."* Oxford: Oxford University Press, 1942.

Lewis, W. H. *The Splendid Century.* New York: Sloane, 1953.

Liljegren, S. B. *Studies in Milton.* Lund, Sweden: Gleerup, 1918.

Lindenbaum, Peter. "John Milton and the Republican Mode of Literary Production." In *Patronage, Politics, and Literary Traditions in England, 1558-1658,* ed. Cedric C. Brown, 93-108. Revised. Detroit: Wayne State University Press, 1993.

Loewenstein, David. *Milton and the Drama of History: Historical Vision, Iconoclasm, and the Literary Imagination.* Cambridge: Cambridge University Press, 1990.

———. "Milton and the Poetics of Defense." In *Politics, Poetics, and Hermeneutics in Milton's Prose,* ed. David Loewenstein and James Grantham Turner, 171-92. Cambridge: Cambridge University Press, 1990.

Low, Anthony. "Milton's God: Authority in *Paradise Lost.*" In *Milton Studies IV,* ed. James D. Simmons, 19-38. Pittsburgh: Pittsburgh University Press, 1981.

Marcus, Leah Sinanoglou. "The Earl of Bridgewater's Legal Life." *Milton Quarterly* 21 (December 1987): 13-23.

———. "Milton as Historical Subject: Milton Banquet Address, Chicago, 1990." *Milton Quarterly* 25 (October 1991): 120-27.

Martz, Louis L. "Eden Restored: Milton's Prophetic Voice." In *Of Poetry and Politics: New Essays on Milton and His World,* ed. Paul G. Stanwood, 1-16. Binghamton, N.Y.: Medieval and Renaissance Texts and Studies, 1994.

Masson, David. *The Life of John Milton.* 6 vols. 1881. Reprint, Gloucester, Mass.: Peter Smith, 1965.

McColley, Diane. *A Gust for Paradise: Milton's Eden and the Visual Arts.* Urbana: University of Illinois Press, 1993.

———. *Milton's Eve.* Urbana: University of Illinois Press, 1983.

Miller, Leo. *John Milton's Writings in the Anglo-Dutch Negotiations, 1651-1654.* Pittsburgh: Duquesne University Press, 1992.

Milton, John. *Complete Prose Works of John Milton.* 8 vols. Ed. Don M. Wolfe et al. New Haven: Yale University Press, 1953-83.

———. *Milton's "Paradise Lost": with Fifty Illustrations by Gustave Doré.* New York: J.B. Allen, 1884.

———. *The Works of John Milton.* 18 vols. Ed. Frank Allen Patterson et al. New York: Columbia University Press, 1931-38.

Parker, William Riley. "The Date of *Samson Agonistes* Again." In *Calm of Mind,* ed. Joseph A. Wittreich, 163-74. Cleveland: Case Western Reserve University Press, 1971.

———. *Milton, A Biography.* Oxford: Clarendon Press, 1968.

Patrides, C. A. "Milton and Arianism." In *Bright Essence: Studies in Milton's Theology,* 63-70. Salt Lake City: University of Utah Press, 1973.

———. "Milton on the Trinity: The Use of Antecedents." In *Bright Essence: Studies in Milton's Theology,* 3-14. Salt Lake City: University of Utah Press, 1973.

———. "Something Like Prophetic Strain: Apocalyptic Configuration in Milton." In *The Apocalypse in English Renaissance Thought and Literature: Patterns, Antecedents, and Repercussions,* ed. C. A. Patrides and Joseph Wittreich, 207-39. Manchester: Manchester University Press, 1984.

Phelps-Morand, Paul. *The Effects of His Political Life on John Milton.* Paris, 1939.

Quint, David. *Epic and Empire: Politics and Generic Form from Virgil to Milton.* Princeton: Princeton University Press, 1993.

Radzinowicz, Mary Ann. "How Milton Read the Bible: The Case of *Paradise Regained.*" In *The Cambridge Companion to Milton,* ed. Dennis Danielson, 207-23. Cambridge: Cambridge University Press, 1989.

———. *Milton's Epics and the Book of Psalms.* Princeton: Princeton University Press, 1989.

———. *Toward "Samson Agonistes": The Growth of Milton's Mind.* Princeton: Princeton University Press, 1978.

Revard, Stella P. *The War in Heaven: "Paradise Lost" and the Tradition of Satan's Rebellion.* Ithaca: Cornell University Press, 1980.

Richmond, Hugh H. *The Christian Revolutionary: John Milton.* Berkeley and Los Angeles: University of California Press, 1974.

Ross, Malcolm MacKenzie. *Milton's Royalism: A Study of the Conflict of Symbol and Idea in the Poems.* Ithaca: Cornell University Press, 1943.

Rumrich, John Peter. *Matter of Glory: A New Preface to "Paradise Lost."* Pittsburgh: University of Pittsburgh Press, 1987.

Schwartz, Regina M. *Remembering and Repeating: Biblical Creation in "Paradise Lost."* Cambridge: Cambridge University Press, 1988.

Shawcross, John T. *"Paradise Regained": Worthy T'Have Not Remain'd So Long Unsung.* Pittsburgh: Duquesne University Press, 1988.

Small, Jesse G. "Author-Functions and the Interpretation of Eve in *Paradise Lost.*" *Milton Quarterly* 26 (October 1992): 63-64.

Spencer, T.J.B. "*Paradise Lost:* The Anti-Epic." In *Approaches to "Paradise Lost,"* ed. C. A. Patrides. London: Edward Arnold, 1968.

Stavely, Keith W. *The Politics of Milton's Prose Style.* New Haven: Yale University Press, 1975.

Steadman, John. *Milton and the Renaissance Hero.* Oxford: Clarendon Press, 1967.

Stein, Arnold. *Answerable Style: Essays on "Paradise Lost."* Minneapolis: University of Minnesota Press, 1953.

———. *Heroic Knowledge: An Interpretation of "Paradise Regained" and "Samson Agonistes."* Hamden, Conn.: Archon Books, 1965.

Swaim, Kathleen M. *Before and After the Fall: Contrasting Modes in "Paradise Lost."* Amherst: University of Massachusetts Press, 1986.

Tanner, John S. *Anxiety in Eden: A Kierkegaardian Reading of "Paradise Lost."* New York: Oxford University Press, 1992.

Tillyard, E.M.W. *Milton.* London: Chatto and Windus, 1930.

Turner, James Grantham. "The Poetics of Engagement." In *Politics, Poetics, and Hermeneutics in Milton's Prose,* ed. David Loewenstein and James Grantham Turner, 257-75. Cambridge: Cambridge University Press, 1990.

Ulreich, John C., Jr. " 'Incident to All our Sex': The Tragedy of Dalila." In *Milton and the Idea of Woman,* ed. Julia M. Walker, 185-210. Urbana: University of Illinois Press, 1988.

Van der Zee, Henri, and Barbara van der Zee. *William and Mary.* New York: Knopf, 1973.

Von Maltzahn, Nicholas. *Milton's "History of Britain": Republican Historiography in the English Revolution.* Oxford: Clarendon Press, 1991.

West, Robert H. *Milton and the Angels.* Athens: University of Georgia Press, 1955.

Wilding, Michael. "The Last of the Epics: The Rejection of the Heroic in *Paradise Lost* and *Hudibras.*" In *Restoration Literature: Critical Approaches,* ed. Harold Love. London: Methuen, 1972.

Williams, Charles. Introduction to *The English Poems of John Milton,* ed. H. C. Beeching. Oxford: Oxford University Press, 1940.

Wittreich, Joseph. *Feminist Milton.* Ithaca: Cornell University Press, 1987

——. *Interpreting "Samson Agonistes."* Princeton: Princeton University Press, 1986.

Wolfe, Don M. *Milton and the Puritan Revolution.* New York: Humanities Press, 1941.

Woodhouse, A.S.P. *The Heavenly Muse: A Preface to Milton,* ed. Hugh MacCallum. Toronto: University of Toronto Press, 1972.

Woods, Suzanne. "How Free Are Milton's Women." In *Milton and the Idea of Woman.* Ed. Julia M. Walker, 15–31. Chicago: University of Illinois Press, 1988.

Woolrych, Austin. "Debate: Dating Milton's *History of Britain.*" *The Historical Journal* 36 (1993): 929–43.

——. "Milton and Cromwell: 'A Short but Scandalous Night of Interruption.'" In *Achievements of the Left Hand, Essays on the Prose of John Milton,* ed. Michael Lieb and John T. Shawcross, 185–218. Amherst: University of Massachusetts Press, 1974.

Wooten, John. "The Metaphysics of Milton's Epic Burlesque Humor." In *Milton Studies XIII,* ed. James D. Simmons, 255–73. Pittsburgh: University of Pittsburgh Press, 1980.

Worden, Blair. "Milton's Republicanism and the Tyranny of Heaven." In *Machiavelli and Republicanism,* ed. Gisela Bock et al., 235–42. Cambridge: Cambridge University Press, 1990.

Zagorin, Perez. *Milton, Aristocrat and Rebel.* Rochester: D. S. Brewer, 1992.

Index

Abdiel, 27, 49, 94, 125n.4, 141, 175
  debate with Satan. *See* Satan
Abraham, 110
Adam and Eve, Chap. 5
  equality, 6, 9-10, 17, 98, 101, 106
  inequality, 12, 16, 104-6
  mutual love, 102-3
  separation scene, 10, 10n.11, 98-101,
    108-12
Addison, Joseph, 26
Aitzema, Leo ab, 37
Algiers, 4
Allen, Don Cameron, 175n.20
Almansor, 106
Anne, Queen (France), 5, 6, 7, 10, 12, 13
Apocalypse, the, Chap. 7
Aristotle, 171
Ascham, Anthony, 76
Augier, René, 8

Babylonian Captivity, 110
Barberini, Cardinal Francesco, 37
Barker, Arthur, xiiin.9
Batista Nani, 11n.12
Bauman, Michael, 93n.17
Beëlzebub, 66, 68, 72, 86, 95, 122, 128, 129,
    130
Belial, 63, 67, 69, 86, 163
Bennett, Joan, xvii, 20n.25, 33-34, 61n.16,
    62-63, 175, 176n.23
Bible, the. *See* Holy Bible, the
Blake, Admiral Robert, 73
Blake, William, 26n.1, 60
Bradshaw, John, 65
Bradshaw, Richard, 65, 76, 98, 132, 133, 166,
    167

Brandenburg, 75
Bremen, 4, 75, 77, 152
Buhler, Stephen, 46-47n.29, 49n.31, 62n.17
Butler, James A., xvii

Caesar, Julius, 106
Campbell, Gordon, xvn.13
Cantor, Georg, 30n.6
Capp, Bernard, 158-59n.9
Chaos, xi, xvi, 5, 6, 8, 11, 13n.15, 16, 18, 36,
    57, 69, 73, 75, 78, 80, 83, 84, 85, 88, 97,
    116, 129, 141
  bridge over, 78, 94-95, 130-31
Charlemagne, 106
Charles I (England), xiii, 2, 4, 23, 33, 61, 70,
    91-92, 111, 116, 126, 126nn.7 and 8,
    176
  and God, 20, 27
Charles II (England), 19, 23, 32, 64, 71, 87,
    91n.15, 111, 120, 126, 181
Charles V (Holy Roman Empire), 106
Charles X (Sweden), 32, 38, 75, 77, 87, 120,
    121, 126n.7, 134, 135, 144, 152, 166
Charles XII (Sweden), 126n.7
Christ
  and David's throne, 110, 163-64, 166
  and Last Judgment, 146
  as man, 163-65, 169
  as the Son, 162, 165, 166
  defeat of Satan, 148, 150, 164
  reign, 146-47
  Resurrection. *See* Resurrection
  second coming, 146-51
Christian Doctrine, xiv-xv, 13, 26, 29, 42, 43,
    44, 47, 52, 97, 137, 146, 150, 155, 158,
    164n.3, 181
  and *Paradise Lost. See Paradise Lost*

Christina, Queen (Sweden), 31-32
Cohen, Kitty, 27n.3
Commonwealth, structure, 4
Corns, Thomas, 70n.29
Council of State, vii, 35, 37, 64, 71, 116, 120, 137
Cromwell, Oliver
  and God, 27, 41
  and Protestant league, 87, 134
  and Satan. *See* Satan
  and Western Design. *See* Western Design
  in the Commonwealth, 64, 120
  in the Protectorate, 19, 27, 40-41, 77, 163
Cromwell, Richard, 127
Curland, Duke of, 167

Danielson, Dennis, 45n.26, 46n.28, 125n.5, 152n.6
Dante Alighieri, 14, 25, 89, 115
Danzig, 134
Davies, Stevie, 13, 33, 62, 69n.27
Denmark, 4, 32, 75, 120, 134
Divine love, 84, 87-96, 102, 114-17, 140, 151, 157-58, 177
  disobedience, 89, 92, 116, 148
  obedience, 91, 92, 140
Dobbins, Austin C., 145n.2
Doré, Gustave, 73
Dorislaus, Isaac, 76
Dunkirk, 39, 127, 130, 134n.15, 137n.18

Elizabeth I, 15, 134
Empson, William, 23n.29, 29n.4, 31n.7, 33, 56n.2, 58n.7, 60, 66, 122, 123n.3, 128, 155n.8, 175n.19
Erlanger, Philipe, 11n.12
experience and art, viii-ix, 18-24, 71, 176-77

Fairfax, General Sir Thomas, 3, 68
Fauconberg, Viscount Thomas, 39
Ferrara, 1
Fish, Stanley, 57n.4
Fixler, Michael, 145n.2, 159n.10
Fleming, Sir Oliver, 37
Florence, 1
Fogle, French, 3
France, Chap. 1, 120, 130
Frank, Joseph, 123n.2
Fraser, Antonia, 19n.21, 41n.17, 126n.7, 153n.7
Frederick III (Denmark), 32, 87, 134, 144
Frederick William (Brandenburg), 38, 77
Frye, Roland, 46n.27

Gabriel, 25, 27, 28, 29, 74, 76, 77, 84, 115, 164, 175

Geneva, 1
God
  and Adam and Eve, 11, 12, 113-14
  and Charles I, 20, 27
  and Cromwell, 27, 31
  and Satan, 96
  and the Son. *See* Milton: Arianism
  as All in All, 146-47, 155-59
  as king, 5, 20, 26, 31, 34-37, 53, 77, 89-90, 124
  creation *ex Deo,* 14, 35; differentiation and reintegration, 88-89, 155-59
  in *Paradise Regained,* 164
  omnipotence, 29, 30-31, 66, 127-28
  omnipresence, 29, 51-52, 67
  omniscience, 29, 58, 114, 125
Goldberg, Jonathan, 20n.26
good and evil
  as God and Dagon, 169, 172, 175
  as spiritual conflict, 119, 140-41, 161, 178-79
  similarities, 59, 78, 93-96
  war between, Chap. 6; and England vs. Spain, 130; and English Republic, 137; and France vs. Spain, 129; and modern, 130n.12; and Restoration, 137; and Resurrection. *See* Resurrection; and Western Design. *See* Western Design; outcome, 139-40, 144, 156-57
  war in Heaven, 30-31, 53, 119, 121, 125-26, 156
governing principle, 14-17, 84-85
  Chaos, 83, 103
  Earth: postlapsarian, 84, 103-4; prelapsarian, 84, 102
  Heaven. *See* Divine love
  Hell, 59, 83-87, 103
Gustavus Adolphus (Sweden), 126n.7

Hamburg, 4, 37, 75, 98, 137, 138
Hampton Court, 40
Hardin, Richard F., 10n.10, 35n.13, 36n.14, 60n.9, 85n.2
Hazlitt, William, 57
Helgerson, Richard, viii-ixn.4
Henrietta Marie, Queen (England), 19
Hill, Christopher, viii-ixn.4, xvn.13, 3, 3n.2, 20n.26, 28, 155, 177-78n.27
Holstein, 75, 137
Holy Bible, the
  Acts 1:9, 149
  1 Cor. 15:4, 149
  Eph. 4:8, 8, 10
  Gen. 3:16-19, 113n.19
  John 3:16, 92-93; 16:12, 149; 18:36, 164n.2, 166n.5

Judges 13-16, 170n.13; 13:1, 171n.14; 14:4,
    173n; 14:20-15:8, 176n; 16:31, 171n,
    176n.18; 17:6, 171n.14; 21:25, 171n.14
Luke 4:1-13, 164n.2; 24:6, 150n.5; 24:15,
    149
Mark 16:6, 150n.5; 16:19, 149
Matt., 149; 28:6, 150n.5
Psalms, 40
1 Sam. 8:1-16, 171n.14
Holy Spirit, x, 13-14, 17-18, 44, 88, 137-38,
    150
Holy Trinity, xvi, 11, 14, 19, 23, 44, 94
Honourable Artillery Company, 126
Hughes, Merritt Y., xvii, 94n.18, 177-78n.27
Hunter, William B., xvn.13, 13n.16, 43

Jacobus, Lee, xvii
Jamaica, 130
Jephson, William, 38, 75-77, 152
Job, 178
John IV (Portugal), 32

Kelley, Maurice, xvn.12, 42-43, 48n.30
Kerrigan, William, xviii
Kleinman, Ruth, 6, 7, 11
Knoppers, Laura, 21n.28, 29n.5, 87n.7,
    111n.16, 171n.14

Labriola, Albert C., 96n.21
Lambert, General John, 68, 86
Landry, Marcia, 58n.6
Last Judgment, 139-40
Lawrence, Henry, 65
Lewalski, Barbara K., xvn.13, 40, 61n.14,
    119n.1, 168n.7
Lewis, C. S., 58n.6
Lewis, W. H., 7n.5
Licensing Act, xiii
Lieb, Michael, xvii
Liljegren, S. B., xii
Lindenbaum, Peter, 177-78n.27
Loewenstein, David, viiin.2, xiiin.10, 20n.25
Louis XIII (France), 1, 91
Louis XIV (France), 5, 7, 11, 12, 19, 32, 35,
    39, 91n.15
Low, Anthony, 45n.25
Lübeck, 75

Machiavelli, xiii, 1, 80
Mammon, 63, 67, 68, 86, 115, 129
Manso, Giovanni Battista, 37
Marcus, Leah, viii-ixn.4
Marlowe, Christopher, 55
Martz, Louis L., 112
Mary II (England), 10n.10

Masson, David, 27n.2
Mazarin, Cardinal Jules, 5, 7, 10, 12, 39, 40,
    49, 68
McColley, Diane, 9, 9-10n.9, 90n.13, 100n.7,
    101, 105, 152n.6
Meadows, Philip, 77
Medici, the, 1
Mephistopheles, 56
Mercurius Britanicus, 123n.2
Michael
    as archangel, 15
    as diplomat, 12, 16, 99, 105-8, 114-15, 132,
        136-38, 147, 153-54
    as soldier, 12, 27, 46, 77, 122, 133, 134,
        140, 141, 175
Milan, 1
Miller, Leo, 37
Milton
    and Charles I, 23, 174, 123-25
    and Charles II, 19, 23, 77
    and Cromwell, 19, 23, 56, 79-80, 112
    and Mary Powell, 175-76
    and Restoration, xiii, 107, 111, 175-76
    and Samson, 175-76
    Arianism, 5, 8, 42-53, 88, 93, 117
    as Secretary for Foreign Languages: duties,
        vii, xii, 4-5, 7, 37-40, 75-77, 132; office,
        vii, 79; treaties, 4, 120
    on God, 26, 29-31, 43
    on governments, x-xi, 97, 102, 107-13, 174
    on kings, 20, 31-34, 41-42, 60, 91-92
    on marriage, 9-10, 107
    private life, 1-2, 120, 175-76
    quietism, 21, 56, 177-79
WORKS
    A Defence of the English People, 111, 124
    A Second Defence of the English People, 1,
        18, 32, 79, 92, 109, 112
    antiprelatical tracts, 123
    Areopagitica, xi, 2, 93
    Christian Doctrine. See Paradise Lost.
    Declaration of the Parliament of the Com-
        monwealth of England, 120
    Eikonoklastes, xiv, 20n.25, 21, 61, 123
    Nativity Ode, 136, 149
    Of Education, x, 2, 108
    Paradise Lost. See Paradise Lost
    Paradise Regained, 21, 106, 127, 136,
        161-69
    Samson Agonistes, 169-79
    Sonnet 17, 3
    Sonnet 19, 178
    The Art of Logic, xv
    The Character of the Long Parliament, 2
    The History of Britain, 2

The Passion, 149
The Readie and Easie Way, 19, 21, 29, 32, 41, 107, 108, 144
The Tenure of Kings and Magistrates, 123
Trinity Manuscript, 25
Upon the Circumcision, 149
Moloch, 66, 67, 69, 85, 86, 129
Monk, General George, 19
Montezuma, 106
Morland, Samuel, 133
Morrill, John, vii
Moscovy, Duke of, 132
Moses, 110

Naples, 1
Nedham, Marchamont, 123n.2
New Model Army, 3, 4, 40, 71, 130, 137
Nimrod, 109, 110
Noah, 110

Oedipus Rex, 171n.15
Oldenburg, 4, 32
Orange, House of, 32

Paradise Lost
    and *Christian Doctrine,* xiv-xvi, 29, 42-53, 92-93, 137, 146-47, 149-51, 154, 155
Parker, William Riley, viiin.1, 175n.22
Parliament, vii, 2, 4, 8, 49, 68, 71, 76, 123, 137, 175
Parthia, 162, 163, 166
Patrides, C. A., 50n.33, 158n.9
Penn, Admiral William, 130
Phelps-Morand, Paul, xii
Philip IV (Spain), 32, 73
Piedmont Massacre, 33-34, 87, 110, 133, 143
political imagery
    and Charles I, 123-25
    and Council of State, 63, 65
    and disobedience, 89, 91-92, 116, 140
    and Dunkirk, 137
    and French monarchy, 4-24
    and heirs: Charles II, 126; Louis XIV, 127; Sweden, 121
    and Parliament, 63-65, 70-71, 86
    and Piedmont Massacre. *See* Piedmont Massacre
    and Restoration, 107, 176n
    and wars, 138-39; England and Portugal, 73; England and Spain, 84, 134-35; England and United Netherlands, 116; English civil, 123; modern, 130n.12; France and Spain, 130; Sweden and Poland, 166; Western Design. *See* Western Design

criticism, viii-ix, xii-xiii, xvii, 18, 20-22, 53, 55-58, 60-62, 78n.32
Milton as Secretary for Foreign Languages. *See* Milton
Pope the, 1, 37, 87
Popham, Admiral Edward, 73
Portugal, 4, 32, 70, 76
Protectorate, structure, 4

Quint, David, 21, 56n.1, 58n.6, 61n.16, 77n.31, 78n.32

Radzinowicz, Mary Ann, 40, 165n.4, 175n.22, 177-78n.27
Raphael
    as archangel, 15
    as diplomat, 9, 11, 34, 98, 99, 103, 105, 114, 131-34, 147, 151-53
    as soldier, 69, 77
Resurrection, the, 17, 136-37, 147-51, 165, 168-69
Revard, Stella P., 56n.1, 119n.1
Richmond, Hugh, 177n.26
Rome, 1, 13, 15, 80, 87, 106, 135, 162, 163, 167-68
Ross, Malcolm, 33, 60
Rumrich, John Peter, 90
Rupert, Prince, 174
Russia, 32

Salmasius, 63
    Defensio Regia, 124
Samson, 169-79
    and Dalila, 172-73, 174, 176
    and Harapha, 172, 175
    and Israelites, 170-71
    and the law, 173-74
    and Manoa, 172, 176
    and Philistines, 170, 171
    and "rousing motions," 169-70, 173-74
    and the woman of Timna, 169, 173
    disobedience, 170
Satan, Chap. 3
    and Adam and Eve, 127
    and Charles I, 61
    and Cromwell, 20, 56, 61, 64-65, 68, 70-71, 79, 86, 163, 166-67
    and Death, 5, 9, 72, 76, 84, 129
    and English ambassadors, 75-76
    and Eve, 75
    and pain, 122, 125
    and Sin, 5, 9, 72, 76, 129
    and the Son. *See* Son
    as antagonist of God, 59, 129
    as dictator, 163

as diplomat, 72-81, 162, 163
as fallen man, 59, 79, 85, 139
as politician, 49, 62-71, 86, 128-29, 162-63
as soldier, 56-57, 62, 74, 84, 128, 141n.20
debate with Abdiel, 122-25
second coming, 146-47
Savoy, duke of, 33, 34, 110n.15, 133
Schwartz, Regina M., 88n.9
Shakespeare, William, works, 12, 46, 80, 86, 116
Shawcross, John T., xvn.13, 169n.8, 177-78n.27
Small, Jesse G., 105n.12
Son, the, 42-53
and Death, 144, 168
and Satan, 49, 84, 93, 95-96, 121, 144, 165-66
and Sin, 144
as angel, 49
as Christ. *See* Christ
as heir, 5, 8, 50-51, 121-22, 126-27
as king, 5, 8-9, 28, 30, 48, 50-51, 90, 122
as muse, 13
Spain, 1, 4, 32, 76, 86, 87, 120, 153
State Papers, viii, 5, 97
Stavely, Keith, 20n.26
Steadman, John, 56n.1
Stein, Arnold, 53n.35, 177n.26
Strafford, Earl of, 49
Stuart, House of, 32, 107
Swaim, Kathleen, 131n.13
Sweden, 4, 31, 32, 75, 76

Tamerlane, 106
Tanner, John, 58n.6, 61n.12, 62n.17, 66n.24, 85-86n.3, 91n.14, 94n
Tetuan, 4
The Instrument of Government, 68
Thurloe, John, 8, 79
Tillyard, E.M.W., 177-78n.27
Transylvania, 4
Turner, James Grantham, xiii-xivn.10

Ulreich, John, 175n.19
United Netherlands, 4, 134
Uriel, 15, 28, 74, 75, 80

Van der Zee, Henri and Barbara, 10n.10
Vane, Charles, 76
Venables, General Robert, 130
Venice, 1
Von Maltzahn, Nicholas, 3n.1

wars, 138-39
England, 19, 73; and France, 19, 120; and Ireland, 64, 120; and Portugal, 120; and Scotland, 64, 120; and Spain, 63, 120, 130; and United Netherlands, 120
English civil, 1-2, 119, 123
France and Spain, 130
modern, 130n.12
Spain and United Netherlands, 134
Sweden, 120; and Denmark, 120, 134, 135, 144; and Poland, 120, 134, 166; and Russia, 132, 166; and United Netherlands, 134
Western Design. *See* Western Design
West, Robert, 15
Western Design, 86, 87, 130, 153
Whitehall Palace, 40
Wilding, Michael, 78n.32
William III (England), 10n.10
Williams, Charles, 58n.6
Wittreich, Joseph A., ix, 9-10n.9, 169-70n.10, 171n.14, 173n.16
Wolfe, Don M., xiiin.9
Woods, Suzanne, xvii, 98n.1
Woolrych, Austin, 3n.1
Wooten, John, 53n.35
Worcester, battle of, 120, 126n.7
Worden, Blair, 56n.2

Zagorin, Perez, 51n.34, 56n.2, 125n.4, 177-78n.27
Zeno of Elea, 30n.6

DATE DUE

Demco, Inc. 38-293